MW00985942

AVID

READER

PRESS

ALSO BY JAMES WHITFIELD THOMSON

Lies You Wanted to Hear

A BETTER ENDING

A Brother's Twenty-Year Quest
to Uncover the Truth
About His Sister's Death

JAMES WHITFIELD THOMSON

AVID READER PRESS

New York   Amsterdam/Antwerp   London   Toronto   Sydney   New Delhi

AVID READER PRESS
An Imprint of Simon & Schuster, LLC
1230 Avenue of the Americas
New York, NY 10020

Copyright © 2025 James Whitfield Thomson

Names and identifying characteristics of some individuals have been changed.

All rights reserved, including the right to reproduce this book
or portions thereof in any form whatsoever. For information, address
Avid Reader Press Subsidiary Rights Department,
1230 Avenue of the Americas, New York, NY 10020.

First Avid Reader Press hardcover edition March 2025

AVID READER PRESS and colophon are trademarks of Simon & Schuster, LLC

For information about special discounts for bulk purchases,
please contact Simon & Schuster Special Sales
at 1-866-506-1949 or business@simonandschuster.com.

The Simon & Schuster Speakers Bureau can bring authors to your live event.
For more information or to book an event contact the Simon & Schuster Speakers Bureau
at 1-866-248-3049 or visit our website at www.simonspeakers.com.

Interior design by Ruth Lee-Mui

Manufactured in the United States of America

1 3 5 7 9 10 8 6 4 2

Library of Congress Cataloging-in-Publication Data

Names: Thomson, James (Writer of A better ending), author.
Title: A better ending: a brother's twenty-year quest to uncover the
truth about his sister's death / James Thomson.
Identifiers: LCCN 2024011517 | ISBN 9781668062869 (hardcover) |
ISBN 9781668062876 (trade paperback) | ISBN 9781668062883 (ebook)
Subjects: LCSH: Thomson, James (Writer of A better ending)--Family. |
Suicide. | Siblings of suicide victims. | Siblings--Death. | Homicide investigation.
Classification: LCC HV6545 .T545 2025 | DDC 362.28--dc23/eng/20241227
LC record available at https://lccn.loc.gov/2024011517

ISBN 978-1-6680-6286-9
ISBN 978-1-6680-6288-3 (ebook)

For Meg, Brian, Brett, Kelly, and Kevin

And in memory of Darryl Carlson

Author's Note

Memoirs are founded on an unspoken bargain between the author and the reader—the author purports to tell his story truthfully and the reader agrees to believe him. There are, of course, countless memoirs in which the writer lies and exaggerates and twists the facts for myriad reasons, but no matter how truthful the author tries to be, there is an inherent problem with the genre. Simply stated, a memoir, by definition, is rooted in memory, and numerous scholarly studies have proven how faulty our memories can be. In this book I quote extensively from letters, police reports, and court records, which are in my possession, so I had no trouble getting that content right. Re-creating dialogue, on the other hand, is a much bigger challenge. During the course of my investigation I took extensive notes, kept a journal, and consulted with others whenever possible in an attempt to record the words and emotions of various conversations as accurately as possible. Still, anyone who has ever rehashed an argument with a friend or loved one knows how difficult it can be to agree on what was said yesterday, let alone fifty years ago. I have tried my best to write the dialogue and every other aspect of this memoir without bias or embellishment. But, in the end, readers are usually the best arbiters of truth. You will tell me if this is a story you believe.

I have changed the names of a number of people in the book and have done so without annotation. Using their real names would not alter the story in any way. 6313 Dunblane in San Bernardino, where the shooting took place, is a fictional address.

I have my dead, and I have let them go,
and was amazed to see them so contented,
so soon at home in being dead, so cheerful,
so unlike their reputation. Only you
return; brush past me, loiter, try to knock
against something, so that the sound reveals
your presence, Oh don't take from me what I
am slowly learning.

RAINER MARIA RILKE

PROLOGUE

I GREW UP on the North Side of Pittsburgh in the 1950s in a typical lower-middle-class family—mother, father, sister, brother—and by the time I was forty-six they were all dead. My mother was the last to go, adrift in a gentle fog of senility that seemed to spare her the heartache of outliving two of her three children. She and I were close and I missed her terribly, but as the years rolled by it was my sister Eileen's suicide at the age of twenty-seven that nagged at me like a pebble in my shoe. Eileen had been working as a secretary in San Bernardino, California, and was married to her high school sweetheart, Vic Zaccagnini, a police officer. They had no children. I had always known her as a happy, bubbly girl, the brightest smile in the room. Then, suddenly, she was gone.

Details about Eileen's death were sketchy, nothing much more than the fact that she had died from a self-inflicted gunshot wound. But we also knew that Vic was in the house when the fatal shot was fired, and I wondered how we could be certain that she had committed suicide and Vic had nothing to do with her death. My parents, who were nearly catatonic with grief, asked me to talk to him and try to sort it out. I had known Vic since he was sixteen years old. His mother was my mother's best friend. When he arrived from California for Eileen's funeral, the two of us sat down in my parents' kitchen and talked. The story he told me was long and sad, but the gist was simple—Eileen had been having an affair with her boss, and when that fact was revealed, she shot herself in a fit of remorse. Vic met my eyes openly, his face filled with bewilderment and grief. He answered all my questions, never stumbling or contradicting himself. In short, I believed him. I told my family what he had told me and we got on with our lives as best we could.

Nearly three decades later, I started to write a novel about Eileen. I assumed the book would be fiction, my imagination filling in the blanks in the story I'd been parroting to myself and everyone else for so many years. But everything changed when I uncovered the police reports from the San Bernardino County Sheriff's Department. According to those reports, Vic had beaten up Eileen shortly before she died, called her a "whore," and threatened to kill her in front of another cop; moreover, the lead detective appeared to have made up his mind about the case before he ever left the office and never bothered to interview the two women Eileen had talked to on the telephone in the last hour of her life. To me, what had been ruled a suicide now looked like a cover-up, the Sheriff's Department protecting a fellow officer.

I have spent years searching for the truth about my sister's death. This is the story of my quest. In the TV world my tale would unfold like one of those true-crime dramas where a dedicated cold-case investigator tracks down every lead and suspect, forensic experts unravel the mysteries of blood and fibers and bullets, and a verdict is rendered with the tap of a judge's gavel in a court of law.

But I do not live in the TV world.

The last leg of my journey took me to a motel room near the Seattle airport. I was sitting by the desk, one knee bouncing nervously while I doodled on a message pad, waiting to go to a meeting with Vic. I hadn't seen him since the day of Eileen's funeral. The meeting had been arranged by Darryl Carlson, a private detective who had become my guide and unflagging companion on my quest. Darryl had said we should go to the meeting empty-handed, no briefcase or notebooks— no hidden recording device—and I agreed. The only exception was a copy of Eileen's letter in my shirt pocket, the one she wrote to our parents on the day she died. I was certain Vic did not know the letter existed, and I wanted to see the look on his face when he read it.

Darryl glanced at the big Rolex on his wrist and said, "Time to go."

"Okay. Should I leave the police reports here in the room or take them in the car?"

"You got extra copies, right?"

I nodded.

"Let's take them. Maybe he'll want a set."

"You think?"

Darryl twisted one corner of his mouth in doubt, or maybe it was hope, but didn't say anything. We put on our coats and walked out to the rental car. It was a dank February evening, pink haze around the arc lights in the parking lot. I pulled out onto the road and asked him how far it was to the restaurant.

"About three miles. You can't miss it. It's up on the right."

"What's it called again?"

"Thirteen Coins."

"That's a terrible name. Sounds like bad luck."

Darryl grinned, then explained it was from an old wedding custom. The groom gives his bride thirteen coins for Jesus and his disciples.

We stopped at a red light, the windshield wipers mewling as they cleared the mist. I asked him if we should have some sort of signal in case I got nervous and went off track.

"Sure, I'll just stab you in the leg with my fork?"

My turn to grin. Darryl had a way of talking me down off the ledge. The driver behind me tapped his horn. I looked up and saw the green light and eased ahead.

"Is Vic definitely bringing his wife?" I asked.

Darryl said he thought so. "We *want* her there. Helps keep things in balance."

Another mile up the road, Darryl pointed at the sign for 13 Coins, and I found an empty parking spot about fifty yards past the entrance. I turned off the engine and let out a long breath like a runner before a race.

Darryl put his hand on my shoulder. "We've come a long way, Jim. You're gonna be fine. Just take it nice and slow."

As we walked toward the restaurant in the chilly night air, my feet felt sluggish while my mind rushed ahead. I caught a glimpse of Vic the moment I stepped through the door. He was standing alone near the hostess station, his face in profile. He turned and saw me and lifted his chin in recognition. As I walked toward him, he gave me a wary smile. More than thirty years after Eileen's death, my journey had come full circle, taking me back to its beginning—I, a jury of one, trying to decide if the hand he held out to me was the hand that had held the gun.

PART ONE

PART
ONE

1

I WAS ALONE, standing in line at a Pirates-Phillies game, waiting to buy a soft pretzel and beer, when I thought I heard my name on the public address system. Just a flicker of consciousness, the kind of thing that comes and goes and never crosses your mind again—unless there's a reason. My name is Jim Thomson. It's a common name, short and easy to remember. Still, when I meet people, they often get it wrong. I'll introduce myself and the person will smile and shake my hand and end up calling me Tim or Tom, last name Thomas or Johnson. It's the kind of mistake we all make now and again. We get preoccupied; we're daydreaming half the time, even when we're looking someone straight in the eye. I remember my mother scolding me when I was a boy, saying, "You hear what you *want* to hear." Which is exactly what happened that night at the ballpark, my name blaring from the loudspeakers, the PA announcer asking Jim Thomson to please report to the information booth, and I, distracted by who knows what—a girl in a low-cut halter? a sudden roar of the crowd?—ignored the summons.

It was mid-September 1974, a balmy evening at Veterans Stadium in Philadelphia. I was a third-year graduate student at the University of Pennsylvania, working on a PhD in American studies. Born and raised in Pittsburgh, I was a loyal Pirates fan and went to the Vet in South Philly a few times each season to watch them play. That night the Pirates took an early lead but couldn't hold it. I'm sure I stayed until the last out as I always do, a lesson I'd learned as a kid when my older brother, Keith, and I left a Cubs-Pirates game in the top of the ninth and missed an improbable game-winning rally.

I drove home from the stadium and parked in front of the house. My wife, Connie, and I had recently moved to a small duplex in Narberth, a suburb on the Philadelphia Main Line, with our two-year-old daughter, Meg. As I was getting out of the car, Connie turned on the porch light and came out the front door in a sleeveless yellow dress.

"Didn't they page you at the game?" She crossed her arms, clutching her bare shoulders as if it were cold out. "I called and asked them to page you."

I was standing on the sidewalk. I couldn't tell if she was angry or worried.

"Why? What is it?"

"I didn't know what to *do*. I kept waiting and waiting for you to call." Connie sobbed and covered her face with her hands. I ran up the steps and put my arms around her, panic in my head—*Not Meggy. Anything but Meggy.*

"Tell me," I said.

"It's Eileen. She's dead."

It was just words for an instant, the news of my sister's death an abstraction. As if I were suddenly living in a world without cats or trees. A world without Eileen.

"How?"

"She killed herself."

"No. She *wouldn't.*"

Tears rolled down Connie's face. "With a gun," she said.

I let out a howl of grief and rage and disbelief, a guttural sound I'd never made before—or since. Our mailbox was a wooden case that had once held some weather instruments on my ship in the Navy. I punched the box and skinned my knuckles on the sturdy louvered slats.

Connie looked frightened, helpless.

"Did she leave a note?" I said.

"I'm not sure. I don't think your mom knows much yet. Your dad's still at work. She said she was going to wait for him to get home before she told him."

I felt a sudden pang of conscience, trying to remember the last time I'd called Eileen or written her a letter. I hadn't seen her in nearly four years.

"I better go call," I said, sucking blood from my knuckles. Such a welcome and curable pain.

My parents' line was busy. So was my brother Keith's. Connie and I sat down at the kitchen table. She told me Mom had called from Pittsburgh around seven thirty. The conversation had been short, a blur of emotion and chaos that had left Connie thinking Eileen had been killed in an automobile accident. It wasn't until she'd spoken to Keith's wife, Alide, that she found out it had been a suicide.

Connie told me she'd put Meg to bed soon after, then called the stadium to page me. "They didn't want to do it," she said. "I don't know why. But I just kept pleading with the guy until he promised."

I thought back to that moment in the concessions line at the ballpark, that flicker of recognition. Why hadn't I inquired about the page? Did I think only doctors got summoned? The parents of lost children? Or did I have some subliminal understanding that this message could lead only to heartache, to some life-changing event? Whatever the reason, it earned me two and a half hours of not knowing, a period of time when the most important thing on my mind was the outcome of a baseball game. I pictured Connie sitting there alone with that horrific news, waiting for my call.

I phoned my parents again and my father answered.

"Hello?" It was a question—one-half hope, as if this might be the call that would undo everything, Eileen on the other end of the line, telling him it was all a mistake; the other half dread, as if he expected another blow, some new weight added to his unbearable sorrow.

"It's me, Dad."

"Jim," he said, relief and disappointment in a single syllable.

"I can't *believe* this."

"No, neither can I. I keep thinking maybe . . . if only I . . ." The words caught in his throat. "I'll let you talk to your mother."

"Hi, Jim," Mom said. "Connie told me you went to see the Pirates."

"Mom, I'm sorry. I should have—"

"Oh, no, honey, that's all right. I had the game on the radio. It was a comfort, knowing you were there."

The way she said it made me feel like a little boy again, and I let go and cried.

2

THE FIRST DAY of school in September 1953 was a big occasion for my brother and sister and me. For Keith it was the start of junior high—walking five blocks to a new school, changing classes each period, eating in the cafeteria instead of coming home for lunch. For Eileen it was the first day of first grade. *Real* school, I reminded her. No more snacks and games and coloring books like they have in kindergarten. For me, the new year meant leaving my best friend, Joey, and going into an entirely new grade from him. When I finished the second grade in June, my teacher recommended that I skip a grade, which meant I would be joining Miss Wyman's class. (Actually, it was only a half grade; I'd be going into 3A instead of 3B. The half grades were an anomaly in the Pittsburgh public school system, which meant I eventually graduated from high school in February rather than June with my original class.)

It was a warm, sunny morning; a light breeze was coming through the open window. Keith had already left for school, and Eileen and I were eating breakfast with tea towels fastened around our necks to protect our new school clothes—a white dress with red polka dots for her, an embroidered brown cowboy shirt with green piping for me. As always, we were bickering. No doubt I'd been kicking her chair under the table or teasing her about the way she ate her Cheerios, one O at a time.

"*James*," my mother said from the sink, and I knew right away it was something important. "I want you to walk Eileen to school today."

"Okay, Mom." I smirked at Eileen. Last year either Keith or our cousin Joanie, who was in fifth grade and lived in the apartment upstairs, had walked her to kindergarten. Now it was my turn.

"This is such a special day for you," Mom said to Eileen, straightening the ribbon in my sister's hair, which was brown with blond highlights from the summer sun. Mom had put it up in curlers last night, so it fell in ringlets around her face. "First grade! You're gonna have so much fun." (Because I skipped and Eileen's birthday was just past the cut-off date for first grade, she ended up being two and a half years behind me in school even though we were only fifteen months apart.)

Eileen was quiet. I knew she didn't like this new arrangement, but she wasn't putting up a fuss.

When it was time to go, Mom walked us out the front door. She wet her fingertip and wiped a smudge off the white toe of Eileen's saddle shoe.

"Oh, yinz look *nice*," she said. "I wish I had a camera." (*Yinz* is the Pittsburgh equivalent of the Southern *y'all*. It wasn't until I went away to college that I learned that this word and several others that I used were unique to Pittsburgh—*redd up* for tidy up, *nebby* for nosy, *jumbo* for bologna. As for pronunciation, a young man from Pittsburgh *warshes* his hands in the sink, buys *flires* for his girlfriend, and tries to *pool* himself up by his bootstraps.)

Eileen and I started down the front steps.

"Hold your sister's hand when you cross the street," Mom said to me. "And make sure you take her all the way to her classroom. Eileen, you wait for Jimmy by the door at lunchtime."

We lived at 911 Wettach Street, half a block from the Schiller

School. Eileen and I walked down the sidewalk past the two redbrick duplexes identical to our own. The safety boy was waiting at the curb on the corner, a clean white patrol belt across his chest. There was no traffic at the intersection, but he spread his arms to block our path. I didn't look back, but I knew my mother was still watching as I took Eileen's hand to cross the street.

Inside the school door, I walked Eileen down the hall. "You're in Miss Gilliland's class," I said. "She's real nice." I loved Miss Gilliland. She wore perfume that smelled like my mother's lilac talcum powder, her blond hair marcelled in perfect waves.

Eileen hadn't said a word since we left the house. The door of her classroom was propped open. Two steps into the room she burst into tears.

"What's the matter?" I said.

"I want . . . to . . . go . . . *home*." Big tears were rolling down her cheeks, snot coming out of her nose, red welts forming around her dark eyebrows. Normally, this would have been my chance to laugh and call her a crybaby, but I was so surprised I missed my cue and put my arm around her shoulder.

"Why do you want to go home? You *like* school." I looked around the classroom and pointed out her friend Elaine Silver.

Elaine was sitting at her desk watching us, uncertain whether she should smile at Eileen or join in the wailing. Miss Gilliland rushed from the back of the room, where she had been arranging some books, and squatted down in front of Eileen, her blue dress fanning out around her feet.

"Hey, sweetheart, what's the matter? Is your brother picking on you again?" She gave me a wink.

Eileen shook her head and pressed closer to my side.

"That's one of the first things you learn in the first grade," Miss Gilliland said. "How to get back at your big brother." She pulled a tissue from her pocket and started wiping Eileen's face.

Eileen gave one last shuddering sob and let the teacher take her in her arms.

"Thanks, Jimmy," Miss Gilliland said with a smile. "She'll be fine."

I felt a knot in my stomach as I made my way up the stairs to Miss Wyman's classroom on the second floor. This was big-kid territory, a place I'd rarely been. I walked into the room apprehensively and looked around. There were a few familiar faces of boys I knew from the playground, but no one who was a friend, no one inviting me to take a seat beside them. I eased my way to the back of the classroom and found an empty desk next to a girl with a giant green ribbon in her hair.

Shortly after we'd recited the Pledge of Allegiance, Miss Wyman passed out pencils and paper and told us to write about what we had done over summer vacation. I printed my name carefully at the top of the white lined paper and began a story about our family trip to the Allegheny County Fair. I'd seen a horse jump off a tower into a swimming pool, a man shot out of a cannon, a zucchini as big as a baseball bat. As I paused, trying to remember the name of the Indian who threw knives at a woman strapped to a board, I noticed the girl with the green ribbon was writing, not printing; so was the boy on the other side of me, each word a continuous line of loops and swirls. I wanted to emulate my classmates, but I didn't know how to make all the letters and string them together, so I raised my hand.

"Would you please tell me how to make a writing *S*?" I asked Miss Wyman.

"A what?"

"A writing *S*." I drew a squiggly line with my finger in the air. "Not printing, the other kind."

The class burst out laughing. Now *I* was the Thomson kid who was about to cry. Miss Wyman came over to my desk and quickly saw my problem. She told me to go ahead and print my composition. Then, before I left to go home for lunch, she pulled me aside and said she didn't have time to teach me *cursive*.

"Ask your mom and dad to show you," she said matter-of-factly. "You'll pick it up fast. You can print all your work for the next two weeks, then you'll have to write in longhand like everyone else."

She knew I was smart, and I did too. I was usually the kid whose hand went up first when the teacher asked a question, even when it meant getting teased by boys who thought that being smart made me a weakling and a coward, which was my own secret fear because my big brother fought all my battles for me.

Eileen was waiting for me by the door of her classroom, smiling, happy.

As we crossed the street on the way home, she said, "Don't tell Mommy I was crying this morning, okay?"

"Okay."

"Promise?"

"Promise," I said. But I told anyway.

3

THE MORNING after Eileen's death I called my parents again. They said her body would be flown back to Pittsburgh, but no other arrangements had been made. Connie and I loaded up our station wagon for the five-hour drive, Meg happily ensconced in the wayback with her books and toys, a blanket and pillow. Two months shy of her third birthday, she was talkative and curious, already reading books like *Hop on Pop* and *Go, Dog. Go!* Meg had a round face, brown hair, and dancing brown eyes. My parents often said she looked like Eileen at that age. The two had never met, so Connie and I told her that her aunt had died in a car accident. How could we explain Eileen's suicide to a small child? We couldn't explain it to ourselves.

After a stop at a HoJo's on the turnpike for gas and lunch, Meg fell asleep, which gave Connie and me time to talk openly about Eileen. Connie had one of Meg's dolls on her lap, absent-mindedly snapping and unsnapping the big plastic buttons on its dress. (Since she'd stopped smoking, she had never been quite sure what else to do with her hands.)

"Do you think it had something to do with work?" she said.

"I don't know, Con. I thought she loved her job." Eileen had been a secretary for the San Bernardino County school system. She could take shorthand and type like a demon.

"Yeah, and they just bought that new house."

"Mom said Vic didn't want to do it, but Eileen kept pushing him. Found the new house and filled out all the papers herself."

"She's such a little dynamo," Connie said, then let out a sigh, realizing the present tense was no longer applicable.

Eileen had told me about the house on the phone. She had been so pleased with herself, telling me how they'd managed to buy the new house and hold on to the old one, which they were renting out. Teasing her, I said she was on her way to becoming a real estate mogul.

"Well, a mogulette, anyway," she'd said, laughing at her own expense. She had been a majorette in high school, a position she'd coveted dearly, spending hours perfecting her baton twirling in the alley behind our apartment.

Connie and I had been married the day after Christmas in 1969, then spent much of the year apart—I on my Navy ship in the South China Sea, she teaching fifth grade in a Boston suburb. I was a lieutenant junior grade and the navigator of the USS *Procyon*, which supplied food to the ports of South Vietnam and the gunships and aircraft carriers that patrolled the coast. When the *Procyon* returned stateside in the late summer, Connie joined me in California. We lived in an apartment in Oakland and saved every penny we could, determined to spend a year traveling in Europe when I got out of the Navy—or at least until the money ran out. On the day of my discharge, we headed for the East Coast via San Bernardino to visit Eileen and Vic.

The town felt a little depressing to me—a drab, sprawling grid—but Vic and Eileen loved it. They drove us around and showed us the sights. A recent fire had left a black swath across the mountains, and a charred smell still hung in the air. The weather was chilly. Connie took a photograph of Eileen and Vic and me in our jackets, standing on a hill with the mountains in the background. We all went out to dinner, then bowling, and had a good time. Eileen and Vic were sweet and playful with each other. Sometimes I'd catch her looking at him the way she did back in high school, giddy with love.

A few weeks later, Connie and I left for Europe, our odyssey taking us from Wales to Turkey. We came home after seven months because Connie was pregnant. I found a job with a publishing company as a college textbook salesman in the Philadelphia area. Meg was born in November 1971. The next fall I started grad school at Penn. Money was tight, California three thousand miles away. I never saw Eileen again.

Connie said, "I can't believe she *shot* herself." She undid a snap on the doll's dress. "I hate guns. They're so . . . *irrevocable*."

I didn't respond immediately. I knew that Eileen could handle a gun. Vic was a cop; he'd taught her to use a pistol and they kept one in the house for her protection. She'd told me about going to the firing range once. Laughed and called herself Annie Oakley. It bothered me a little, picturing her with a gun, but I didn't say anything. Growing up, Keith and I had had pop guns, cap guns, squirt guns. But a line had been drawn when we asked for a BB gun—our parents said no, not even if we bought it with the money we'd saved from our paper route. My father was a city boy who had never gone hunting in his life. To him, guns were just a way for us to get into trouble.

My mother felt the same. Her younger brother Frank had been a gun enthusiast. When he was twenty-three, he got into an altercation over a pistol with the owner of a gas station. The details of the incident were unclear. The newspapers said it was an attempted robbery, but family members maintained it was more of a prank, Frank acting on a dare, trying to recover a gun that had been taken away from one of Frank's friends. What's clear is this—Frank was shot during the incident, and the bullet shattered the bone in his upper right arm. After a long stay in the hospital, he was released on bail. Frank had worked in CCC camps as teenager and had never been in trouble with the law before. People said he used to be happy-go-lucky, but when he came home from the hospital, he was desolate at the prospect of going to prison. Babush, my Polish grandmother, told him he'd brought shame on the family. He became sad and withdrawn, taking long, solitary walks. My mother recalled how he'd walk from Babush's in Penn Hills to the North Side to visit her, twelve miles away. One day, on the way to see an attorney, Frank jumped off the Sharpsburg bridge.

No, there would be no guns for the Thomson boys. By the time Keith and I were adults we agreed. Neither of us ever owned a gun. But Eileen had one, and she used it.

When I'd spoken with my mother the night before, she told me Eileen had been depressed. She said Eileen and Vic had been separated since the beginning of the summer but didn't want anyone to know, so my parents had kept it a secret. I felt hurt that Eileen hadn't told me about her troubles. I would have been on her side no matter what.

In the car I said to Connie, "Mom said Eileen had been depressed. It's just so strange. I didn't know she had any problems."

"Well, there were all those miscarriages. Maybe that had something to do with it?"

Eileen had had several miscarriages, none of the pregnancies lasting more than three or four months.

"Yeah, okay. But that isn't enough to make you *kill* yourself."

"It's not just losing the baby, Jim. Your whole world is turned upside down. Every hormone in your body going off like popcorn."

"Do you remember when she had the last one?"

"Around Thanksgiving, I think. Maybe she had another one and didn't tell anybody."

"Maybe," I said. "Obviously there were a lot of things we didn't know. I wish she and Vic had adopted, but I guess he wasn't interested."

"That's ridiculous," Connie said. "Why do some people think it has to be their own flesh and blood? Either you want children or you don't.

You hold that baby in your arms for two seconds and it's *yours*. That was probably one of the reasons why they separated."

I shrugged. "I just don't get it. It seemed to me like she spent all her time worrying about everybody else."

"Maybe that was the problem. She kept everything bottled up inside." Connie snapped and unsnapped a button on the doll's dress.

Annoyed by her fiddling, I snatched the doll away and tossed it into the back seat. "Well, she sure found a *fucking* melodramatic way to let it out."

Connie flinched as if she'd been slapped.

"I'm sorry," I said, my eyes filling with tears. "I'm just so *angry*."

"It's okay." She gave me a sad smile. "You're allowed to be upset."

We drove in silence for a while. I didn't like myself much at the moment. I'd always prided myself on my even-temperedness and self-control; now I was uncertain where my emotions would take me from one minute to the next. I'd been up much of the night, staring at the thin trapezoid of light from the streetlamp coming in past the window shade, trying to process my feelings. I'd never had anyone close to me commit suicide. People who did so were obviously desperate, but it seemed like such a selfish act. I remembered talking with my friend Cody in the middle of the night while we were on watch in the South China Sea, one of those times when men tell each other things they would never say in the light of day . Cody's father and brother had both committed suicide, and he was having a tough time coping with the loss.

"It's like they leave a coin for you to carry around in your pocket," he said. "Heads is anger, tails is guilt."

4

WHEN WE were kids, Eileen and I couldn't spend five minutes in a room together without quarreling, and would often end up
slapping and kicking and pulling each other's hair. One time she bit
my arm so hard she left purple teeth marks in my skin. My mother resorted to all sorts of punishments to get us to stop—a wooden Fli-Back
paddle was usually her first choice, no time spent trying to figure out
which of us was at fault—but nothing seemed to work. I'm fairly certain I was the primary instigator. Eileen's very existence seemed like an
affront, and I wished she would disappear. I couldn't remember when
she wasn't there, bugging me.

Living in a three-room apartment, we had a hard time getting
away from one another. The house on Wettach Street was owned by
my father's cousin Charles Thomson, who lived upstairs with his wife
and three children. Originally built as a single-family dwelling, the
house had been divided into two apartments by converting one of the
second-floor bedrooms into a kitchen. Our apartment on the first floor
consisted of the kitchen, my parents' bedroom, and the "front room."
During the day the front room served as our living room; at night, Keith
and I slept on the foldout couch, Eileen on a single bed in the corner. I was a bed wetter until I was ten or eleven, which made things

uncomfortable for my brother, but he never upbraided me or teased me about it, as he had been a bed wetter himself. We had no bathroom in our apartment, just a toilet down in the cellar. Saturday evenings we children would troop upstairs one by one to bathe in our cousins' tub.

Lying in bed at night, Keith and Eileen and I would talk and tell stories. We'd pretend we were cowboys trying to hold off a band of marauding Apaches, or GIs driving the Japs out of Iwo Jima. As we prepared for battle, Keith would announce that somebody had to play the bad guy—it wasn't any fun if we were all on the same side. Eileen and I were natural enemies, and Keith said we couldn't have two boys against a girl, so most of the time it was me against them. Once the battle was underway one of two things would happen—either we'd have a pillow fight and make so much noise that Mom would come in and yell at us, or Keith would hold me down so Eileen could tickle me, and one of my flailing limbs would whack her and she'd start to cry and Mom would come in and yell at us.

All in all, we had a happy childhood, with one notable caveat—my father was a drunk. One minute he'd be laughing and bouncing you on his knee, the next minute he'd grab you by the throat, sputtering with rage. In perhaps my earliest memory at the age of three or four, I was acting silly, trying to steal a few extra minutes before I went off to bed. When I tried to crawl onto my dad's lap, he threw me across the room like a rag doll and I struck my head on the iron stove in our kitchen. My mother screamed at him as I sobbed in her arms, a huge lump forming on the back of my head. (Conventional wisdom said you should never let children go to sleep after a hard bump on the head or they might never wake up, so Mom was determined to keep me awake for an hour or two.) Not long after that incident, my mother decided to leave my dad. She told me I was going to have to stay with my aunt Mil and uncle Norb for a while because there wasn't enough room for me at Babush's, who lived with Aunt Pauline (my mother's youngest sister), Uncle Pete, and their two children in a tiny four-room house. Mom,

Keith, and Eileen stayed at Babush's for about a week, but the situation was untenable. Soon we were all back together on Wettach Street, Dad maudlin and contrite, Mom vowing to leave him again as soon as she could find the means.

My father was a dry cleaner. He picked up clothes from his customers and brought them to a dry-cleaning plant that serviced independent drivers, then returned the clothes to his customers the following week. Dad was six feet tall, bald, with a big belly and short, powerful arms. He wore thick, wire-rimmed glasses that left deep indentations on the sides of his nose when he took the glasses off to clean them. His teeth were brown and broken—Mom said it was the result of brushing too hard, one of his many excesses—and he lost them all by the time he was fifty. He had a deep voice with a booming laugh, but the scariest times were when he was silent and brooding. The rest of us would sit nervously at the dinner table, eyes fixed on our food, waiting for an eruption. My father drank red wine, which he bought in half-gallon jugs. He kept one jug under the kitchen sink, another in his truck. I remember sneaking sips, trying to discover the magic it held, but I winced every time I took a taste.

He finally quit drinking when I was eight. Years later, when he was dying of cancer, I suggested he take a shot of whiskey to help ease the pain.

"Nah, Jim," he said, flapping his hand to dismiss the suggestion. "Beating the bottle may be the best thing I've ever done in my life. I'm not giving in now."

My family was poor, but I don't think I ever realized it when I was growing up. We wore hand-me-down clothes and put strips of cardboard in our shoes when they got holes in the soles, but so did lots of other kids. Keith started a paper route when he was ten, delivering the afternoon edition of the *Pittsburgh Sun-Telegraph*, and I was his helper. We had 110 customers over an area of about four city blocks. I was six years old. I had a job, which I was proud of, and I loved being with my brother every day. All the money we earned from the paper route went to the family budget, which my mother managed. Keith got an allowance of a dollar a week and I got a quarter.

Frugality was the watchword in our house. We scrimped on everything—clothes, food, toilet paper, haircuts. When the TV broke, we'd wait for a year or more before we got it fixed or bought another. I don't remember being hungry, but I loved milk and resented having to drink the powdered stuff my mother mixed with water, which tasted like liquid chalk. I remember telling my mother when I was about ten or eleven, "When I grow up, I'm going have real milk at my house all the time." She gave me a wistful smile and said, "I hope you can."

Our family moved from the apartment on Wettach Street when I was twelve to a new apartment on Voskamp Street. We kids liked the place. Eileen got her own room on the second floor while Keith and I shared the room with steep eaves in the attic, but my parents thought the wooden building with its balky furnace was a firetrap. A year later we moved to a first-floor apartment of a brick building on Chestnut Street, near the corner of a busy intersection two blocks north of the Allegheny River. This was a railroad apartment, the rooms connected like cars on a train—living room in front and kitchen in back with the bedrooms in between. The only way in or out of the kitchen was through the bathroom, unless you went out the bulkhead doorway in back and walked around the building. Our solution if someone was in the bathroom—my father spent an inordinate amount of time reading the newspaper while "sitting on the throne"—was to tap on the door, say, "Coming through," and turn your head away in deference to the person on the toilet. There was no central heat in the apartment, just electric space heaters in the bedrooms and a gas stove in the living room. The lights would flicker every time one of the space heaters kicked on, and we had a box of fuses handy for the inevitable overloads. When we crawled out from under the mountains of blankets on the beds on winter mornings, we could see our breath.

For Keith, Eileen, and me the best thing about moving to Chestnut Street was having the Sarah Heinz House, the local Boys & Girls Club, one block away. Affiliated with the nearby H. J. Heinz Company, Heinz House had a swimming pool and gymnasium, game rooms with Ping-Pong and pool tables, a lobby with a fireplace and the latest issues of numerous magazines—*Life*, *Time*, *National Geographic*, *Popular Mechanics*. As Eileen and I got older, Heinz House became the center of our social life. It was the place where I learned to dance, where I got my first kiss.

In 1959, a year after we moved to Chestnut Street, Keith graduated from high school and joined the Air Force. For Eileen and me, now both in our early teens, it was almost as if he'd flipped a switch on his way out the door, his departure triggering dramatic changes in our lives. Eileen stopped growing—stuck permanently at five feet, one half inch—got braces on her teeth, and developed large breasts that drew sidelong glances from my pals. I grew six inches and gained forty pounds in one year. My voice got deeper and my body sprouted hair. We both had severe acne. With our new bodies, Eileen and I became somewhat shy and awkward with each another—and we finally started to get along. Maybe we knew, on some intuitive level, that the stakes were much higher now, our pubescent egos forever dangling on the edge of insecurity and self-loathing. Or maybe we simply stopped acting like children. One thing for certain, with Keith gone we were no longer vying for his attention, and that alone had a big effect on the dynamic between us.

When we were children, my parents used to refer to me as Eileen's "little brother." It was an endearment, a way of distinguishing me from Keith, but I didn't like it. I think that's why I have such a vivid memory of walking Eileen to school the day she started first grade. That morning my mother made it clear, and Miss Gilliland confirmed, that I was Eileen's big brother too. It simply took six more years and Keith's leaving for the Air Force for Eileen to grant me that role and for me to start acting the part.

The peculiar thing about the childhood hostilities between Eileen and me is that they were an aberration. Truth was, we were both good kids, more alike than different. We rarely got in trouble and were mortified when we did. Everything about us was geared toward making people like us, especially the adults in charge. Unabashed teachers' pets, we brought home report cards from elementary school with near perfect grades for our academic work and gold stars, literally, for conduct. Not so with Keith. One marking period when he was in the sixth grade, his teachers gave him straight As in his subjects, straight "poors" in behavior. The teachers were making a point, I suppose. Then again, so was he. He was a rebel and proud of it, less an outlaw than a provocateur. He was suspended from elementary school for refusing to sing in music class; he wrote his senior thesis in high school English on gonorrhea. He was six foot one, handsome, a varsity swimmer with a cocky grin and a swagger in his walk. He got the highest math score at Allegheny High School on the College Board test. Eileen and I idolized him, but his defiance puzzled us. Why *not* be good, we wondered. It seemed like its own reward.

When Eileen and I became adults, the difference between Keith and the two of us became even more profound. She and I were plodders, overachievers. Content with our quiet, mundane lives, we were both advancing slowly in our careers, earning the adult equivalent of gold stars. Keith, on the contrary, seemed to grow angrier and more frustrated with each passing year. A womanizer at heart, he was married with four children. Despite his expertise in computer technology, he could not advance in his job at IBM for lack of a college degree. He loved to go to bars and drink, and when he did, he wore an attitude like a plume in his cap, ready to fuck or fight, whichever opportunity came first.

In our letters and infrequent telephone calls, Eileen and I discussed Keith's problems. It was a comfort, having her to talk to. At least one of my siblings was stable and happy. Or so I thought.

5

Traffic on the turnpike was light except for the big tractor trailers. As Connie dozed off, I could feel the pressure in my ears as I drove up into the mountains.

And then.

Eileen is dead.

The thought came to me all at once, a simple, incontrovertible fact announcing itself without warning or regard. It felt like a punch in the chest, a blow against which I had no defense. I would never see her again, never talk to her. How could that be possible? I tried to rewind the film in my head to earlier, happier times, but I couldn't get past an image of my little sister—her eager brown eyes focused on *what*?—with a gun in her hand. I'd had that same vision many times as I lay awake last night. There was no way to shake it. I knew it would keep coming back again and again until I got used to it. In the most rational part of my mind, I told myself it didn't matter *how* Eileen had died—only that she was gone. Still, I couldn't stop wondering, *What was her last thought before she pulled the trigger?*

This wasn't the first time my life had been touched by a gun.

At football practice my senior year of high school I had been one of the ring leaders in a hazing. A boy named Roger Kinney had hung back after the first day's practice and avoided the gauntlet of fists in the shower room, the price each rookie paid for being part of the team. A few of us veterans warned Kinney he was going to get some extra licks after practice the next day for skipping the traditional hazing, and told him not to come back unless he got his shaggy hair cut. He chose to defy us.

We pummeled Kinney in the showers the next day; then six of us dressed quickly and waited for him in the parking lot. Eddy Radzik brought a pair of scissors just in case we needed them. Kinney sauntered toward us with a gym bag in his hand, a friend walking beside him. We made a wide circle around the two boys, and Eddy approached Kinney with the scissors in hand, snipping them menacingly. When Eddy tried to grab Kinney by the hair, everything seemed to speed up. Kinney reached into the gym bag and there was a sharp cracking noise. Eddy stumbled backward. Chip Andraitis rushed in and slammed Kinney across the cheek with a vicious forearm. Kinney fell, rolling over onto his back, then got up on one knee, a small pistol in his hand. Chip retreated, his hands up, until his back was against a fence. Ten feet away, Kinney fired at him twice.

We stood there transfixed as Kinney rose to his feet and held the gun on us, a stillness in the air, no sound except the echo of the gunshots. Kinney and his friend turned and ran down the path on the side of the hill. I was more enraged than frightened. I couldn't believe the punk's audacity. I figured he must have had a starter's pistol. If the gun had been a real gun, surely Chip would be dead. But Eddy said his leg was burning, and when he pulled down his pants, there was a small red dot the size of a pencil eraser on his thigh.

Someone took Eddy to the hospital. The next morning, I learned that he had been shot by a .22 pistol, the bullet so small the doctors didn't bother trying to take it out. That afternoon, two plainclothes detectives came to the practice field and took my teammates and me to a juvenile detention center. We sat for hours in a large room with about thirty other boys, most of them in faded brown jumpsuits, a television mounted high on the wall playing at full volume.

For the first time, I felt myself getting anxious. The guards wouldn't tell us anything, and I was late for work as a doorman at a movie theater and didn't want to lose my job. When I asked a guard if I could use the telephone, he grinned and said, "You think everyone gets one phone call? That's TV bullshit, kid. Go sit your ass down. I'll tell you when you can call your mommy."

The investigators came and got us one by one. When it was my turn, a bald, burly detective kept asking me the same questions again and again. Why had we been bullying Kinney? Had I punched him in the shower? Who brought the scissors? I couldn't understand why he was being so hostile. Kinney wasn't a victim. He was the one who shot my friend.

They let me go home about nine thirty that evening. I went back to football practice the next day and life returned to normal. In the second game of the season, I ran a punt back seventy-five yards for a touchdown. Against Carrick, I scored three more touchdowns. It was Eileen's first semester of high school. I could see the look of pride in her eyes when we said hi to each other in the halls, her girlfriends whispering and giggling when I walked by. I was a star and I knew it.

Midway through the season there was a trial in juvenile court. My friends and I were charged with assault and battery, Kinney with assault with a deadly weapon—no lawyers, no jury, just a judge asking questions. My friends and I stood before him, listing our accomplishments—honor roll, student council, National Honor Society. Kinney had no feathers in his cap, nothing that made him stand out from countless other boys except for the fact that he'd shot someone. He kept mumbling and the judge had to ask him to speak up.

While I was in the courtroom, it never occurred to me that the judge might convict me or order the school to drop me from the football team. My friends and I hadn't done anything unlawful. We were just trying to initiate a new player, following a tradition of high school football teams all across America.

The judge agreed. He dismissed the charges against my friends and me and sentenced Roger Kinney to a year in reform school. Kinney, who had not been in custody while waiting for the trial, was told to report to authorities in one week. The night before his incarceration, he got a hunting rifle and put a bullet through his head.

When I heard the news in school the next day, I felt nothing but contempt for him. My teammates concurred. *Fuck him*, we said to one another. He was a loser. He wanted the glory of being on the football team but didn't want to pay the price.

We ended up having a mediocre season—four wins and three losses—but I scored a bunch of touchdowns, was named most valuable player, and got my picture in the paper. College coaches started sending me recruiting letters. Flattered as I was, I knew I wasn't as good a football player as my press clippings made me seem. I soon learned that some of the more prestigious colleges based their scholarships on financial need. This meant I could keep my scholarship even if I didn't make the football team. Colgate University sent me a ticket to visit the campus and I had my first airplane ride to Binghamton, New York.

I visited Rutgers, then Harvard. Alumni slipped me twenty-dollar bills for spending money on these trips. I knew that I was being recruited for something more than football. I was second in my class with a 3.9 average, but my College Board scores were mediocre compared to most applicants at these top-rated colleges. What made me different was my background. In their eyes I was a tough, inner-city kid, dodging bullets as well as tacklers as I scrambled to escape the North Side. To college administrators, I was the picture of affirmative action before it had a name. Which was fine by me. I was ready to don a black leather jacket and motorcycle boots, stand on a chair in the dining hall, and sing "Leader of the Pack" if they'd only let me in.

Three colleges offered me scholarships. I was leaning toward Harvard—the name alone was hard to resist—but my dad wanted me to go to Colgate. He was an FDR-hating Republican and didn't like the politics of Harvard professors, the liberal Democrats JFK had brought to Washington. Besides, Colgate had offered me a full scholarship; Harvard expected my family to pony up three hundred dollars a year. As the deadline for making a decision approached, my father and I were at odds over my options. Finally, I asked him how much he was going to contribute to my education. He shook his head and said he couldn't give me a dime. I looked into his eyes, not an easy thing for me to do, and simply nodded. I didn't say a word, but he knew what I was thinking. *No money, no say.*

I chose Harvard. A few weeks before school started, I broke my leg in a touch football game and couldn't play on the college freshman team. The injury proved to be a stroke of good luck as it gave me more time to study. I was a painfully slow but enthusiastic reader, awed by the beauty of works like *The Iliad* and *Paradise Lost*. My roommate, a dyed-in-the-wool wonk, encouraged me to go to Lamont Library with him after supper and we'd study until it closed. In the final assignment for freshman composition, I wrote about the incident with Roger Kinney—a clear, cold-eyed account. When I got the paper back, the instructor's comment on the last page read—"Good job. A powerful, gripping story. You need to work on your punctuation. A-" It was the first A of my college career. As I walked across Harvard Yard, the weather was cool, the sky gray and dreary, but I felt as if I'd died and gone to heaven.

Then, in that moment, it hit me—I was alive; Roger Kinney was dead. He was sixteen years old, a boy who only wanted to be himself. Why, I wondered in my shame, had my friends and I needed to break him? Not just beat him with our fists, but take away some harmless thing that made him different? How could I have been a part of that? How could I have been so callous about his death? I had written an entire paper about him, mining his pain and tragedy for material, and gotten a good grade. But what was missing was an acknowledgment of my role in Kinney's death—a simple admission of guilt.

This was my epiphany, sudden and unshakable. When I went home to Pittsburgh that summer, I didn't have the courage to look up my old teammates and try to convince them we were wrong. Still, I knew in my heart that we were. The incident with Roger Kinney made me a watcher not a joiner, wary of any group that defined the world in terms of *us* and *them*. It is a wariness that I have carried with me my entire life.

6

I ALWAYS FELT a surge of pride when I came back to Pittsburgh. I loved the brown rivers busy with tugboats and barges, the medley of bridges, the streets and houses zigzagging up the sides of the hills. In recent years, great swaths of my old neighborhood had been torn down to build a highway connecting the northern suburbs with the business district downtown. But the government had run out of money to finish the project, leaving hundreds of families displaced and block after block of vacant lots filled with weeds and feral cats.

Once a bustling shopping district, East Ohio Street reflected the North Side's steady decline. The street had always had its fair share of bars and pawnbrokers, but the supermarkets and restaurants and clothing stores were all gone, a number of storefronts boarded up entirely. We drove past the barber school where Eileen had worked while Vic was overseas in the Air Force. She'd brought her Cairn terrier, Cal—short for California—home with her. Eileen sent me a photograph of our pet-phobic father sitting in a chair holding the dog, a picture so out of character she might just as well have sent one of the old man in drag.

I hadn't thought about Eileen for the past ten or fifteen minutes. Now that memory brought her back. I could picture her sitting across the kitchen table from my father, the two of them locked in a fierce game of 500 rum. Cards were a blood sport in our family, no quarter asked for or given. Dad would never let us win. "When you finally beat me," he'd say, "you'll know it's for real." Each of us in turn savored that first victory. When Eileen got hers, she taped the score sheet to the wall next to the kitchen table as Dad beamed with pride and a touch of chagrin.

Chestnut Street was too busy and narrow to park in front of the apartment building. I found a space on a side street, and Connie and I walked around the corner with Meg. I went up the stone steps, put the suitcases down in the vestibule, and reached in my pocket for my keys. I hadn't spent more than a dozen nights in my parents' apartment in the past seven years, but I still kept the key on my chain, as if I might suddenly find myself back home on Chestnut Street one day with no one able to hear my knock on the door.

I opened our apartment door and stepped into the living room with Connie and Meg. "We're here," I called out.

Homecomings were always joyful for me, but gloom had already enveloped the apartment, the window shades pulled down to the sills in the mid-afternoon. Thankfully, Meg was unaware of the somberness of the occasion as she ran ahead through the bedrooms. Mom was holding her in her arms when Connie and I got to the kitchen. Dad was sitting at the table, drinking coffee with their friend Carol McBee.

I gave my mother a hug, my chin resting on top of her head. Everyone was fighting back tears. Sensing that we might want some time alone, Carol said she had to run along and told my mother she'd call her in the morning.

"Are yinz hungry?" Mom said. "Carol brought some nice cold cuts."

Neither Connie nor I wanted anything. My mother gave Meg a cookie. Unable to make herself sit down, Mom started cleaning the kitchen. She was five three with a broad face, a thin, turned-up nose, and pale green eyes, which she did not pass on to any of us children, and a small gap between her front teeth, which made her smile pretty and unique. In early middle age she had always been a little chunky, but after menopause she had gotten quite thin. She liked to cook but rarely seemed interested in eating herself.

We made small talk for a while. No one mentioned Eileen. I asked when Keith was coming, and my father told me that he was taking a flight from Albany that would get in around eight that evening. I offered to pick him up at the airport when the time came.

"Yes, that would great," he said. "I'll go with you." It was a sweet gesture, not wanting me to be alone.

Connie took Meg into the living room to watch *Sesame Street*, and Mom finally sat down. It was time to talk.

I asked my parents what they'd heard from California.

"Vic called twice today," my mother said. "He's taking a late flight that doesn't get in till tomorrow morning."

"Have you made arrangements with a funeral home?"

"I talked to Bea. They're going to use Brady's on Cedar Avenue."

Bea, whom I called Mrs. Z, was Vic's mother, a short, fat woman with a loud voice and a hearty laugh who had become my mother's best friend over the course of Eileen and Vic's courtship and marriage. The two of them spoke on the telephone every day, and my parents spent most holidays with her and her twin sons, Mark and Paul, who were two years younger than Vic. Bea had been divorced from the boys' father for a long time. She had a bawdy sense of humor and was the only person I ever knew who could needle my father and get away with it. Eileen had been the daughter she'd never had. She loved to visit San Bernardino and go to Las Vegas and gamble at the casinos with Eileen and Vic.

"What about the funeral?" I said. "Do they know when that's gonna be?"

"Not till Monday," Mom said. (It was Thursday afternoon.) "Saturday's too soon, and they don't hold funerals on Sunday."

"I think that's better," Dad said. "That way people will have plenty of time to come to the viewing."

"The *viewing*?" I said. "Is that what Vic wants?"

"Sure," my father said. "We all do. We need to see her and tell her goodbye."

I winced, the taste of bile in my throat. We had not discussed *how* Eileen had shot herself, but I'd assumed she had put the gun to her head. Isn't that what you did when you wanted to end your own life? I wondered what kind of gun she had used, how gory the wound had been. I imagined the undertaker washing the blood from Eileen's hair and patching her skull.

"Can they *do* that?" I said. "Fix her up, I mean?"

My father looked confused by my question, but my mother understood what I meant. "She shot herself in the *heart*, Jim."

That one word seemed to freeze us in place for a moment. Eileen had so much heart. We needed her smile and her boundless optimism. How could she take that away from us?

Dad looked down at his hands and shook his head. "I should have listened better. She kept asking for help, but I didn't listen."

"You *did*," Mom said. "She just couldn't tell us."

"Tell you what?" I said.

"We don't know, really. We knew she was unhappy, but not that she . . ."

"But she never told you what the issue was?"

"Well, it was her and Vic," Dad said. "They were separated. I tried to get her to talk about it, but all she would say is that they'd grown apart."

"How long were they separated?"

"A few months," Mom said. "Pretty much all summer. I was worried sick, but I didn't want to stick my nose in. I talked to Bea and she said the same thing. You try and fix somebody else's problems and you just end up making things worse."

Eileen started going out with Vic Zaccagnini in her senior year of high school. Vic was a junior. I was away at college when they began dating so I didn't see them together, but by all accounts, they were crazy about each other. "He hangs around here like a lovesick puppy," my father told me one day on the phone, laughing. "We have to chase him home at night or he'd sleep on the floor by the stove in the living room."

The co–head majorette in the school band, Eileen was pretty enough, but what made her stand out was her energy, her desire to get things done and make the most out of every day. She had no time for teenage angst. Her dark brown eyes were radiant with delight, the simple joy of being alive. She'd had a few dates before she met Vic, but he was her first real beau. I'm not sure why she wasn't more popular with boys. Maybe they just saw her as a friend. That was certainly the case with my pals from the neighborhood. They liked to tease Eileen and flirt with her, but none of them asked her out.

When Vic came on the scene, Eileen changed. It wasn't just that they were going steady—his high school ring on her tiny finger, loops of string lacquered with nail polish to keep it from falling off—but that she took the relationship so seriously. My best friend, Al Kehren, a commuter at Duquesne University, used to get Eileen to type his term papers. One day he came to the house and she reacted coldly when he tried to kid around with her. He gave her a poke, hoping to get a laugh, and she got angry and stomped out of the room. Al turned to my mother, who rolled her eyes and said, "She's got a boyfriend now, Al. You're not even supposed to *look* at her."

Where did that come from, the need for Eileen to make sure other boys knew she was already spoken for? She had so little experience; she was never sexy, never a flirt. Perhaps she thought that this was what you did when you were going steady. Or was this something Vic demanded? Maybe he was the kind of guy who would sulk and interrogate her and fly into a jealous rage if he caught her talking to another boy in the hall? I can't say that I ever saw this sort of behavior in Vic, nor did my parents ever mention it. But Eileen had definitely changed. Once she put that ring on, she *belonged* to him.

A lineman on the football team, Vic Zaccagnini was about five ten with a thick torso and broad, powerful shoulders. He had brown eyes and dark brown hair, swarthy skin with acne scars on his cheeks, and a concave nose. He was far from handsome, but his smile was quick and disarming. Conversations around our kitchen table tended to be lively and opinionated, but Vic rarely had much to say. To me, he seemed entirely average, not someone I would have expected my sister to fall madly in love with. Initially, I kept that opinion to myself, but as their relationship grew more serious, I began to chide her, telling her she was too young to be acting like this and needed to date other guys. She told me to mind my own business, which is exactly what I would have done if the shoe were on the other foot. On one occasion our discussion became so heated, she stomped out of the room and didn't talk to me for several days. I don't know if Eileen told Vic about my disapproval, but if she did, he never showed any resentment toward me.

In a much gentler way, my parents tried to convince Eileen and Vic to go more slowly, but the young couple could not be deterred. They were married in February 1967 at St. Peter's, the Roman Catholic church next door to Allegheny High School. Eileen, in her white, once-in-a-lifetime gown, had just turned twenty; Vic, in his blue Air Force uniform, was still eighteen. My dad had tears in his eyes as he walked her down the aisle.

Religion was not a touchy subject in our house—my mother had been raised Catholic and converted to Lutheranism when she married Dad—but my father's mother, Mum, from dour German Protestant stock, had not been pleased when her son married a Catholic and a lowly Pole to boot. To Mum, Eileen's conversion was something she could store in her vault of grudges. There was much Sturm und Drang over her threat to boycott the wedding, but she showed up in the end, and rumor has it that someone actually saw her smile. Meanwhile, my Polish relatives, who were all Catholic, turned the reception at the VFW into a lively party with polkas and giant platters of pierogies and kielbasa and pastries. Eileen was still Eileen to them no matter where she went to church.

My mother lit another cigarette and Dad refilled his pipe.

"Are they gonna have the funeral at St. Peter's?" I asked.

"I guess," my mother said. "That's where Eileen would want it."

"I'm not sure they'll . . ." I stopped and shook my head to dismiss the thought.

"What?" Dad said.

"I don't think you can get buried in a Catholic church if you commit suicide. They believe it's a mortal sin."

My father slumped in his chair, another worry creasing his brow. Why had I said that? I'd given myself a chance to dismiss the notion, then gone ahead and said it anyway.

"Times have changed, Jim," my mother said. "They're not that strict anymore."

"I hope you're right," my father said.

"It's such a tragedy," Mom said. "I wish Eileen could've had a baby. I think that would have changed everything."

"Yeah," Dad said, "she took that last miscarriage really hard. She had her hopes so high."

I said, "They should have adopted. I don't know why Vic was so dead set against it." My voice echoed the frustration Connie had expressed earlier in the car—*You hold that baby in your arms for two seconds and it's yours.*

My parents exchanged a puzzled look. "Is that what she told you?" my father said.

"Yeah, she seemed pretty upset about it, but I guess Vic wouldn't budge." It seemed strange that they didn't know this.

"No," my mother said. "He was all for it. Eileen was the one who kept saying she wanted to have her own."

It was my turn to look puzzled. In that moment I began to question

everything I thought I knew about my sister. I remembered talking with
Eileen about adoption and commiserating with her about Vic's obsti-
nance. But she had obviously lied to me. Mom talked to Vic's mother
on the phone every day, so she would have known the truth. Did Eileen
want me to think Vic was the bad guy in this disagreement? Or was she
afraid I'd try to talk her into doing something she didn't want to do?
My head was spinning, trying to make sense of it. What other lies had
she told me? Told herself? No doubt there were more lies and secrets
to uncover, contradictions that made her into someone I really didn't
know—a troubled woman alone in a room with a gun in her hand.

I asked my mother if Eileen had left a suicide note, just as I'd asked
Connie shortly after I learned of Eileen's death.

"I don't know," Mom said. "I didn't ask."

Why *not*? I wondered. Isn't that one of the first things people
want to know when there's been a suicide? I wanted *an explanation*. As
if my sister, so despondent she'd put the muzzle of a gun to her chest,
might have had the wherewithal to sit down with pen and paper and
tell us *why* she felt the need to take her own life, providing us with the
answers to all of our questions and absolving us of any blame—some
proof that she'd thought about us before sailing off to never-never
land.

I said, "So, it was the police who called to tell you she was dead?"

"Yes," Mom said. "Vic got on the line and tried to talk, but he was
too upset. The poor kid. He feels responsible. I could barely talk myself."

"So where did she do it?"

"In their house. Vic tried to help her. He called an ambulance and
they took her to the hospital, but they couldn't stop the bleeding."

When my mother told me Eileen had shot herself in the heart, I
had assumed that she died instantly. Now I wondered how long she
had lived. Did she pull the trigger, then change her mind and cry for
help? Eileen died in the middle of the afternoon. Had she left work

early or called in sick? I wanted a timeline, some way to understand how Eileen had gotten to that point of no return, a moment when she felt like death was the only way out.

"Let me get this straight," I said. "She shot herself, but she didn't die right away, and Vic came home and found her?"

"No," Mom said. "He was *there*."

"Where?"

"In the house. He was in another room when it happened. He ran in and she was kneeling on the floor." Mom crushed her cigarette in the ashtray and reached for another. My father was lost in thought, his eyes staring at something that wasn't there.

I was dumbfounded. "But Mom? How do we know *Vic* didn't shoot her?"

Her face collapsed. From what I could tell, the idea had not occurred to her or my dad. They looked confused and appalled, but mostly they looked weary and very old.

In a soft voice Dad said, "You mean you think Vic . . . ?" He couldn't say the rest out loud.

"It's *possible*," I said, my disbelief suddenly morphing into suspicion. In my mind, Vic's presence in the house changed everything.

"No," Mom said. "He'd never . . ." She shut her eyes for a moment and shook her head, trying to expel some ghastly image. "I can't *believe* that. Vic worshipped the ground she walked on."

"So, you can't believe Vic could have shot her, but you *can* believe Eileen killed herself?"

Mom looked hurt and confused by my question. I was challenging her, making her think the unthinkable.

"The police came to the house right away, Jim," my father said. "They know what they're doing."

"But Vic's a *cop*, Dad." I set my jaw. "They're his friends. They're gonna believe whatever he tells them."

He nodded dejectedly. "I see what you mean."

We sat in silence, mulling over the possibility, cowed by the enormity of the situation, bewildered by the implications. If Vic shot Eileen, it would answer one set of questions but leave other questions in its wake. We didn't want the complications of murder. We wanted Eileen back.

Mom said, "Maybe you better talk to him, Jim."

"Talk to Vic?" The knot in my throat was so tight I could barely speak.

She nodded and took a puff on her cigarette. "You know him. You'll know if he's telling the truth."

7

THE CONVERSATION with my parents circled back to Eileen's depression and her separation from Vic. I was still hurt by the fact that she hadn't told me how badly she was struggling.

"I think she was embarrassed about it," Mom said. "Like she was a failure or something."

I said, "Whose idea was it, hers or Vic's?"

"Oh, hers, definitely. She said she just wasn't happy, but she didn't know why."

I asked them when they had last spoken to her.

"It was about ten days ago," my father said. "She called from a hotel room. I don't know where she was. Somewhere out in the desert, I think. Her voice was just so *empty*. I told her, why don't you just come home to Pittsburgh, sweetheart? I'll send you money for the ticket. But she said no, she wanted to work things out for herself."

Mom said, "What about you, Jim? When was the last time you talked to her?"

"About three weeks ago when I was up at Keith's. She sounded fine. Wanted to hear all about Meg."

My parents nodded grimly. They knew all about my visit with Keith. Over the past few years my brother's drinking had spiraled out of control and he had become increasingly violent. My parents and Connie and I would get hysterical late-night calls from his wife, Alide—Keith had blackened her eye, broken her nose, torn a fistful of hair from her head. Once she had found him passed out, slumped over the steering wheel of his car in the driveway, a cigarette burning between his fingers.

The previous summer Keith had gone to California on a business trip and stayed with Eileen and Vic. While he was there, he got arrested for a DUI driving a rental car. Shortly thereafter Connie and I received a letter from Eileen. The letter was dated August 11, 1973, thirteen months to the day before she died. In the first part of the letter, she talked about the golf lessons she and Vic were taking and how badly she played. She wrote with an ingenuousness that was both refreshing and oddly childlike. She'd scratch out a word and write "oops" in parentheses, put "HaHa" next to her jokes. Turning to the subject of Keith, she said she and Vic wished that "he'd straighten up." She told me she was grateful that Alide had been able to confide in Connie and me. Then she said, "I told Mom it's a shame that we can't coach Eddie [Keith's thirteen-year-old stepson] to take a frying pan & knock Keith out cold when he starts on Alide."

I remembered thinking there was something utterly ridiculous about Eileen's suggestion. It's the kind of thing you see in the movies or in a cartoon—a boy whacks his father with a frying pan and somehow that solves the problem. But in reality the aftermath of such violence would no doubt be horrific.

We had hoped that the arrest and stiff fine for the DUI would help Keith get control of the situation, but things only got worse. By the following summer the calls from Alide had become more frequent and more frantic, his anger and violence continuing unabated. One night, in a drunken rage, he had awakened the four children—ages six to thirteen—and gathered them in the living room, ranting about how there were going to be some changes around the house. At one point, he grabbed the family cat by the scruff of the neck and threatened to kill it in front of his terrified children. My parents offered to send Alide what little money they had so she could leave him, but Alide could not bring herself to make the break. I wanted to intervene, and the only thing I could think to do was to go see my brother and try to talk him into getting some help.

When I was a kid, Keith had been my idol. It was he, rather than my father, who had played catch with me, and he'd let me join in baseball and touch football games with his friends, always making sure I was on his team. If anyone bullied me, his revenge was swift and brutal. We worked the paper route together. He took me to see the Pirates at Forbes Field, seventeen cartoons at Garden Theater on Saturday mornings. The first time he came home on leave from the Air Force, I wept with joy. I was fifteen at the time, proud of the fact that I had grown nearly as tall as he in the year he'd been away, but the moment I saw him I began sobbing like a little boy. I held him in such awe then. Now I was mortified by the turn his life had taken.

When I told Connie about my plan to go see Keith unannounced and confront him about his drinking, she was skeptical. She worried that my plan might backfire and Keith would hurt Alide even more once he realized how much she'd been telling us.

Her words made me pause, but I pressed on. I felt like I had to try to do *something* before my brother ended up in jail. Or dead.

I got to Kingston about twelve thirty on a Saturday afternoon. When Keith saw me, he did a double take.

"Just passing through," I told him. But he knew something was up.

We went to a bar and played knock rummy with his pals for a nickel a point. Keith introduced me to everyone, proudly announcing that I had gone to Harvard and was working on my PhD.

"He got the brains in the family," he said with a chuckle. "I got the looks."

By the time we got into a booth to talk, he'd had three or four shots with beer chasers. When I broached the subject of his drinking, Keith told me smugly that he didn't have a problem and never missed a day's work.

"Great," I said, rolling my eyes, frustrated by his unwillingness to admit to his problems. "But what about the rest of it? You get drunk driving tickets. You beat up Alide. You can't smack your wife around just because you're pissed off at the world."

"I'm not pissed off at the world. Just her."

"So you *hit* her?"

"It's one of the options." He gave me a disdainful grin. "Unless you're pussy-whipped and just stand there like a wimp."

"That's bullshit."

"Look, she *asks* for it. She knows what I'm like, but she can't keep her fucking mouth shut. Just keeps yapping and yapping till she gets what she wants." He clenched his fist.

"Nobody wants a black eye."

"Yeah, well, it's not like she's some victim. You know that Rolling Stones song? 'You can't always get what you want.' I'm telling you, Jim, she gets what she *needs*." He grinned, pleased with his repugnant analogy, and held up his empty bottle. "How 'bout another beer?"

I said, "Daddy was a drunk, but at least he never hit Mom."

Keith scoffed. "Right."

"What?" I said. "You're saying he *did*?"

"Why don't you ask him? Better yet, ask *her*."

I didn't push back much at that point. Frankly, I was overwhelmed, disgusted by his casual brutishness, reeling over the possibility that he was just repeating history. I shuddered at the thought of my mother cowering in fear as my father came at her, another petty tyrant asserting his will.

Back at the house, Keith told Alide why I had come. She reacted angrily and told me to mind my own business.

"Fine," I said. "I'll keep out of it. But do me a favor, okay? The next time he beats the shit out of you, don't call my parents and don't call me."

Somewhere in the middle of all this Eileen phoned from California to say hi to Keith and his family, and she was surprised that I was there. In a low, guarded voice, I told her of my mission. She thanked me profusely for trying to help. The irony, of course, was that Eileen needed help even more than Keith did. Her suicide a few weeks later made that all too clear. But what I would *not* know for another twenty-seven years was that her own marriage had become so volatile that it would soon cost her her life.

When I left Keith and Alide's the next morning I was as anxious to leave as they were to be rid of me. Driving home, I kept thinking about what Keith had said about Alide asking for it, that the violence was something *she* needed. And what about my father and mother? I could remember my dad throwing me across the room, whipping Keith with a belt, punching Eileen when she was a little girl, but I had always been certain he'd never struck my mother. Yet how likely could that be, given his Vesuvian temper? Maybe this was what *I* needed to remember—or *not* remember. But to what end? How could I believe that my father, for all his volatility, would have never crossed that line when I had done so myself?

A few months before my surprise visit to Keith's, Connie and I had had a terrible row. It started as a fight about money. Connie's father and mother had loaned us five thousand dollars for the down payment on a house, but there were additional expenses to consider and our budget was extremely tight. As a graduate student, I got a monthly stipend from the GI Bill, which I supplemented by mowing lawns, driving a taxicab, and filling an officer's billet with a Naval Reserve Unit in Philadelphia. Connie had spent the school year working part-time as a teacher's aide, looking after an emotionally disturbed child who was causing havoc in a third-grade classroom. Now she planned to take the summer off. She wanted us to go on a vacation and rent a place on the Jersey shore, but I said we couldn't afford it and she grew peevish. At the core of Connie's resentment was a feeling that our marriage was something less than she had bargained for, that there was a world of privileges and pleasures she had been expecting and was now being denied. Several of her college friends had husbands who had already moved up a few rungs on the corporate ladder while I, with my Harvard credentials, had seemingly pulled a bait and switch. Defensive and self-righteous, I told her I thought we were doing fine. We had plenty of food, we were buying a house, we had two functional cars and a healthy, happy child. What else mattered? Why keep score? We had more than enough.

To make my point, I brought up JD, a fellow Connie and I had known in the early days of our courtship. He'd worked as a carpenter, and he and I had played rugby together. I knew Connie had always admired him, a man who worked hard and didn't have much but was happy in his own skin. As I continued talking about him, I noticed a hesitation in Connie's voice, a guardedness I'd never heard, or never let myself hear, before. Then it dawned on me. JD had visited us in California once while I was in the Navy. He and Connie had gone horseback riding in the hills while I was off at work on the ship. That night, the three of us got stoned and stayed up late, talking and laughing. Now I felt a pain as sharp as a fish bone in my throat.

"You slept with him, didn't you?" I said. She dropped her eyes for a second and didn't deny it. I stood there not knowing what to do. Two thoughts kept running through my head—one was the image of Connie and JD fucking; the other was the fact that Connie and I were scheduled to sign the purchase-and-sale agreement on a house in two days.

"Say something," Connie said.

I swung my open hand and caught her flush on the cheek. She yelped and began to cry, and I took her in my arms. In that moment I'm not sure which feeling was worse, knowing she had been unfaithful or the shame I felt in having struck her.

Connie and I never talked about that ignominious moment. I believed that our transgressions—her infidelity and my slap—were an aberration, singular misdeeds to be forgiven or, at least, rationalized away. I did not think of myself as a hypocrite for chastising Keith for abusing his wife, but the difference between him and me was much smaller than I was willing to admit. Denial, blindness, call it what you will. It took me decades to see that there was a legacy of violence that had touched my brother and sister and me, erupting in each of our lives that summer.

Did my father ever hit my mother? Keith said all I had to do was ask. But I never did, preferring my truth to his. Years later, when I was finally ready to ask the question, they were all dead.

8

Mom started making spaghetti sauce for supper and asked me to go to the bakery to get a loaf of bread. I took Meg with me, carrying her on my shoulders; on the way we ran into Mrs. Stackline, who lived next door to Mum. When she saw me, she gave me a big smile, which quickly fell away as she remembered the news about Eileen—as if a smile might be inappropriate.

"Oh, Jimmy, I *heard*," she said, her fingertips touching her cheek in dismay. "I'm so sorry."

"Thank you." For a moment I wondered if this was the proper response or if there was another, still-unlearned phrase with which to accept someone's sympathy.

When I introduced Meg, she thought I said Mae, my mother's name, and I didn't bother to correct her.

"She's *so-o-o* cute," Mrs. Stackline said. "She looks so much like Eileen."

"A lot of people say that. It's the brown eyes, I guess."

"Yes, and that sweet, round face. Same as you, Jimmy. When you and Eileen were little, you practically looked like twins." Mrs. Stackline glanced down at her feet, then back up again.

"How are your parents holding up?"

I shrugged one shoulder. "Still in shock. We all are."

"It's so tragic. I can't imagine what they're going through. Was it sudden?"

It was an odd question. "What did Mum tell you?"

"Cancer. I saw her in the backyard this morning and she told me Eileen had passed away. She was too upset to talk about it."

My face flushed with anger. The lie was typical of my grandmother.

"Eileen didn't have cancer. She shot—" I caught myself, suddenly remembering that I had Meg on my shoulders. I made a finger pistol and pointed it discreetly at my chest.

"Oh dear. Oh my Lord!" Mrs. Stackline put her hand on my arm. "Don't worry, Jimmy, I won't tell anyone."

"That's all right. There's no shame in it. We're just sorry she's gone."

"Yes, no. No shame at all."

I couldn't tell if she meant it or was just trying to convince herself. Suicide clearly carried a stigma in some people's minds. It had never occurred to me *not* to tell the truth, and my parents had not suggested it either, as if we knew without saying it that a lie that was too big to contain could only lead to a different kind of shame. But this was not our story alone, and I wondered if Vic and his family would also settle on some lie they'd want everyone to tell.

After supper my father and I went to the airport to pick up Keith. As we drove down the parkway, I could see how much Dad missed being out on the road. He used to put twenty thousand miles a year on his truck as a dry cleaner. Now he was a doorman at the Stanley Theater downtown, the same job I'd had in high school, and walked to work or took the bus. We didn't talk much, lost in our own thoughts and grief. At one point he started singing softly, "My funny valentine, sweet comic valentine," and I glanced at him and smiled. My father's father died in 1954, the first death of anyone close to me. One evening on the way to the funeral home I was riding in my father's truck, just the two of us, and Dad began to sing. He had a deep voice that was rarely in tune. Most of the time I don't think he was even aware that he was singing. For him, it was almost like breathing, but that evening it seemed strange and irreverent to me. In the few days since my grandfather died, I had been trying to act as solemn as possible, hands and eyes squeezed tight when I said my bedtime prayers, trying never to smile or look happy, not even when my great-aunt Marie gave me a dollar at the funeral home. Curiosity got the best of me, and I said, "Daddy, why are you singing?" He turned and looked at me as if he hadn't remembered I was there. Then he smiled sadly, an ocean of love in his eyes, and said, "I'm singing because my father died." I was just a boy, but I knew exactly what he meant—*Everybody mourns in his own way, son. Don't judge me on mine.*

We got to the airport early. I parked the car and we went inside to wait for Keith at the gate. As the passengers from his flight began to come off the plane, I felt uneasy. I hadn't seen or spoken to him since my surprise visit to his home a month before and wondered if he would still be angry with me.

Keith came off the plane, put his bag down, and lit a cigarette. When he saw Dad and me, he smiled. We went over and shook hands with him and I took his bag. As we walked down the corridor, Keith gave me a soft kick in the butt, his way of showing me that he bore no resentment for the things I'd said to him a month ago. If any hard feelings remained, they were mine.

On the drive home none of us had much to say. Later in the evening I pulled Keith aside and told him what I'd learned about Eileen's death.

Keith stared at me and shook his head. "It's hard to imagine."

"Which part?"

"The whole scene. Little Miss Sunshine in the middle of that psychodrama." There was a smirk on his face, a touch of disdain in his voice as if to say, *See, everybody's fucked-up, even a Goody Two-shoes like Eileen.*

"Did you know she and Vic were separated?"

"No."

"Neither did I. It all seems so crazy with Vic being in the house when it happened." I told him about my conversation with our parents and Mom saying I should talk to Vic.

"Yeah, somebody needs to talk to him. You want me there too?"

"No, that's okay. I think he'll feel less threatened if it's just me. Maybe he'll open up more. If we're both there, it'll look like an interrogation."

Keith gave me a shrug. Time to move on to something else.

I lay awake that night, wondering why he had given in so easily. We were dealing with the last days of our sister's life. There must have been questions he wanted to ask. Perhaps he was still harboring a grudge at me for coming to his home and chastising him for beating his wife. Or maybe I was the one with the grudge? Did I really believe that Vic would reveal more if I talked to him myself? Or did I relish the notion that it was my responsibility and my mother had chosen *me*? Whatever the reason, Keith wouldn't be joining me and I would be talking to Vic alone.

9

In the morning Keith and I walked down to the florist on East Ohio Street and ordered a funeral basket with a ribbon that said "SIS-TER" and another that said "AUNT." On the way home Keith asked me if I ever went golfing and I said no, I'd gone only a few times when I was a teenager. He suggested we find a driving range—they'd have clubs we could borrow.

It seemed like a selfish, irreverent thing to do, but we were both anxious to escape the gloom at home and we knew our parents wouldn't object. Keith and I drove out to the range near North Park and got two buckets of balls. By the time we were finished I had blisters on my hands; still, it relieved some of my tension and helped me feel closer to Keith again.

Shortly after we got home from the driving range, Vic arrived. He came in the door with his head bowed and his shoulders slumped.

"Hi, Mrs. T," he said to my mother.

"Oh, Vic." She opened her arms and embraced him.

My father and brother and I each shook his hand. His face looked haggard, his eyes hollowed with sadness. Connie said hello and introduced him to Meg. There weren't enough chairs in the living room, so I sat cross-legged on the rug with Meg on my lap. We asked Vic about his flight, asked after his mother and brothers. There was an eight-by-ten framed photograph of Eileen and her dog, Cal, sitting on the harvest table in front of us, but no one cried or mentioned her name. We were awkward and hesitant with one another like survivors of a shipwreck, uncertain why we were the only ones left alive, not knowing where we were or how we were going to get through this. Mom brought some food into the living room from the kitchen, but no one was hungry. Time dragged on. My father asked Vic about the dogs.

Choking up, Vic said. "Topi's fine, but Cal keeps *looking* for her."

We all got tears in our eyes, as if the dog gave us permission to miss her too.

Keith said he had to run some errands, which was a euphemism for going to a bar. Connie took Meg to the playground. My father asked Vic about the visiting hours at the funeral home and he gave us the details.

"You can go early if you want," he said. "You know, to be alone with her."

"Yes, I'd like that," Dad said. He got a handkerchief from his pocket and took off his glasses and started cleaning the lenses, rubbing them over and over. My father was slow and methodical in almost everything he did; now he clung to his rituals more than ever, trying to keep his whole world from spinning out of control.

"Vic?" my mother said hesitantly, trying to be gentle with him. "Jim has some questions for you. Some things he wants to talk about."

Vic's body slumped, a look of resignation on his face, as if this were something he had been expecting; then he nodded. He and I stood up, and he followed me out to the kitchen.

I closed the door behind us. The window was half-open; we could hear two men outside by the gasoline pumps talking about the Steelers.

I asked Vic if he wanted something to drink.

He shook his head, then said, "Maybe some water."

I got ice from the refrigerator and filled two glasses, then sat back down at the kitchen table, across from him. The conversation of the men outside the window drifted away, and for a minute we made small talk about football, which we both would have gladly continued without ever mentioning Eileen. But it was time.

"So how you holding up?"

Vic shrugged. "Okay. I don't think I've had more than two or three hours' sleep since . . ." His eyes drifted away from mine. "I keep hoping I'll wake up and everything will be different."

"Vic, I don't have any agenda here. I'm just trying to find out what happened. This whole thing was a total shock to me. I didn't even know you two were separated."

"Yeah, since the beginning of summer. We just got back together."

"I thought you two were crazy about one another."

He smiled sadly. "Me too." He took a sip of water. "I guess our problems go back to last winter, after Eileen had the miscarriage. She wanted to buy a new house, which was fine with me. I'm thinking we can move to a better neighborhood. Have more room, get a garage. Yard for the dogs. We started looking at places and found a few we liked." He paused. "Next thing I know she says she wants to hold on to our old house and rent it out. She talked to some guy in her office who owns six or seven houses, and he convinced her it was a sure thing. Retire at fifty if you want and live off the income. But I was skeptical. I didn't want to carry two mortgages. Plus, I wasn't too keen on being a landlord, worrying about the tenants not paying their rent, somebody calling me up in the middle of a ballgame to come fix his toilet. I guess I still think of myself as a street kid from the North Side and the whole real estate thing . . . that's just not *me*. But Eileen wouldn't let it go. You know how stubborn she could be. She had the numbers all laid out on a spreadsheet. Rental income, expenses, interest rates. Told me she had a friend who would be a perfect tenant. She finally wore me down, man. I just figured, hey, she's smarter than me. I said my piece. Either it's gonna work or it isn't."

He took another a sip of water.

"I really liked the new house after we moved in. Great place, bad timing. Me and Eileen were both swamped at work. I had gone under-cover, which was nights mostly. Nothing heavy-duty, but long hours. One evening we went out to dinner with friends and it seemed like Eileen was a million miles away. Plus, she lost a lot of weight. One time I gave her a hug and her whole body was tight as a guitar string. Nothing but skin and bones. She started getting rashes. I could see how unhappy she was. She wasn't picking on me, she was just . . . *distant*. Moody. I kept asking her what was wrong, but she wouldn't talk about it. After a while she told me the problem was us, we didn't *connect* anymore. I tried to get her to be more specific, but it was all this vague stuff, like: We're so *different*. We've grown apart. We don't have anything in common anymore. Bullshit like that."

There was a touch of spite in his voice, putting all the blame on Eileen. I drank some water, determined not to fill in the silence or take sides. I wasn't being coy. I just wanted to hear more before I asked any questions.

Vic said he thought the problems might have something to do with her job. Back in March, Eileen had taken a different position with the school system—a promotion of sorts with more responsibility, but without a pay raise. She really liked her boss, and Vic suspected she had a crush on him. When he brought it up, Eileen became so defensive Vic figured it must be true.

He went on. "At the end of May she said she wanted a trial separa-tion. I didn't want to do it, but I was worn-out, man. I felt like I was drowning. I figured maybe it would do some good if we spent some time apart."

As I listened, I thought about the last time I'd seen him and Eileen in San Bernardino, married four years and still giddy with love. I tried my best to hold on to that thought—but lurking behind that memory was the feeling I'd had since they first started dating—that Vic was too ordinary for Eileen and sooner or later she would want something more. Which, I assumed, was exactly what happened. Vic was Vic, stalwart, devoted, boring. Eileen couldn't say it out loud, but Vic was no longer enough.

"So you moved out?" I asked.

"Yeah, I went to stay with a buddy, a guy I knew from the Air Force."

"Did you and Eileen see each other much?"

"Off and on. We'd talk on the phone. Once in a while we'd go out to eat or something. We had a couple of real good times, like we were on a date. Then I'd call her the next day and it was back to square one. She couldn't wait to get me off the phone. In early August we had a big blowout. I got off work on a Saturday night and went over to the house to see her. She wasn't home and I figured I'd wait. I fell asleep in my car on the street outside the house. Eileen didn't come home until early Sunday morning and said she'd been with this salesman she knew from work. She claimed nothing happened between them; they were just out real late and she slept on his couch because she was too tired to drive home. I told her I thought the separation was supposed to be about us trying to work out our problems, not her sleeping around with other guys. She accused me of spying on her, saying I didn't trust her, and I said, Why *would* I trust you? We were screaming at each other, both of us crying. It got real ugly."

"Did you hit her?"

"I just grabbed her by the arms and shook her real hard." Vic's eyes and voice were filled with regret. "I was so *hurt* and angry. Just trying to find some way to get through to her."

How could I condemn Vic? A month before, I had slapped Connie and condoned it in my own mind as an acceptable action for a man whose wife had cheated on him. The feeling I had at this moment was one of empathy with Vic, so much so that I assumed, as he did, that Eileen was lying when she said that nothing had happened between her and the salesman.

"I know it was wrong," Vic said. "I told her how sorry I was. Funny thing is, in a way that argument seemed to help. A big jolt that made us both see how bad things had gotten." (His rationalization wasn't much different from the one I'd used myself—a slap that served as a catalyst for reconciliation. Something we both *needed*, as Keith would say.) "The next day," he said, "we started talking about getting back together. We went to see a marriage counselor and tried to sort things out. Then we decided to go to Vegas, just to get away for a night. You know how much Eileen loved to play blackjack." He smiled for a second at the memory.

"When was this?"

"Saturday, Labor Day weekend."

"Okay." I wanted to make sure I had the timeline right. Eileen died on a Wednesday, eleven days later.

"While we were in Vegas, Eileen got moody a couple of times, then she'd catch herself and snap out of it. By the time we left, everything seemed good. Then on the drive home she asked me to pull over— there were some things she needed to say. We were in the middle of the desert. I could feel my heart pounding—like I knew my life was about to change, but I didn't know how. Eileen asked me not to say anything until she was finished. She said she'd been doing a lot of soul-searching, trying real hard to be honest with herself and figure out how things had gone wrong. She was sorry for the way she'd been treating me, she kept pushing me away and didn't know why. She hoped I could forgive her." He stopped for a moment, refocusing his attention on me.

"I won't lie to you, Jim, it meant a lot to me hearing her say that. I felt like *she* was the one who went off the rails. I was just laying low, keeping my head down. She told me she was tired of being tired all the time, tired of being unhappy. She said she was thinking about quitting her job, which really floored me. That was the last thing I expected her to say. I was still trying to process that when she tells me she wants me to come home—move back in—and we can sign the adoption papers and start a family. I can still remember that look in her eyes. She was so full of *hope*, man. I was too. My whole body shaking. I just put my arms around her and we both broke down and cried."

I nodded compassionately. It was heartbreaking to think of all that hope, tragedy just around the corner.

Vic and Eileen kept talking that week and she said she was definitely going to quit her job. He told her he thought it was a good decision. He felt like she needed a break and he still had suspicions about her relationship with her boss. To Vic it seemed as if a big weight had been lifted off her shoulders. Eileen said she wanted to spend some time decorating their new house and she was going to offer to babysit for a friend, who was divorced and had custody of his two-year-old son. Vic moved back into the house and they went to see the marriage counselor.

"He told us we needed to get everything out in the open, all our dirty laundry—that if we had anything to confess, now was the time to do it. Eileen said she had nothing to hide. She knew how jealous I was, but she swore she had not been sleeping around, she had always been faithful. She said she flirted sometimes and went out on a few dates, but that was it."

"Did you believe her?"

Vic shrugged one shoulder. "I *wanted* to. It didn't fit with all the stuff that had been going on, but she kept insisting."

Vic went to work around ten o'clock Tuesday night, then came home in the early morning and took a nap. When he woke up, Eileen told him her conscience had been bothering her. She said she hadn't been telling the truth. She had slept with her boss.

"She said it only happened one time. That she went to a campground with him and he got her drunk. I flew into a rage. I was yelling, swearing, throwing stuff around the room. Bad as it was, in one way it was almost a relief to have her admit it. At least I knew I wasn't crazy and all my suspicions weren't something I'd just dreamed up in my head."

He was talking fast, more urgency in his voice than anger, as if he were afraid he wouldn't be able to start again if he stopped. "I was actually more mad at *him* than her. I tried to call him at his office but he wasn't in. We were in the bedroom. Eileen and I kept talking, and after a while she admitted that it had been a full-blown affair. She had all this guilt built up inside of her and everything started pouring out. She told me what they did, all the places they made love. I asked her if they had done it right there, in our bed. She said yes, and it felt like someone stuck a hot knife in my gut. I told her I couldn't live with her anymore and Eileen said she knew it. She ran into the bathroom and started swallowing a bunch of pills. I went in and grabbed her throat and made her spit them out."

I closed my eyes for a second, trying to dispel the image. Poor Eileen, so utterly distraught and exposed. So ashamed. "What kind of pills?"

"Aspirin. I don't know how many she actually swallowed. Not enough to really hurt her. She was completely hysterical, thrashing around, screaming at the top of her lungs. I never saw her like that before. I made her sit on the bed and got her calmed down and we kept talking. I asked her if she had told me everything and she said, 'Yes, isn't that enough?'"

Vic ran his fingertips lightly across his lips. "Eileen said she hated herself for hurting me and ruining our marriage. She said she wished she was dead. I put my arms around her and said I still loved her. I told her it's like the counselor said, you can't solve your problems unless you get everything out in the open. I said I thought we could still work things out. She didn't believe me at first, but I just kept saying it over and over. It seemed like everything was under control, but she was still shaky. Then I told her I needed to call someone. I figured if I could just have a nice, normal conversation, everything would be fine, and the first person I thought of was Mrs. T. When I told Eileen I was going to call her, she said, 'No, Vic, don't, please don't tell my mother.'

She was pleading with me, getting hysterical again. I said I wasn't going to tell your mom about the affair; I just needed to talk to someone. The phone was right there next to the bed. I tried to dial but I was so upset I couldn't remember the number. I probably called that number a hundred times, but I got all mixed up. I asked Eileen for the number, but she kept shaking her head, begging me not to call. I said, 'Look, I'm not going to tattle, okay? I just need to talk to someone. Just tell me the phone number.' But she wouldn't do it. Finally, I said, 'Fine, I'll just go in the den and get the address book.'"

He shook his head.

"I went to the den to look up the number. There was a phone right there in the other room. When I picked it up and started to dial, Eileen shouted, 'Vic!' Then I heard a shot. I ran back to the bedroom and she was on her knees. There was a dark spot on the front of her blouse. I called 911 and started doing CPR on her. The ambulance got there real fast, but . . . ." His eyes filled with tears and he looked straight at me.

I was leaning forward in my chair, forearms on the table, a trickle of sweat running down my neck. I pictured Eileen with a look of surprise on her face, blood starting to bubble from her chest. A car horn outside and startled us both. Someone at the gas pump called out to the attendant.

I said, "Was she conscious after she shot herself?"

"No."

"How long did she live?"

"About an hour. The bullet tore her up inside. She died on the operating table."

"Did she use your service revolver?"

"No, another one. A .357 Magnum with .38 bullets." He had a rueful look on his face. "Those guns are made to kill people, Jim." There was something about the way he said it that had a ring of unqualified truth. I did not believe it could have come from the mouth of a murderer.

Vic said they kept the gun in the house for Eileen's protection. But it was unloaded and had been in a case on a high shelf in the closet.

"I don't know how she could have gotten it down and loaded it so fast. I couldn't have been out of the room for more than thirty seconds."

"Did you go to the hospital in the ambulance with her?"

"No, I was home . . . with the police. They questioned me and I told them everything. I went crazy when the call came from the hospital saying she was dead. I was glad they were there with me. I don't know what I would have done if I had been by myself."

Vic was puddled in the chair, exhausted. I sat there considering the story he had told me, not looking for contradictions but simply trying to absorb it. I kept thinking how Eileen had screamed out his name just before she pulled the trigger—the last word she ever spoke.

"I can't understand why Eileen didn't want you to call my mother," I said. "Even if you *had* told her about the affair, Mom would have understood."

"Yeah, Mrs. T has a great outlook on things. She makes everyone around her feel so calm. That's why I wanted to call her. My head was pounding so hard I thought it was going to explode. I kept thinking everything would be okay if I could just talk to her."

Vic's voice was filled with regret, but he did not seem guilty or defensive. To me, it sounded like he had made what he thought was a good decision in a moment of crisis and it turned out to be the wrong one. I did not presume to second-guess him. I knew he had already been through the what-ifs in his own mind a hundred times over.

"How often did you go see the marriage counselor?" I said.

"Twice, I think. Maybe three times."

"And Eileen never said anything about her affair?"

"Nothing. When the counselor asked her about that sort of thing, she got all tearful and acted like she was being unjustly accused." There was an edge to his words. "She hated dealing with anything unpleasant, anything that made her feel uncomfortable. If a cashier in a store gave her the wrong change, Eileen couldn't look them in the eye and tell them they made a mistake. She'd just turn around and walk out the door."

"*Really?*" I said, a bit puzzled. The Eileen I knew was feisty and had no trouble standing up for herself.

"Thing is, she wanted everything to be *perfect*. Perfect wife, perfect employee, perfect friend. I think that's one reason why the miscarriages were so hard on her, like they were a personal failure, a black mark on her character or something."

"So she didn't want to adopt a baby?"

"No. That was fine for other couples. She said we had to have our own." His bitterness was palpable. "It was like pulling teeth to get her to talk about our problems. She never wanted to confront *anything*. She didn't even want to tell your parents we were separated, but I said it wouldn't be right, lying to them all the time, making up excuses about why I wasn't there when they called the house. Plus, my mom knew, and I didn't want her to have to lie to Mrs. T."

"Did your friends out there know about the problems you two were having?"

"Not really. Except the guy I was living with, of course. But Eileen? I don't think she told anyone."

"I don't understand why she had to keep everything a secret."

"I don't either. She kept everything bottled up inside. When she finally told me all that stuff about her boss, the way it all came out pouring out, it was almost like she was finally admitting it to *herself*."

"Maybe she was just starting to come to grips with what she'd done?"

"Yeah," Vic said, his face filled with regret. "That's why Eileen didn't want me to call Mrs. T. She didn't want her mother to find out she'd been a bad girl."

Vic and I looked at each other and shook our heads. There was nothing left to say.

After he left, I related Vic's story to my parents and Keith and Connie. They listened carefully, trying to understand, but there was no skepticism. Asking for more clarification would have cast doubt on Vic's story, suggesting that it was insufficient and, perhaps, not entirely true. No one was ready to deal with that possibility. Vic was one of *us*—bereft, disoriented, struggling to make it through the day. It was easy to believe his story. The hard part was believing Eileen was dead.

10

Brady funeral home was a ten-minute walk from our apartment, one block west of Latimer Junior High, where my siblings and I went to school, one block south of Allegheny General Hospital, where we were all born. My parents and Keith and I arrived a half hour before regular viewing hours began. The funeral director greeted us in the foyer. We introduced ourselves and he told us he was sorry for our loss.

"Would you like to see Eileen now?" he said. I liked hearing him use her name.

"Please," my mother said.

He pushed open double pocket doors. The casket was on the far side of the dimly lit room. There were three tall stands of candles in red glass containers and at least two dozen baskets of flowers, the cloying smell so strong I thought I would gag. As we approached the casket my dad let out a heart-wrenching moan and I grabbed his elbow to steady him. Eileen was wearing a pink dress with black onyx rosary beads in her crossed hands.

"Oh, she looks so *pretty*," Mom said, then bent over the coffin and gave her a kiss. And I found myself thinking, *No she doesn't. She looks dead.* Horribly, maddeningly, irredeemably dead.

Vic and his family arrived a few minutes after we did and we exchanged hugs and handshakes and tried to offer one another solace. Mom had told me that when she first spoke with Vic's mother, Mrs. Z had said, "Well, I guess this is the end of our friendship," and Mom said, "No. Whatever went on between Vic and Eileen was their business. You and I will always be friends."

Our extended family and other mourners began to arrive. People were solemn and compassionate, some weeping openly. They said, "She was so young!" "She was always smiling." "I can't believe she's gone." Several well-meaning souls tried to assure me that Eileen was in a better place now. The *how* of Eileen's death did not come up often, but when it did, I simply told people that she had been depressed and took her own life.

The next few days of mourning were a blur, and I began to wish there were a formalized ritual for these occasions—some sort of call-and-response—the same words and gestures repeated over and over, no one having to think about what we said.

Sometimes during the lulls I would stand by the coffin and stare down at Eileen. I had never touched a corpse and the idea revulsed me, but it wasn't hard with her. I brushed my hand over her hair and ran my fingertips lightly across her cheek. Her skin was cold and thin and dry like the felt top on an old pool table, her body hard as slate underneath. In life she was always talking, laughing; now her mouth seemed too serious. Too grim. At one point I took her hand and discovered the boneless web between her thumb and forefinger, that prehensile curve. The flesh there still had a little elasticity, a little *give*, and I began to massage it gently, trying to make myself believe that Eileen knew I was holding her hand.

When we gathered on the morning of the funeral, Vic went up to Eileen's coffin first. He knelt down and prayed, then staggered, sobbing, as he tried to rise to his feet, and his twin brothers rushed forward to support him. One by one we approached the coffin, first my parents, then Keith, then me.

"Goodbye, little sister," I said. I bent down and kissed Eileen on the forehead. The kiss left a cool, waxy film on my lips, but I didn't wipe it off.

As the pallbearers were lining up, Keith hurried back to the viewing room. When he returned, he said to me, "I saw you kiss her goodbye. I didn't want them to close the casket and regret that I didn't."

My mother was right; the Catholic Church did not banish Eileen for being a suicide. The funeral was held in the same church where she and Vic had been married. All through the mass and later at the cemetery, the words the priest spoke seemed utterly rote, Eileen's name filling in the blanks in a leaden, generic ceremony. I found myself wondering why he didn't say something about the real Eileen, that vibrant, happy girl we remembered. I wanted to speak up as we stood by the grave, but I didn't. No one did. Maybe the *way* she died had shocked us into silence, making us disbelieve our memories, at least for the moment, as if no one was quite certain who she had been. I placed a flower on top of her casket and walked back toward the cars.

As we were milling around, waiting to leave the cemetery, I overheard an exchange between my father and one of his old drinking buddies.

"Hang in there, George," the man said. "Call me if you feel like talking."

"Thanks," Dad said.

"I mean it. Don't be a stranger," his old friend said kindly. "Things will probably get worse before they get better."

My father nodded. "Spoken like a true optimist."

Dad's friend looked puzzled, but I understood what my father meant. Only an optimist would believe that things would *ever* get better.

• • •

Friends and family gathered at my parents' apartment after the funeral. When the guests had gone in the late afternoon, a friend took Keith to the airport, and Connie and I packed our bags for the long drive home. We took the luggage up the street and got Meg settled in the car, and I went back to the apartment one last time to say goodbye to my parents. Dad was sitting at the kitchen table with a sad, faraway look in his eyes, Mom standing by the sink, her face ashen, with a letter in her hands.

"This just came in the mail," she said.

It was an envelope with familiar blue-and-pink flowered edges, familiar handwriting. A letter from Eileen.

My mother handed me the envelope. "I'm afraid to open it."

The envelope was postmarked the day Eileen died. I took a knife from the drawer and slit it open. My feelings were a peculiar mix of anticipation and trepidation. I'd been longing for a suicide note, but now I wasn't sure if I wanted to read it. I unfolded the letter, a single page of lined notebook paper addressed to my mom and dad. Eileen said that the past three months had been "a nightmare," but she and Vic were back together. She told them she had quit her job the day before and would be watching the two-year-old child of a friend, which "will be good practice in helping me be a housewife." After thanking them for sending some photos of Meg, she says she often thinks about Keith and hopes he finds a way to straighten out his life. In closing, she thanks them for sticking by her and hopes these hard times will make her a better person. Most important, she realized, "*I still love Vic—after all of this—& that means a lot to me. I think it's taught me what a prize I have!*" The letter is signed with "Lots of Love" from her, Vic, and their two dogs.

I handed the letter to my mother. "It's okay, Mom," I said. "There's nothing terrible in here. It's just Eileen."

Mom read the letter, then looked up at me, a single tear running down the side of her nose. "Oh, Jim," she said. "She sounds so full of hope."

In the weeks and months that followed, I sometimes wished that I could talk to the people Eileen had known in California, if only to get a better understanding of her life and how it had all come undone. But this desire to talk to others was, at best, a vague longing, and I never attempted to call anyone. No one tried to encourage me or embarrass me into finding out more about Eileen's death—a testimony, I suppose, to the taboo that surrounds a suicide, the notion that this is a topic that is best kept secret and the less said the better. Or maybe it was a true measure of the height of the wall I had built around myself. People understood that the subject was inherently off-limits.

Still, I thought about Eileen often, and I was haunted by the letter. I asked my mother if I could have it, and she gave it to me without hesitation. From time to time, I'd take it out and read it. *I'd picture Eileen sitting at the kitchen table as she would at home, writing in a spiral notebook, one foot tucked up under her rump, the tip of her tongue protruding from the corner of her mouth in rapt concentration. Her pen moves quickly as the words come in a rush. She thinks she has it all worked out. She'll babysit the little boy and get "good practice" being a housewife. The morning sun slants through the window, glinting off the faucet of the sink in the new house, the house that was supposed to be part of her bright future. Her future with Vic. She wonders why she lost that focus. How did things go so wrong? Never mind. She won't let herself dwell on it. She's quit her job and put the affair with her boss behind her. She's had a bad summer, but everything is okay now. She pauses for a moment and taps the pen on her chin. The kitchen cabinets are well stocked, the canisters on the counter perfectly aligned. She stayed up late the night before, cleaning and polishing, making everything perfect now. She loves this house, loves her dogs. Loves Vic, her prize. She's put him through so much with her moods. Her infidelity and her deception. What made her think she needed something more than him? Did her boss seduce her or the other way round? It doesn't matter one way or the other. She's put all that behind her now. An audible click from the AC startles her and snaps her out of her reverie. She tears the pages from the spiral notebook, trims the ragged perforations with a pair of scissors. Folds the letter and puts it in the envelope and writes the address on the front. She can do this; she knows how to be happy. She catches her reflection in the window and practices a smile. It's a beautiful morning. Today is the first day of the rest of her life. She walks to the mailbox down the street and drops the letter in the slot. On the way home her feet start to feel sluggish; there's a sour aftertaste of coffee in her mouth. She's told her parents the nightmare is over, but she knows it isn't. Not until she tells Vic the truth.*

11

I FINISHED MY dissertation in the spring of 1977, a few months after my son, Brett, was born. The dissertation was a study of the works of Raymond Chandler, creator of Philip Marlowe, the quintessential wisecracking, hard-boiled detective. PhD in hand, I accepted an appointment with the English Department at the University of Miami and we moved to Coral Gables, Florida. At Miami I taught introductory courses in American literature and several electives of my own design, including History of the Detective Novel and Sports in Literature. I liked teaching but quickly realized I was not cut out for the publish-or-perish grind of academia. I was determined to strike out in an entirely new direction, but I was struggling to explain to myself (and to my patient, baffled wife) why, after I'd spent so much time pursuing a degree, I could turn around and junk it so easily.

As I was searching for a new career, I met a neighbor who had just started a business selling microprocessors to keep track of photocopies in professional firms. He needed someone to open the Atlanta market. I didn't have any business experience, and he didn't have any money to pay me, but we quickly negotiated a deal in which I would trade my first six months' salary for a small equity stake in the company. Connie and I moved to Atlanta. I bought two suits and a slab of rich brown cowhide along with some leather-making tools and fashioned my own briefcase. Our product filled a niche in the market, and I discovered I had a knack for sales.

It was a time of enormous changes. We had been in Atlanta for less than a year when my father died in August 1979. A month later our daughter Kelly was born. While all this was going on, I agreed to open a new branch of the company in Boston. In November, we left Atlanta in a two-car caravan and headed for New England, our third move in three years. Our lives had been so hectic; pregnancy and childbirth had restricted Connie's ability to travel, and she did not see the house we bought in the suburbs until the day we moved in. I worked tirelessly to build my business, which was flourishing, but I became involved in a disastrous love affair and my marriage fell apart.

Connie and I agreed on a custody arrangement in which the children spent half their nights with me and half with her. I'd drive to my old house after work, pack a bag of clean clothes for the kids, and take them to a fast-food restaurant. In the morning I'd deposit them at various locations on school days; on weekends we'd embark on a hubbub of activities—sports, birthday parties, sleepovers, numberless G- and PG-rated movies at the local cineplex. Much as I tried to be a good father, the divorce weighed heavily on me.

One winter evening, after driving home to my apartment in a snowstorm, I knew I had to find a way to rid myself of all the anger and self-loathing I felt over the failure of my marriage. That night I sat down at my kitchen table and began to write a letter to my kids. I did not attempt to justify what had happened or tell my side of the story, though I did acknowledge the guilt I felt over the breakup with their mother.

The writing proved to be good therapy, and I found I wanted to keep it going. I copied the letter into three journals with a stitched binding, one for each child—Meg, Brett, and Kelly—then began to write to them individually, chronicling their successes and failures, describing holidays and birthday parties, ruminating on my ideas about parenting, agonizing over the Red Sox. Although my entries dealt with what the children were doing at their current ages, I wrote to them as if they were adults. I wanted the journals to have the tenor and immediacy of a letter, so I did not go back and reread past entries for fear I would start editing and deleting them, trying to rewrite the past.

For much of my life I'd harbored a secret ambition to become a writer. I had a file folder filled with ideas for short stories—newspaper articles, characters names, opening paragraphs, a list of titles—but I'd never found the time, or the spunk, to follow through. Still, the journals for my children put a pen in my hand and got me into the habit of sitting at my desk. Then, in 1985—the year I turned forty—two things happened that would change the course of my life. The first was writing a short story called "The Spice of Life"; the other was meeting Elizabeth McCarthy, a divorcée with two boys. I wrote the story as a tribute to a friend who had recently died of AIDS—a way to help me cope with the loss. I sent it out to various magazines, collected a fistful of rejections slips, and put it away in a drawer. But the spark had been lit. Elizabeth and I met through a dating service called LunchDates and spent our first date at a sandwich shop in Boston, talking about Woody Allen movies. It didn't take long for us to fall in love.

A few years later I joined a workshop led by the esteemed short story writer Andre Dubus, and Elizabeth and I bought a rambling Victorian farmhouse where we were married with all five of our children participating in the ceremony. My biggest problem was finding time to write. The company I had helped to found was an unqualified success, and my salary and commissions seemed like a small fortune. In business it's called "golden handcuffs," those precious shackles that keep you from venturing away from the fold. But they are still handcuffs. A year later, with complete support from Elizabeth and a generous severance package from my business partners, I retired.

• • •

As the years passed, I remained open when it came to talking about Eileen's suicide. If the subject came up in conversation—someone's curiosity trumping the tendency to shy away from a topic that is intrinsically taboo—I would tell my pat, unreflective story with no more emotion than if I were reading an article from a newspaper. The feelings I had about Eileen's death came over me in rare, unguarded moments, like the time Elizabeth and I went to Pittsburgh to sort through the belongings in my mother's apartment.

Mom had declined rapidly after falling and breaking her hip and had gone to live in a nursing home. The apartment was clean and well organized. My mother was not a pack rat except when it came to us kids; she saved our drawings, letters to Santa Claus, school papers and awards. I went through drawer after drawer, separating out the things I wanted to keep for myself or give to Keith, discarding the rest in a large green trash bag.

"Look at this," I said to Elizabeth, holding out Eileen's elementary school report cards. "Straight As." The report cards were covered with gold stars, the teachers saying what a joy it was to have Eileen in their classes. "She was everybody's favorite." I took one last look at the report cards and tossed them into the trash bag. "But she blew it."

Elizabeth looked me, careful not to react.

"She should *be* here," I said, tight-lipped, seething.

I missed Eileen. I wanted her there with me, sitting on the floor, sifting through the keepsakes of her life and mine. I wanted us to laugh and tell stories, to remember our family and the children we used to be. The rental truck parked outside was slowly filling up with old furniture and mementos and unresolved emotions. This was the end of an era. When I closed the door of Mom's apartment at the end of the day, there would no longer be a place in Pittsburgh that I could come home to.

• • •

In the years after Eileen's death, weeks, even months, would roll by when she never crossed my mind. But I always remembered her birthday—February 4—and the date of her death. When my mother was still living, I would call her on those days and make small talk, pretending it was just an ordinary day, and wait for her to mention Eileen, hoping she might want to reminisce. Certain anniversary dates were more poignant than others, like the tenth anniversary of her death, her fortieth birthday.

Then an odd thing happened. With the start of the New Year in 2001, Eileen seemed to become a daily presence in my life. I began looking through boxes of old photographs and rereading the random letters and cards my mother and I had saved over the years—everything from a photo of Eileen and me as toddlers, holding hands on the sidewalk in front of the house on Wettach Street, to the letter she wrote the day she died. Now it almost seemed like she was beckoning me, daring me to write her story. I didn't try to analyze it. Didn't ask why. I simply plowed forward—boldly, foolishly—unaware of the truths and dangers that lay ahead.

The book I began writing was a novel narrated by the dead girl's brother. Like me, he had interviewed his brother-in-law immediately after his sister's death and accepted the idea that his sister had committed suicide. But, unlike me, the narrator was vexed by doubt. Did he really believe it was suicide? Or, he wondered, did he simply take the easy way out, too busy or lazy or cowardly to challenge his brother-in-law and the crooked police department, who may have let one of their fellow officers get away with murder? At some point I realized that my narrator would need to go to California and start digging around if he was ever going to find out the truth. I can remember exactly where I was when this thought came to me—riding my bicycle on a rolling road in Puerto Rico, a brown horse and its foal standing in the shade of an almond tree, the sturdy, white Rincón lighthouse posing for a postcard at the edge of the sea. As I began to pedal up a long, steep slope, I wondered how my protagonist would go about his search. Were police records available to the public? Would they even exist in a case this old? Should my narrator hire a private detective to help him? Then it dawned on me. It wasn't a character in my novel who needed to make this journey—I did.

Elizabeth smiled when I told her of my revelation. She had watched me try to write my way back to Eileen by telling stories, but she had known all along what I was only beginning to understand—that I had to be a part of this story, not some fictional narrator conjuring up characters he had never met.

It was time for me to confront Eileen's death head-on. Time to go back and answer that page on the public address system in the ballpark, a voice loud and clear calling my name.

PART
TWO

12

THE REVELATION I'd had on my bicycle in Puerto Rico did not immediately launch me into action. Back home in the States, I was still dawdling, not quite sure how to proceed, when I logged on to the Internet one day and typed "private investigators Los Angeles" into the search engine. Logistically, it would have made sense for me to look for a private investigator in San Bernardino, a city of nearly two hundred thousand people, which lies sixty miles east of LA, but I knew that many retired police officers eventually became private investigators, and I didn't want to run across anyone who might have known or worked with Vic. Not yet, anyway. (Besides, I was taken by the irony of the situation, searching for a PI in Marlowe's hometown to guide me along the way.)

I scanned the first twenty sites from my Google search, eventually landing on one for Darryl Carlson—Avatar Investigations in Century City on the Avenue of the Stars. The photograph showed a man in a pale-colored suit with a black briefcase in one hand, sunglasses in the other. He looked big and fit, with a halo of white hair and an easy, reassuring smile. The dates outlining his experience put him in his early sixties. He had started out as a policeman in Oregon, then spent ten years with the US Border Patrol before becoming a private eye. His write-up stated that he helped his clients prove their innocence, avoid unjust deportation, and recover lost property while maintaining their "integrity, credibility and ethics" and keeping them "centered through difficult times." *Perfect*, I thought. Marlowe with sensitivity training.

I printed out the web pages and dialed his phone number. He answered on the first ring.

I introduced myself, explaining that I wanted to find out more information about my sister's suicide in San Bernardino twenty-seven years ago. He asked me to tell him the story, and I gave him the five-minute version. With cautious follow-up questions he began probing to gauge whether I had a grudge against Vic or hoped to prove that he had murdered Eileen. I assured him that all I wanted to do was to find out more information and get some details for the novel I was writing.

"Where's your brother-in-law today?" Darryl asked. "Is he still on the police force?"

"I'm not sure," I said. "He remarried and had a kid, then quit the police sometime in the eighties to go into private security work. I haven't spoken to him myself since my sister's funeral."

"Not at *all*?" The way he said it sounded like an accusation, and I got a little defensive.

"No. I never really thought about it. I mean, we were never that close. His mother still lives in Pittsburgh and was best friends with my parents before they passed away. They saw each other all the time, spent the holidays together. She'd keep them updated on what Vic was doing and they'd tell me. I guess I wasn't that interested. Like I said, we were never close."

"But you have no reason to suspect him of foul play? Chest wounds are pretty rare in suicides."

"Not really. He looked me straight in the eye when he told me the story. He and Eileen were high school sweethearts. They were crazy about each other. If he killed her, even if it was an accident—the two of them struggling over the gun or something like that—I have a feeling his life has been a living hell. Waking up every morning with all that *guilt*, he's probably suffered more that way than if he'd gone to prison."

It must have sounded strange, but this wasn't the first time I'd said something like this. Whenever I talked about Eileen's death in the past, occasionally a listener would feel comfortable enough to play the devil's advocate and try to implicate Vic in her death. I didn't try to counter these arguments with protestations of Vic's innocence. My reply, like the one I gave Darryl, was simply to say that if Vic shot Eileen, I was certain that the regrets he had endured would be punishment enough. When I said it, it didn't *seem* like a rationalization—an excuse for my having accepted Vic's story at face value and not probing deeper—but I suppose it was. What I know now, of course, is that I had more doubts about Vic than I was willing to admit to a private investigator or anyone else. I didn't think I was lying when I told Darryl I didn't suspect Vic of foul play and simply wanted to get more information for my novel. But maybe I was lying to myself.

"I don't want to talk you out of a job," I said to Darryl, "but could I get the kind of documents I'm looking for on my own? Police reports, the coroner's report, the autopsy results, things like that?" It was a simple question, and Darryl seemed to welcome it.

"Sure, you could probably get a lot of it. But only a professional is going to see what's *not* there—all the stuff between the lines. Like a GSR, gunshot residue test. The police should have done one on your sister's hands to see if she fired a gun. If they didn't, that would raise a red flag for me, but you might not even notice it was missing."

I liked his answer. I wanted to trust him. His voice was gravelly and kind and put me at ease. He told me his fee was a hundred dollars an hour plus expenses—fifteen hundred up front—with the assurance that he didn't "keep a tight clock." I said I'd send him the retainer along with a letter detailing everything we'd discussed about Eileen, and he told me to be sure to include factual information such as exact names, dates of birth, the address where Eileen and Vic had been living when she died.

I hung up the phone and stared out the window into the backyard. It was twilight, the last day of March, a patch of snow lingering in the shady part of the lawn, a rafter of a dozen or more turkeys pecking at the grass.

Elizabeth came to the window and stood beside me. "You okay?"

I nodded. "It's really strange. I haven't even found out anything yet, but I feel like I've stepped across some invisible line and there's no turning back."

"Oh, Jim, you crossed that line a long time ago."

The packet of information I sent to Darryl included the information he asked for, along with a copy of the letter that Eileen wrote on the day she died and a sympathy letter written to my parents by one of Eileen's coworkers, Betty Clay. Betty was the only one of Eileen's friends in California whose name I knew and I was hoping Darryl could find her.

I had discovered Betty's letter when Elizabeth and I were cleaning out my mother's apartment. My parents had no doubt received a number of sympathy cards and letters, but this was the only one they'd saved. Betty said that she and Eileen had gotten close despite the difference in their ages (Eileen was the same age as Betty's oldest daughter) and the two of them had spent a great deal of time together that last summer. She told my parents that Eileen had been active in the Child Welfare Fund, providing clothes, shoes, and glasses for needy children, and since Betty and her friends could not come to the funeral, they were making a gift to the fund in Eileen's name.

My mother had kept the letter in a drawer with her most important papers, each of the two handwritten pages sealed in plastic laminate. Betty said, ". . . even though I knew that she [Eileen] had changed and was quite depressed, I never dreamed of such an ending. But if I had, I don't know how I would have handled it differently." Betty had obviously been trying to come to terms with the flip side of the suicide survivor's coin—*tails is guilt*—and she was wise enough to understand that my parents might be struggling with the same thoughts as well. "I have worried that you are both blaming yourselves for what happened to Eileen," she wrote, "but you never need do that. She felt so close to you both and talked of you often—so much so that I felt as if I knew you both. One of the things she told me during the summer was that she had the happiest childhood that was possible, and she realized how lucky she was for that. When she felt troubled, her first instinct was to call home."

It was easy to see why my mother had cherished this letter. Betty's compassion was deeply touching, but what struck me most was the irony of that last sentence. In a moment of trouble unlike any she had ever known, Eileen had chosen to end her life rather than face a call home. It was heartbreaking, and I couldn't understand why Eileen hadn't known my parents would have stood behind her no matter what. I remembered being a teenager, snickering about some girl getting pregnant and having to drop out of school, and Mom said, "Don't *talk*! Everybody makes mistakes. That could be your sister someday."

Ten days after I sent the packet, Darryl phoned and said that he'd located Vic through his social security number. He was living in Kent, Washington, a suburb of Seattle. Darryl told me where Vic worked and how much money he made. When I asked him how he'd found all this out, he said, "I got an old friend who works for the Feds. Cost a hundred bucks but saves me a ton of time."

I wasn't sure if it was a matter of knowing where Vic was—that he could be just a phone call away—or the specificity of Darryl's information, but I felt a little spooked.

"Seattle, huh? My son, Brett, lives there."

"Oh yeah, what's he doing?"

"He just got out of college. Evergreen State. He's a drummer. Wants to be a rock 'n' roll star."

Darryl laughed. He said he liked Seattle and had been there often. Then he launched into a story about two deputy sheriffs from LA who were involved in a love triangle with a woman. "One night one of the deputies is driving home from work and his brakes give out and he slams into a wall. Killed instantly. The other guy puts in his time and retires and moves up to Seattle, but I guess the case always seemed a little fishy, and a police detective started looking into it again about fifteen years later. There's no statute of limitations on murder, so the detective locates the retired deputy who's living in Seattle, and he calls him up and says he wants to come to talk to him. The guy says sure, okay, and they arrange a time to meet. The day the police detective was supposed to arrive from California, the other fellow went out in the woods and shot himself."

"Jesus, I don't want something like *that* to happen."

"No, no, of course not. It's just, you can't always control these things. You open the lid on Pandora's box and . . . well, you see what I'm saying?"

"Yes, of course." Part of me wanted to tell him to lay off the melodrama, but he'd made his point. This was a real person we were talking about. Vic had a job, a family. A life. No one could predict what ugly truths we might uncover once the investigation got rolling, or where those truths might lead.

Before we hung up, I said, "What about Betty Clay? Any luck finding her?"

"I got a few leads but nothing yet."

"Well, keep me posted."

13

I WAS ON the board of directors of a small digital imaging company in San Francisco run by an old friend and had to go to a board meeting in late April. That seemed like a perfect opportunity to take a detour to Los Angeles and meet Darryl. I called him to discuss the plan, and he said that would be great, he was really looking forward to it. He wanted us to drive out to San Bernardino and get a feel for the place. Maybe talk to Betty Clay if he could find her.

A few days later he called back to say he had found an address for Betty, but when he phoned the number a teenage girl answered and told him Betty, her grandmother, had passed away. Darryl asked the girl to have her mother call him back. When she did, they quickly determined that the Betty Clay who had died was not Eileen's friend, just someone with the same name. The woman on the phone—Cheri Flint, a paralegal—seemed curious and started asking Darryl about the case.

"I'm not sure why she was so interested," Darryl said. "But she's lived in San Bernardino her whole life and her house is real close to where Vic and Eileen lived. She told me she has a friend who works in the coroner's office who might be able to help us, so I faxed her the information you sent me and she's going to see if her friend can come up with anything."

"Boy, what a lucky break. That really *is* a strange coincidence."

"Yeah," Darryl said. "But you know what? In my business, this kind of thing happens all the time. You can't ignore *anything*. You have to go after every little shred of information. Sometimes it's something you thought was completely irrelevant, then you check it out and before you know it, the whole case starts to fall into place."

The night before I left for California, Elizabeth said to me, "Are you going to take your computer?"

"Yes, of course," I said. I did all my writing on my laptop and rarely traveled without it.

"Maybe you should stop writing your novel for a while and start keeping a journal instead." She gave me a guarded smile. "I think it might help if you tried to record your feelings, unedited, right now. You know, stop being a writer and just be . . ."

"A human being?"

"Be Eileen's *brother*, Jim."

I found an old ninety-nine-cent composition book in my desk and slipped it into my briefcase.

Darryl's office in Century City was located in one of the many modern twenty-story office buildings lining both sides of the Avenue of the Stars. He wasn't listed on the directory in the lobby, but I took the elevator up to the suite number he had given me and found the name of a law firm on the door. The receptionist smiled warmly when I asked for Darryl and said he'd be right out. Darryl greeted me like we were old friends. He was wearing a colorful open-collared shirt and a thick gold chain around his neck. He had wide shoulders and enormous hands, a silver-and-gold-plated Rolex on his wrist. His thinning white hair was combed straight back over a suntanned pate, wispy tendrils hanging over his collar. With his big smile and white horseshoe mustache, he looked like an older version of the popular wrestler Hulk Hogan. I followed him into a small conference room.

"This is what I got so far," he said, laying some papers out on the table. "Why don't you look this over while I go make a couple of phone calls, then we'll talk."

On top of the stack was a legal document from 1981, in which Vic was named as a codefendant in a wrongful termination suit after he had left the San Bernardino police and gone to work for a large retail chain. But it didn't seem relevant to the case and I moved on. Next was a photocopy of the directory of employees for the San Bernardino City Unified School District for 1973–74, which showed that Mrs. Eileen Zaccagnini worked as the meeting and conference secretary under Dr. Thomas Dwyer, associate superintendent, along with three others. Executive Secretary Betty Clay was at the top of the list. The next document, the 1974–75 directory, was nearly identical, except for the blank where Eileen's name had been. Darryl had made photocopies of various other school department literature, including a piece on the retirement of Eileen's boss, Dr. Dwyer, the man Vic told me had been her lover. The article featured a photograph of Dwyer, a mildly handsome man who had started teaching in San Bernardino upon graduation from San Diego State in 1941. I did a quick mental calculation: he would have been about fifty-five in 1974, the same age I was now. I tried to imagine myself having an affair with a twenty-seven-year-old, tried to imagine Eileen being drawn to a man who was twice her age. I wondered if they had been in love, who broke it off and why, how he felt when Eileen killed herself, if his wife knew about the affair. I had asked myself these questions when Eileen died, but now they felt more urgent, more critical.

I couldn't help but be reminded of the affair I'd had about a year after Connie and I moved to New England. The woman had worked in my office—my *only* employee—which had given us ample opportunity to indulge in our lust. I was thirty-five; she was twenty-nine, married with a young daughter. The affair was stormy and tawdry and utterly mesmerizing. We both left our spouses and got divorced, but happiness eluded us. She wanted to get married and buy a house; I begged for time alone to settle into a routine with my children. We fought constantly—two adulterers who didn't trust each other. Unable to move forward or to break it off, we lived in a soap opera of our own making, a cliché of love-gone-wrong. Things became so untenable at work that I fired her; she hired a lawyer and threatened, justifiably, to sue me and the company. This should have been the end of it, but we kept raging on for another two years—never moving in together, never able to stop the cycle of bitter argument and fevered recoupling—until we finally broke it off.

Sitting there looking at the photograph of my sister's lover, I realized that I had never thought about the similarities between my affair and the one that Eileen had had with her boss, not even when the therapist I was seeing at the time warned me that if things kept going the way they were, either my lover or I was going to end up in the emergency room, or worse.

My thoughts were interrupted by Darryl, who had returned to the conference room. He told me he had just spoken to Cheri, and she was going to get the records from the coroner's office later today. She'd already tracked down Eileen's death certificate and Vic's marriage license for his second marriage, which she had just faxed over along with a list of questions based on Eileen's letter and the other material I'd sent him.

"Seems like she's a real natural at this," Darryl said. "She's already started thinking like a professional investigator."

He put the papers on the table in front of me. The death certificate was on top. It stated that Eileen had died from a "self-inflicted .38 caliber gunshot wound," the injury occurring at approximately 1:45 p.m., death at 3:10. I felt a ripple of sadness. With its ornate border and official seals, the death certificate seemed so coldly factual.

Vic's new marriage license, eerily, had the same border and seals. I glanced from one type-written box to the next. Vic Zaccagnini didn't have a middle name. His father had been born in Italy. His mother's maiden name was Kovalik; I'd always assumed that she, too, was Italian, but now realized she was probably Polish or Croatian. In another box: "Age: 27." In another: "Number of this marriage: 2. Date last marriage ended: 9-11-1974. Last marriage ended by: _Death_." His new wife's name was Yvonne Marie Burdette. She was twenty-two years old; this was her first marriage and her occupation was special deputy sheriff. Vic's profession was listed as "policeman." The form was signed by the recording clerk, Marcia J. Brickley: "Subscribed and sworn before me on: _Sept. 11, 1975_. Date license issued: _Sept. 11, 1975_."

I did a double take.

"Did you _see_ this, Darryl?" Nothing I'd seen up to that moment had given me pause. Now it felt like I'd heard an ominous footfall, my synapses suddenly on high alert.

"The date?" He nodded. "Cheri mentioned it in her notes."

"Vic got a marriage license on the first anniversary of Eileen's death? _Jesus!_ What the hell do you think _that_ means?"

"I have no idea."

"It couldn't be a coincidence, could it? Something that just slipped his mind? Both dates are right here on the form."

"Yeah, it's pretty strange," Darryl said. "Maybe he was trying to make a point."

"Which was?"

"I don't know." He bit his lower lip. "That's what we're trying to find out."

14

THE NEXT morning traffic on the freeway was light heading east; the other side of the road was backed up for miles. I found a good rock 'n' roll station, turned up the volume, and drove 80 miles per hour like everyone else. Darryl and I had planned to meet at a restaurant in West Covina just off the freeway. I arrived early and the hostess led me to a booth by the window. As I waited, I looked over the documents Darryl had given me the day before. One set, which I had not read carefully in his office, concerned Vic's second marriage, to Yvonne. From my mother, I had learned that they had had a daughter and the marriage ended in divorce. According to the documents, the child, Christina Jane, was born on Vic's thirtieth birthday in 1978. In 1993, Yvonne filed a petition with the superior court in San Bernardino seeking back payment of $2,300 in child support. Several months later the issue was resolved. In a subsequent petition, Yvonne stated that she had "reluctantly agreed to relinquish the back payments . . . only as a means of stopping the defendant's harassment, and demanding and manipulative phone calls."

I turned to the documents we'd gotten from Cheri Flint, which I had read the night before. Along with Vic's marriage license and Eileen's death certificate, Cheri had included four pages of typewritten notes. At the top of the first page she'd made a note: "WHERE WAS 'FREDDY' THE DAY OF THE DEATH?" Freddy was the two-year-old Eileen mentioned in her last letter to my parents, the child of a friend she'd agreed to babysit. When Cheri read Eileen's letter, she concluded that Freddy was actually in the house at the time Eileen wrote the letter. The "verbiage of the letter," according to Cheri, "indicates immediacy, 'I am watching *a little 2 yr. old boy.*' Not I've started watching or have been watching." This was an interesting deduction. I had read the letter a hundred times but had never considered that possibility.

Drawing on the information that I had sent to Darryl, Cheri had made a list of events leading up to Eileen's death and tried to pick apart the story Vic had told me in my parents' kitchen. She felt that the time frame didn't work. She was skeptical of the notion that Eileen had loaded the gun herself. "Why was he [Vic] home in the middle of the afternoon during the week?" Cheri noted. "Was there a life insurance policy? Why, if he was 'very close' with Eileen's mother would he then take out a marriage license exactly one year to the date of her daughter's death? Where did they go for marriage counseling?"

Her questions unnerved me. I had convinced myself I wasn't out to prove that Vic had harmed Eileen, but *I* was the one who had chosen to unearth this entire matter. Cheri had no trouble trying to implicate Vic in Eileen's death, and I needed to look at the information she had uncovered with the same critical eye that she did. With all this percolating in my head, I got out the composition book that Elizabeth suggested I bring and made my first journal entry.

I'd written only a paragraph or two when Darryl arrived. We ate breakfast, then headed for San Bernardino in his white Camaro. His cell phone rang often and he took some of the calls in Spanish. He told me his first wife was from Spain, but he didn't become fluent in the language until he was in the Border Patrol.

The conversation turned to Eileen. I told Darryl that her death had broken my father. It wasn't just that she was gone but *how* she had died.

Darryl said he thought of suicide as "a permanent solution to a tempo-rary problem." I agreed. I'd always seen Eileen's death as the result of a momentary impulse, a desperate leap into the void, which didn't quite square with what I knew about the subject. According to the various magazine and newspaper articles I'd read over the years, most suicides seemed to be a culmination of a prolonged descent into madness or clinical depression, the actual suicide often preceded by several unsuc-cessful attempts. These attempts, the experts pointed out, were warn-ing signs, cries for help. In the letter to my mother, Betty had said that Eileen was depressed that summer, but I had always considered that to be a normal reaction to the difficult circumstances she had found her-self in. Her marriage was falling apart. She had suffered multiple mis-carriages. Who *wouldn't* be depressed? But even her best friend hadn't thought she was in danger of taking her own life.

I said, "I think everything must have come to a head in that big blowout with Vic. Eileen was out of control, but I don't think she really wanted to *die*."

"She just wanted the pain to stop."

"Exactly." I told him about Elizabeth's friend Debbie, who'd had bi-polar disorder and had attempted suicide six times. Debbie used to joke about it and say that one day she was going to get it right. When she finally did, Elizabeth's mother, a devout Catholic who was very fond of Debbie and thought suicide was a mortal sin, kept saying she didn't know why she did it. Elizabeth tried to explain that Debbie suffered from depression. "Elizabeth told her mother, 'You know how some people have heart trouble and they take medicine for it? Well, some-times the medicine doesn't work and the person has a heart attack and dies. That's what happened to Debbie, Mom. She couldn't help it. She had a suicide attack.'"

"That's a good way to put it," Darryl said. "I've been involved in AA for years—give lectures sometimes, do some counseling, try and work with people on a spiritual level. One time this woman told me how she'd have these bouts where she'd get so distraught, all she wanted to do was kill herself. I told her that was the suicidal self talking, like the devil trying to trick her. You have all different kinds of selves—mother self, sister self, friend self, work self. When the suicidal self starts talking, you have to step back and look at your *basic* self. The real you. The woman who loves her family and goes to work every day and tries to treat everybody with kindness and respect. That woman is a *good* person. Why would you want to murder her? She doesn't deserve to die. You have to get in touch with your creative self and help her find some other solution."

"That's great advice. Unfortunately, people who are suicidal aren't always thinking straight. Like you said, they just want the pain to stop. That's why I hate the idea of having guns in the house. If Eileen hadn't gotten ahold of the gun at that specific moment, I think she'd probably still be alive today."

"Vic was a cop, Jim. There was *always* going to be a gun around." Darryl's voice was matter-of-fact, nothing showing on his face, but I could tell he was puzzled by my naivete.

He was right. I *was* naive. That's why I'd hired him, to help me see Eileen's situation in a different light. Just as Cheri's questions had. My job was to pay attention to what they said and not let my own biases and beliefs blind me from the truth.

The conversation turned to Eileen and Dwyer. I told Darryl I'd always been curious about him. After Eileen died, in those rare moments when I considered the possibility of talking to other people in California, it had been his side of the story that I'd most wanted to hear. Was he haunted by his part in the melodrama? Did he try to get her to leave Vic and be with him, or was he secretly relieved that he didn't have that complication in his life anymore?

I told Darryl we needed to find him. "He'd be over eighty now. I hope he's still alive."

"Alive and in his right mind."

As a man who had once slept with another man's wife in an all-consuming love affair, I was hesitant to cast Dwyer as the villain in this story. "It's gonna be weird talking to him. I wonder what he'll say. It could have ruined his marriage, ruined his life. Or he could just be some asshole who shrugged his shoulders and walked away."

"No way to know how he's going to react. He might deny it ever happened or claim he hardly remembers Eileen, but I don't think so. With most people, the older they get, the more they want to tie up loose ends. Get everything in order before they go meet their Maker."

"You think?"

"Absolutely. That's how *I* feel about it. I've made peace with all three of my ex-wives. Asked them for forgiveness. I don't have grudges against anyone except maybe myself. Sometimes when I think about all the crazy stuff I've done in my life, all the drinking and raising hell . . ." He curled his lip in disdain. "When you're young, it's like you got this demon trapped inside you. You're out there runnin' and gunnin', going after the things you want. If somebody gets hurt, too bad. Lemme tell you, when I go stand before the good Lord, I sure hope He's passing out *mercy*. 'Cause if He's passing out justice . . . man, we'll *all* be vapor."

15

The san Bernardino Mountains were brown but the lawns were green, the city much cleaner and prettier than I remembered from my visit thirty years before. We drove through town and parked on the street next to the public library; ten minutes later Cheri, an attractive woman in her mid-to-late thirties with short blond hair, arrived. After we had introduced ourselves, we went into the library and found an empty table.

Cheri was the first to speak.

"I feel like I have a special connection with Eileen already, Jim."

She opened her briefcase and took out two identical sheaves of paper separated with a large black clip. "Turns out the police reports were attached to the autopsy protocol. I was up half the night poring over this stuff. Some of it's pretty hard to believe."

"Like what?" I said.

"Let's start with the little boy, Freddy. Guess where he was?" She paused for effect. "*In* the house."

I felt the hair rise on my forearms. Cheri's reading of Eileen's letter to my parents had been correct—she was babysitting for the little boy and he was in the house. Now the next logical question was: Where was he when the gun was fired? The idea that Eileen might have shot herself in front of a child was unthinkable.

"And that's just the tip of the iceberg." She handed one sheaf across the table to Darryl and me.

The first police report, written by Deputy G. B. Engel of the San Bernardino County Sheriff's Department, stated that Engel had been assigned to go to 6313 Dunblane, where "a woman shot herself." Deputy Ken Larkin had also been assigned to the scene, Cheri read aloud as Darryl and I followed along. Upon his arrival at the house, Engel saw Deputy Larkin's vehicle parked out front, but Larkin was not in sight. Engel entered the house and "called for Dep Larkin and received no reply."

"You have to ask yourself," Cheri said, "why *didn't* he get a reply from Larkin? Or Vic? I'm sure he went in there and shouted for them. They must have heard him. This was a typical three-bedroom ranch house. Vic and Larkin couldn't have been more than twenty or thirty feet away. What were the two of them doing in the bedroom?"

Engel's report continued:

At this time, R/O left the res [residence] *and searched the exterior of the res for Dep Larkin.* [The individual who is writing the report, the reporting officer, typically refers to himself in the third person as the R/O.] *This was accomplished with negative results. At that time, R/O again approached the front door of the res and was then contacted by a WMA, approx 25 yrs. approx 5-11, 210# wearing only a pair of blue jeans (no shirt or shoes).* [The police reports have occasional typos and misspellings, which I have corrected without notation.]

"Engel worked for the San Bernardino County Sheriff's Department," Cheri said. "Vic was a city cop, but the two departments worked together all the time. Engel was a *friend* of Vic's. We find that out in another report. So why does he describe him like he was a total stranger?"

"What's a *WMA*?" I asked Darryl.

"White male adult."

"Is that standard police reporting for him to describe someone he knows like that?"

"No, not at all. Your report is supposed to be *accurate*. If you know the person's name, you write it down. You can't get any more accurate than that."

[Vic] *demanded of R/O in a very anxious manner, "where's the ambulance?" R/O replied that the ambulance was enroute, and advised this subject to listen and he could hear their siren. R/O at that time entered the res and followed the subject to a bedroom which is located in the northeast corner of the res. R/O noted that Dep. Larkin was present here and was bent over what appeared to be a WFA approx 25 yrs of age. R/O noted Dep Larkin was administering mouth-to-mouth resuscitation and also Cardio-Pulmonary Resuscitation (closed heart massage). R/O was, at that time, advised by Dep Larkin, to leave the res and proceed to direct the ambulance to the res.*

"There's another red flag," Cheryl said. "When Engel first gets there, Larkin and Vic don't respond to his shouts. Then, when he finally enters the bedroom, Larkin tells him to go back outside. Why don't they want him in there? Engel doesn't need to *direct* the ambulance. Those drivers know how to find the house. That's their job. Besides, there's two police cars parked out front."

Darryl and I were silent as Cheri continued to walk us through the report. An ambulance came and took Eileen to St. Bernardine hospital. Shortly after, a sheriff's detective arrived at the scene.

"Now we come to Freddy," Cheri said.

It should be noted that the victim and the R/P [Vic] were babysitting for a Deputy Sheriff and this child was present during the entire incident.

Darryl gasped. "My God. That sounds like he was *in* the room when the shot was fired."

Two detectives from the juvenile division came and took custody of the boy. Engel's report ended abruptly with the arrival of Detective Delaney and Lieutenant Vaughn of the homicide division. In the box labeled "Reporting Officers" at the bottom of the form Engel included Larkin's name and badge number along with his own.

The next report was written by Vaughn. According to him, Detective Delaney went to the bedroom to investigate while the lieutenant proceeded to the kitchen, where "the husband of the victim . . . was being talked to by Deputy Engel, who was a friend of his." Vaughn said that he observed Vic "to be very emotional, to be crying, holding his head in his hands and resting on top of the kitchen table." Although he was "somewhat incoherent," Vic calmed down when Vaughn started to question him, and was able to make a statement.

Vic said that he and Eileen had been having domestic problems. They had been separated for three months and had been back together for about a week. He told Vaughn that Eileen had gotten a new job about six months earlier and that her boss, "Dr. Hal Boring . . . was involved in this."

This was a new twist in the story. Eileen's lover wasn't Dwyer as Darryl and I had assumed; it was Dr. Boring, the assistant superintendent.

I looked at Cheri and said, "The guy's name is Hal *Boring*?"

Cheri nodded, and we laughed out loud. It was a welcome moment of comic relief, but it lasted only a few seconds before we turned back to the report.

Vic told the detective that he had "caught" Eileen with Boring on several occasions while they were separated, but she would "pass this off as coincidence," claiming she had no feelings for him. Although Vic didn't believe her, he said that he still wanted her back. He mentioned that he and Eileen had twice gone to see a counselor named Dr. Mac-Laren.

Lieutenant Vaughn wrote:

He stated that last week his wife had spent all night with Dr. Boring and that she had told him of this yesterday and what had occurred between her and Dr. Boring.

He stated that there was a big argument that occurred at Dr. Boring's house on 33rd Street and that deputies were called to the disturbance.

"Keep that in mind," Cheri said. "There's gonna be more about that disturbance at Boring's house in another report."

He stated that yesterday his wife finally admitted to him that she did have an affair on the night that she spent all night with Dr. Boring. She stated that he got her drunk and she lost control. He stated that as a result of this she resigned from her job yesterday. They went to see the doctor, the counselor, last night.

Vic said he went into the bedroom to lie down at some point, and Eileen came in "and told him she wanted to kill herself." Then she confessed to the affair with Boring, telling Vic "how many times they had seen each other and where." Vic said he couldn't live with her, and Eileen ran into the bathroom and started swallowing pills. Vic thought the pills were aspirins, and choked Eileen to keep her from swallowing them.

"Why did he *choke* her?" Cheri said angrily. "That isn't how you stop someone from swallowing something. Did Vic say that because he was afraid the police would find bruises on her neck?"

He stated that his wife had called Mrs. Boring, her boss's wife, and told her about the affair she had been having with Dr. Boring. He stated that his wife (victim) then called Dr. Boring at the office and Zaccagnini stated that her boss was not there and his wife talked to the secretary and Zaccagnini stated that he was on the extension.

Cheri questioned why Vic had been listening in on the other phone. To her, it was one more indication that he was trying to control Eileen.

> *At about this time Zaccagnini stated that his wife changed Freddy's cloth-ing and he stated, "I guess I did some yelling. I went in the bedroom to call back east to her parents. I walked out of the bedroom and she was sitting on the bed. I was going to get the phone numbers. I was in the den. I heard the shot. She was yelling. She was kneeling against the bed."*
>
> *. . . He stated that he saw a black spot on her blouse and then he called the* [911] *operator.*

I sat there for a moment, stunned, trying to take it all in. The re-port said nothing about some of the key details Vic had told me all those years ago. Nothing about Eileen pleading with Vic not to call her mother. Nothing about Eileen refusing to give him the phone number. Nothing about her having to load the gun or calling out Vic's name. Perhaps these details were unimportant to the police, but they seemed crucial to me—the key to understanding Eileen's state of mind. But what was missing from the report paled next to the new information it revealed—all the things that Vic had *not* told me.

Cheri picked up on my confusion. "It doesn't make sense, does it?" she said. "One minute Eileen's changing Freddy's clothes, the next minute she's pulling the trigger. I just can't see her doing that. Not with that little boy right there in the room."

"I can't either," Darryl said, the first words he'd spoken in a long time.

I said, "That one fact turns everything upside down."

"I guess that's why Vic didn't mention it when he was telling his story to you," Cheri said. With that, she turned to the top of the next page of Lieutenant Vaughn's report.

Reporting officer asked Zaccagnini about the wrinkled papers . . . on the
bed where the shooting occurred (adoption papers) and he explained that
he had crumpled them up after seeing them on the dresser and threw them
at his wife and told her and Hal to go adopt a baby.

"She wanted to adopt a baby and then she goes and shoots her-self in front of a two-year-old?" Cheri said. "I just can't believe that. It doesn't add up."

"A *lot* of things don't add up," Darryl said.

I wasn't surprised by the mention of adoption papers. Vic had told me that Eileen had decided to move forward on that front when they went to Los Vegas and agreed to reconcile. I wondered if Eileen had signed the papers Vic had thrown at her.

We kept going and came to the gun. Vic had said they'd had it in the house for Eileen "to use when he was working." Usually it was kept in a carrying case on the bottom shelf of the nightstand, but Vic told the detective that he had noticed Freddy in the bedroom that morning and instructed Eileen to move the gun case so the boy couldn't get his hands on it.

"What a conscientious guy," Cheri said, her voice dripping with sarcasm. "So worried about the little kid getting hurt."

When Vic was asked if Eileen had ever threatened suicide before, he said he'd had a conversation with Mrs. Boring, who told him that Eileen had called their home saying she wanted to kill herself, and Dr. Boring had gone to see Eileen to help her. (How Vic happened to be talking with Mrs. Boring, Cheri noted, was not explained.) A few para-graphs later Lieutenant Vaughn wrote:

On another occasion where his wife attempted to commit suicide he stated
that his wife grabbed a gun. He said this was on an occasion when he tore
her clothes off, smacked her and beat her and called her a whore.

"Holy shit," I said.

Darryl sighed and ran his palm across his head.

He stated that [on that occasion] *she started taking aspirins and he stopped her and then he went to call his mother on the telephone and at this time she grabbed the gun case and he took that away from her.*

I was too horrified to speak. I felt anguish for Eileen, anger at Vic, shame at the ease with which I had let myself believe his story all those years ago. Along with that, I was dismayed by the tone of the police report itself. Much as I knew, intellectually, that the report was supposed to be a record of the facts and the detective's unbiased observations, I wanted Vaughn to say that what Vic had done in beating Eileen was *wrong*. Yet for him it was simply a piece of a puzzle, which he noted with no disgust or concern. I wanted some sense that the detective was going to use these revelations to probe more deeply into the possibility that there had been foul play. But there was none.

Cheri said, "Vaughn probably patted Vic on the back and told him that is exactly what *he* would have done if he thought his wife was fooling around on him. Give the little bitch something to remember." Her outrage was electric, and so was mine.

A little further on the report said:

He [Vic] *was asked about other suicide threats his wife may or may not have made in the past and he explained that about three weeks ago on a Sunday morning his wife was out all night and he was at the house waiting for her. When she came home he stated that he hit her and she took a bunch of aspirin or something.*

The report went on to say that Vic had told Vaughn that Eileen's best friend was Betty Clay. Then, in the few final lines:

At this time Frank [last name crossed out], *San Bernardino Police Officer, advised Zaccagnini of the death* [of his wife] *and . . . he became very hysterical and made threats against Dr. Boring and on one occasion made a telephone call to the school district relaying this threat to a secretary.*

"Vic was good at making threats," Cheri said. "Remember that blowup at the Borings' house that Vic mentioned to Vaughn? Boring called the sheriff's office that day and the deputies came and wrote it up."

I glanced back through Vaughn's report, trying to find the comment about the argument at the Borings' house.

The confrontation occurred on September 4, exactly one week before Eileen's death. Two deputies, Hughes and Corbett, arrived independently about four fifteen in the afternoon. (Like Larkin and Engel, both deputies worked for the San Bernardino County Sheriff's Department. Vic was employed by the city police, and the reports did not indicate if either deputy knew Vic personally.) Hughes's report said that when the officers arrived, Dr. Boring and Vic were standing in the driveway, Mrs. Boring was also outside, and a "female subject" (Eileen) was sitting in a small pickup truck. Mrs. Boring told Hughes "her husband was having an affair with Mr. Zaccagnini's wife and that she had invited them over to talk." Then an argument between Vic and Dr. Boring erupted inside the house, and Dr. Boring called the sheriff's office. After being confronted by the deputies, Vic got into the truck with Eileen and drove away. Both deputies reported the incident to a sergeant later that evening. Hughes wrote that Deputy Corbett told him Vic "made a threatening statement to him about his wife."

Corbett's report added more details. While Hughes was talking to Mrs. Boring, Corbett spoke with Vic, who told him Eileen was having an affair with Boring. Vic said he knew Dr. Boring had called the sheriff's office, but he'd waited for the deputies to arrive to show Boring he wasn't afraid.

> *At this time R/O [Corbett] advised Mr. Zaccagnini to leave this residence*
> *and go to his own. R/O observed that this subject and his wife were involved*
> *in a heated argument. At this time R/O tried to ascertain from Mr. Zaccag-*
> *nini if there was going to be any further problem between himself and his*
> *wife. At this time Mr. Zaccagnini stated, "Not really, but in a half hour you*
> *can come pick her up off the lawn and you can take me to jail."*

After threatening Eileen's life in front of Corbett, Vic got in the truck, had a brief argument with Eileen, then swiftly drove away.

My mouth was parched, a dull pain radiating from my sinuses into my skull. *At this time*—a phrase that the police reports used ad nauseam—I probably should have taken a break, gotten a drink of water, and walked around the library or gone outside for a few minutes, but I was riveted to my chair, my head spinning as I tried to keep all the names and information straight. According to the last report, Vic knew Eileen was having an affair with Boring a week before she died, but an earlier report had said that he had learned about it only the night before she died. I was certain Vic had told me years before that Eileen's first confession—her revelation about sleeping with her boss, *once*—had come on the morning of her death. As I mulled over these discrepancies in the long months ahead, there would be times when I thought they were crucial, other times when they didn't seem to matter at all.

The lead investigator on the case was Detective Neil Delaney. He wrote two reports. The first, the main report, was a description of his findings at the crime scene. This report was written on September 20, 1974, nine days after Eileen's death. It stated that, upon arrival, Deputy Engel had picked up the gun from the floor and unloaded it. Engel had then placed the gun on a dresser, and put three .38-caliber bullets and one empty shell casing on top of the television.

Cheri looked at Darryl. "Why would Engel pick up the gun and unload it?"

"I have no idea," Darryl said. "It doesn't make any sense."

"Engel was Vic's *friend*," Cheri said. "Now his fingerprints are all over the gun."

Darryl shook his head. "This whole investigation stinks. Maybe there's a reason why the cop picked up the gun, but it looks like the cops are running around, destroying evidence, not following proper procedures."

The pills in the bathroom, according to Delaney, had been identified as Excedrin. A note was on the coffee table in the living room: "Vic, Freddy and I went out for a walk. Love, Eileen."

"She must have written that before she went out to mail the letter to your folks," Cheri said. "The old post office was just a few blocks away."

Next, Detective Delaney added he'd received a call from Dr. Boring saying the San Bernardino assistant police chief—Vic's superior—had contacted him and advised him that Vic had made death threats against Boring. The report also stated that Deputy Corbett, upon learning of Eileen's death, contacted Detective Delaney and told him about the confrontation on the Borings' front lawn and the threat that Vic had made toward Eileen. Cheri turned back to Corbett and Hughes's reports of the disturbance.

"Look at the date," she said, pointing to a line on the page. "These reports were written on September eleventh, the day Eileen died. The confrontation at the Borings' house happened a week before. The cops waited until she was dead before they made any record of it." She shook her head in disgust. "I guess the police didn't bother to write up domestic disputes back then. At least not when a fellow policeman was involved."

"Or until somebody wound up dead," Darryl said.

"Let me get this straight," I said. "What you're saying is, the only reason we even know about the incident at the Borings' is because Eileen died?"

Cheri nodded. "Corbett and Hughes didn't report this incident until *after* they found out Eileen was dead. Delaney just told them to write it up and put it in the file so they could to cover their asses."

"And maybe to point the finger at Vic," Darryl added. "They knew he had threatened to kill her a week before."

It was hard to take it all in, but, for me, the picture of what had happened that day had changed entirely. Vic had viciously beaten up Eileen on at least one occasion and threatened her life in front of another cop. Those two facts alone should have made the police deeply skeptical that she had committed suicide, yet, as far as I could tell, they had let Vic off the hook and never seriously considered that he may have been the one who had pulled the trigger.

Detective Delaney's second report focused on a face-to-face interview with Dr. Harold Lloyd Boring, a "WM," forty years old. The report itself was written on September 19, 1974, eight days after Eileen's death, but did not record the date when the interview took place.

According to Delaney, Boring recalled an incident that had taken place in June or July, when he had gone to Vic and Eileen's house at 6313 Dunblane "in the nighttime hours" to pick up some papers. He said Eileen invited him in for a piece of pie. While he was there, Eileen "yelled her husband was home and 'he's jealous of you' . . ." Boring ran out to the garage, where Vic found him and an argument ensued. On another occasion, Boring's car was parked in front of Eileen's house and Vic drove by. Vic ran the license number to identify the owner, and later confronted Eileen about it. Shortly thereafter, according to Boring, he began receiving threatening phone calls from Vic, saying he'd be beaten up if he didn't leave Eileen alone. Vic had told me none of this in our conversation in my parents' kitchen, nor had he told me about the incident on the Borings' front lawn.

In this interview, Delaney asked Boring about his relationship with Eileen. At first, Boring denied anything improper had occurred, saying only that he was aware Eileen had confessed to a liaison with him prior to her death and was surprised to hear he'd been named:

> . . . he did not know where she could possibly come up with any such story. He stated that nothing ever happened, however later in the interview he admitted spending the night with her in the Lytle Creek campground and that during that incident . . . they had slept in sleeping bags and that he had attempted to have intercourse with her, however [it was] unsuccessful. He stated that the other story she had evidently told was completely erroneous, that there was never any sordid love affair between them in the back seat of the car, in the school yard or anything of that nature.

I said, "In other words, he claims they never had an affair?"
"Yep," Cheri said with a rueful smile. "And that's not all."

> He stated that approximately August [date unreadable] he had talked to the victim and she had called him, she was depressed over different things; he would not elaborate on those things. He stated that the victim had at that time talked about killing herself. He stated that he advised her to go to a marriage counselor or a psychologist and recommended a friend of his who was both. He stated that she had told him that she had gone with a salesman who calls on the school administration by the name of Rick Avery off and on during the month of August and that he is aware of other people in the office that have gone with the victim, but would not elaborate on who they were.

I felt a rush of blood. "Boring's saying she was a slut, running around with lots of different men."

"That's right," Cheri said. "He denies the whole thing."

"And Delaney lets him get away with it," I growled in frustration. "What about Mrs. Boring? What did she say?"

"He never questioned her."

"But Mrs. Boring talked to Eileen on the phone fifteen or twenty minutes before she was shot."

"Jim," Cheri said, a shift in her tone, trying to be gentle, "the police didn't *want* to know what really happened. When Delaney interviewed Boring, he was just going through the motions. Boring told him a story and he wrote it down. He didn't care if there were contradictions. He just wanted to put the report in the file and close the case."

There were more reports. Next was an interview with Freddy's father, A. J. Waering, in which he stated that Vic had moved into his apartment in June. Waering was apparently the divorced friend Eileen had mentioned in her last letter to my parents. Vic had been living with him all summer, but he said the two of them never discussed Vic's "domestic problems."

"Sounds about right to me," Cheri said. "You and your wife just separated? Bummer. How 'bout them Dodgers?"

Waering said Eileen called him on September 10 to say that she had quit her job and could babysit for Freddy if needed. He dropped the boy off at the house about seven in the morning and Eileen seemed "very happy and excited about keeping [his] son."

There was no speculation in the report about where Freddy might have been when the fatal shot was fired. Once again, the police report was maddeningly bland and lacking in curiosity. As a father, I could only imagine how deeply a small child would have been traumatized if he had been a witness to all that chaos and violence, but the detective did not ask Waering what, if anything, his son had said about the shooting. Police are supposed to stick to the facts, but Delaney seemed to be uninterested in asking even the most basic questions to make him understand the case.

The police sketch of Vic and Eileen's bedroom was of little value. It showed the bed was slightly askew, the phone on the bed, the gun on the dresser. On the floor between the bed and the closet—eleven feet, eleven inches from the door—the police had drawn a squiggly circle labeled "blood."

The coroner's investigation, which was a shortened version of Vaughn's police report, offered only one new piece of evidence—that Vic had been "requesting telephone numbers of some of the family" from Eileen and had gone into the "living room" to look for them when he heard the gunshot. This detail corroborated the story Vic had told me, though in my memory he said he was in the den. The report mistakenly listed Eileen's height as five feet, five and a half inches, when, in fact, she was only a half inch over five feet. This fact was corrected in the autopsy protocol, which described Eileen's wounds in detail. Entering just below her sternum, the bullet passed downward through her liver and ruptured her abdominal aorta. Death resulted from internal bleeding. The bullet—"half-jacketed . . . whose nose is markedly flattened"— was recovered by the medical examiner, marked for identification, and turned over to a criminalist from the sheriff's office at the autopsy. In the last line of the protocol, the examiner noted that there was "a rather large concentration of aspirin in the stomach and a significant concentration of aspirin in the blood [which] indicates the subject had ingested aspirin within a few hours," corroborating that part of Vic's story.

Cheri came to the last page of the reports. She hadn't included it in the papers she gave to Darryl and me and was careful not to let us see it as she held it close to her chest.

"This is hard to look at," she said. "You might want to brace yourself."

I shrugged. "Go ahead. At this point I'm ready for anything."

She placed the page on the table in front of us. It was a copy of a grainy black-and-white photograph—Eileen lying on a coroner's table, sprigs of her short dark hair splayed against the crumpled white sheet beneath her head. If you saw the photo with no introduction, you might not think she was dead. Just drugged or drunk perhaps. A spot of light in one open eye. Her lips parted as if she were trying to speak.

16

Cʜᴇʀɪ ꜱᴛᴀʀᴇᴅ at the photograph of Eileen on a table in the morgue. "My friend in the coroner's office took one look at this and said, 'That's not the face of a woman who wanted to die.'" She put the photo in her file and closed the flap. "He also told me that if this were *his* investigation, it wouldn't have been ruled a suicide so quickly."

"Who's your friend?"

"I'd rather not say. The less you know the better. That way, nobody gets in trouble. I just want to help you get to the bottom of this. Like I told you, I feel like I have a special connection with Eileen." There was a resolute look in her eyes as if she'd been working on this case for months. Years. "I'll tell you one thing, there's no way she committed suicide, not with that little boy in the house. And the date on Vic's marriage license? That was like pissing on the grave."

Darryl slid his chair back and said it was time to take a break. I went to the men's room and splashed cold water on my face. When I came back to the main room, Cheri said she wanted to search the files in the library for information about Hal Boring. As a paralegal, she knew how to find things quickly and efficiently. The library had records of marriages and divorces on microfiche. She found that Boring had been married twice—the first time in 1961, then to a woman named Gloria.

"March of '73," Cheri said. "What a scumbag. That means he was only married for a little over a year when he started the affair with Eileen."

The more I thought about him, the angrier I felt about *Doctor* Boring. Eileen was just a plaything for him.

In the literature from the San Bernardino County school system, there was a group picture from 1997 that included Boring. He had a pudgy face, graying hair, a receding chin. He looked so *ordinary*, which, ironically, was my first impression of Vic all those years ago. I wondered what Eileen had seen in him. A mentor? A shoulder to cry on? But she had been so fragile then. Easy pickings.

Another article from 1997 announced Boring's resignation after forty-one years in education, thirty-four of them in San Bernardino. The subtitle of the article—*Harold Boring's announcement comes on the same day a public report is critical of the School District's financial operation*—seemed to suggest that Boring was linked to problems with the budgeting process, but the article went on to say that the School Board president praised Boring's work and said that he was leaving the department on good terms.

Darryl found a current address for him in the San Bernardino telephone book. It appeared that he and his second wife, Gloria, were still married.

"Broadmoor Boulevard," Cheri said. "That's over near the golf course. We can drive by there after we go see Eileen's house."

It was about three o'clock when we stepped out of the library into the warm sunshine. Darryl and I got in his car and followed Cheri to her house, so she could leave her SUV for her husband. She had five children—two from her first marriage, three from the second. When we arrived, the oldest, a slender girl about fourteen, was standing in the driveway, holding a toddler on her hip. The other children came out of the house along with Cheri's husband. She told him she'd be back in an hour and handed him the keys.

I crawled into the cramped space behind the front seats of Darryl's Camaro, while Cheri sat up front. As he drove, she gave him directions and started commenting on various landmarks.

"That's where the old post office used to be," she said, pointing at an unoccupied building on a weedy lot. "Eileen probably walked here with Freddy when she went out to mail the letter to your folks."

A few minutes later we stopped across the street from 6313 Dunblane Avenue. The neighborhood was quiet—no other cars going by, no children playing, no one walking a dog. I had photographs of Eileen and Vic's first house in San Bernardino, a tiny pink box with a pink-and-white-striped aluminum awning out back. This place was considerably more upscale, a well-appointed ranch of beige stucco. There were two lovely trees on the grassy lawn, a high wooden fence enclosing the backyard. I thought about how proud Eileen must have been the day she and Vic moved in—then I realized that buying the new house was probably an attempt to breathe some life into her failing marriage, the way some couples hope that having a baby can keep them from splitting up.

Cheri pointed at a window on the left side of the house. "That's the bedroom on the northeast corner where it happened."

From the position of the front door, it appeared that Engel could not have been more than thirty feet away from the bedroom the first time he entered the house and called for Larkin. Darryl asked me if I wanted to get out and walk around, and I said no.

From there we proceeded to 33rd Street, which was about a mile from Dunblane. Cheri checked the address in her notes and directed Darryl to stop in front of a handsome adobe house with a red tile roof. This was where the Borings were living when the confrontation occurred on the front lawn a week before Eileen's death.

I stared at the house and pictured another sweltering afternoon like this one. *A patrol car is parked next to the curb with its blue lights flashing, while Gloria Boring stands in the doorway, smoking a cigarette. She's wearing a red silk blouse and well-tailored shorts, her makeup flawless, determined to look her best when she meets her husband's lover. Hal glances back at her from the edge of the lawn and makes a gesture with his empty hands like a man falsely accused. Gloria wants to believe he's innocent, but she knows what a good liar he is—she was the other woman once herself. Vic is talking to Deputy Corbett with his fists clenched. He wants to beat the shit out of Boring. He also wants to beat the shit out of Eileen, but he can do that later. Corbett walks Vic across the lawn to the pickup truck in the driveway and tries to calm him down. The truck is a rusty Toyota, the kind tradesmen drive when they come to work in this neighborhood. Vic's eyes blaze with rage as he tells the deputy he can come to the house on Dunblane in half an hour and pick his wife up off the lawn and cart him off to jail. Eileen's in the truck with her head bowed, her hands in her hair. She knows what Vic is going to do to her when she gets home. Chances are she thinks she deserves it.*

On the way to the Borings' current residence, we stopped at a fast-food restaurant to get some cold drinks, then rode along the perimeter of a golf course. The Borings lived a block or two from one of the fairways on a plush tree-lined street. Darryl drove past the house slowly, then turned around. As we eased by a second time, I imagined Hal Boring coming out and flagging us down, asking us what we wanted. I was still reeling with anger and confusion over everything I'd read in the police reports. In some ways he seemed as culpable in this tragedy as Vic. But I wasn't ready to confront him yet.

On the drive back to West Covina, Darryl and I discussed our next steps. Along with Betty Clay, I asked him to try to find Vic's ex-wife, Yvonne.

"I'll bet *she* knows a thing or two," Darryl said. "If there was any foul play, she's probably the one Vic would have told." That said, he was concerned about how to go about initiating a conversation. If he started asking Yvonne about Eileen and she mentioned it to her daughter, chances were it would get right back to Vic. "We don't want to give him a heads-up. If he's still got some friends in the police department, any evidence from the case that's still on file is liable to go missing. Besides, if Vic finds out, you could be in real danger. He might decide to come after you."

Naive as it may seem, I had honestly never considered that possibility until he said it.

When I called Elizabeth later and mentioned Darryl's comment, she wasn't at all surprised. "I've been worried about that since you decided to go out to California. This isn't some novel you're writing anymore, Jim. This is as real as it gets."

17

Dᴀʀʀʏʟ ᴅʀᴏᴠᴇ me to the motel where I had left my rental car, and I made my way to Pasadena to see my old friend Nate Moehrig. He and his wife were both lawyers, and while neither of them dealt with criminal cases, they were flabbergasted by the details of the San Bernadino police reports.

"No question in my mind, this was *not* a suicide," Nate said when I had finished telling the full story. "I'm not going to tell you what to do, but I think you're gonna have to see this thing through to the end and get the case reopened. There's no statute of limitations on homicide. Get the district attorney involved. Someone who can make people give depositions and tell the authorities what they know under oath."

Nate's wife agreed. "The date on your ex-brother-in-law's marriage license, that's like saying, *Ha!* I got away with it."

I didn't agree or disagree. The things I'd discovered the past two days were so much more than I had bargained for, and the responsibility felt overwhelming. I poured myself another glass of red wine, hoping it would help me sleep.

I sat in the board meeting in San Francisco, trying to concentrate on the business at hand, but all I could think about was Eileen's case. One detail that kept coming back to me was Vic's description of her "previous suicide attempt." Vaughn's report said:

> On another occasion where his wife attempted to commit suicide he stated
> that his wife grabbed a gun. He said this was on an occasion when he tore
> her clothes off, smacked her and beat her and called her a whore. He stated
> that she started taking aspirins and he stopped her and then he went to call
> his mother on the telephone and at this time she grabbed the gun case and
> he took that away from her.

The first three or four times I'd read those words I hadn't been able to get past my anger over the beating. The description made it seem like it was a simple fact in their domestic battles, the requisite response when you suspected your wife of cheating. But as I began to look more closely at that first suicide attempt, I realized that it was nearly identical to the one that led to Eileen's death—the only differences being that in this version Vic goes to call *his* mother instead of mine, and Eileen doesn't die.

Anyone who has been in a volatile relationship knows how you can keep having the same argument over and over again. You fight about the kids, money, the dog, *whatever*. There are accusations and threats and promises, but nothing gets resolved or forgotten; the next week you fight about the same thing again. Eileen and Vic no doubt quarreled frequently over the question of her fidelity, but there was something about the description of these two incidents that didn't ring true.

I reread the account of the final argument in the police report. Vic told Vaughn about Eileen trying to swallow the aspirins; then he said he went into the den to call my mother, at which point Eileen started yelling and he heard a shot and found her kneeling by the bed.

Betty Clay had said in her sympathy letter to my parents that when Eileen felt troubled, "her first instinct was to call home." But this time it was Vic, not Eileen, who was trying to make the call. Maybe the police report did not attempt to repeat verbatim everything that Vic had said, but it seemed peculiar that there was nothing about Eileen begging Vic not to make that phone call and expose her adultery. To me, this detail had always seemed crucial, yet somehow this detail had failed to make it into the police report.

I might have been able to accept that it was all just a single case of sloppy reporting; then I remembered what Darryl had said in our first conversation about looking for things that were *not* there. Vic had told me that Eileen had to get the gun case down from the closet and load it before she fired. This seemed like another crucial detail, but there was nothing about it in the police report.

I drifted into a fugue state like the one I had outside the Borings' old house, trying to imagine how the interrogation went down. *Lieutenant Vaughn keeps pressing Vic, asking him about the suicide. "So," Vaughn says, "did your wife ever try to take her own life before?" This isn't a trick question. Vic is a fellow cop; Vaughn isn't trying to trip him up, just fill in the details. Vic wants to give the detective something—something to prove that Eileen had been on the brink—so he starts to make up a story. Like all good liars, he keeps it as it as close to the truth as possible. He remembers the time he beat up Eileen after she'd been out all night. There's a chance she may have told Betty Clay or one of her other friends about that beating, so Vic figures he better reveal it to the police. Then, as he's spinning his tale, trying to turn that bitter quarrel into a suicide attempt, Vic gets confused, one lie leading to another as the two stories become indistinguishable. Eileen tries to take aspirins. Vic goes to make a phone call. His mother, Eileen's mother— what difference does it make? The call never gets made. Eileen grabs the gun, but he takes it away from her. In the first suicide attempt, anyway. In the second one, not so lucky.* Unfortunately, I had no way of knowing if my imagination had brought me any closer to the truth.

Maybe both stories were true. Maybe everything happened exactly as Vic said, but it seemed as if the police weren't interested in probing deeper or trying to catch Vic in a lie. They weren't interested in getting Boring's story straight or resolving any discrepancies either. In his main report Delaney noted:

> [Boring] *related . . . that he had talked to the victim on numerous occasions, that he had dated her and had had an affair with her and that on several occasions she had told him that her husband, Vic, had threatened to kill her . . . He stated that approximately three weeks ago that Vic had beaten her up but he could not remember seeing any bruises or abrasions from that supposed beating.*

Later in the same report Detective Delaney said that Deputies Corbett and Hughes told him about the threat Vic made on the Borings' front lawn. Delaney advised them to write it up as an interoffice memo.

This passage from Delaney's main report seemed unequivocally clear—in the initial phone call with Delaney, Boring admitted he and Eileen had dated and had an affair. Yet when Delaney sat down in a face-to-face interview with him, Boring told a different story, claiming that he and Eileen had spent only one night together in a campground and tried and failed to have intercourse. When Delaney wrote his report on the interview, he made no attempt to resolve this contradiction. Why didn't Delaney say to Boring, *You already* told *me over the phone that you and the victim had had an affair. Which is it? Did you or didn't you?* In the same vein, Delaney never bothered to ask Boring about the incident on his front lawn a week before Eileen's death. If what Boring told Delaney in the personal interview was true and he was *not* having an affair with Eileen, then one is left with the absurd conclusion that she killed herself over an affair that actually never happened.

Perhaps Delaney could have uncovered the truth if he had talked to Mrs. Boring. Also, there was Rick Avery, the salesman Boring said Eileen had "gone with . . . off and on during the month of August."

Avery might have been able to provide a lot of useful information, but Delaney didn't bother to track him down either.

I kept thinking of all the questionable things the police did or did not do. Deputy Engel, Vic's friend, picked up the gun from the floor and unloaded it. The gun was not checked for fingerprints—at least there was no report to that effect—nor were Eileen's hands tested for gunshot residue, a standard procedure that Darryl had mentioned in our first telephone conversation. There was no report by Deputy Larkin, the first officer on the scene, no detailed description of Eileen's clothes or measurements of the blood stains on the floor. Perhaps these things were investigated at some later time by forensic experts, and the reports were not included with those that Cheri had found. But from my vantage point, the entire investigation seemed like an exercise in incompetence and indifference.

Flying back to Los Angeles from San Francisco, I looked over the autopsy protocol and the coroner's investigation. The coroner had written of Eileen's wound, "There was what appeared to be a bullet hole, with tattooing around the hole, approximately four inches in diameter." It continued, "Centered around the gunshot wound is a cluster of red flattened markings 11x11 cms. in size and centered approximately 1.5 cms. below the wound." Darryl had told me that whenever a gun was fired, tiny bits of powder and gases, which he called "spittle," were expelled from the muzzle along with the bullet, which caused tattooing, and I'd assumed that was the case. I started making diagrams in my journal, trying to understand the physics of it. Spittle burst from the muzzle of the gun in a cone-shaped spray like water from the nozzle of a garden hose. A ballistics expert, test firing a gun in a laboratory, would be able to replicate the pattern and determine the angle of the bullet's entry and the distance the muzzle had been from the victim's flesh. If the San Bernardino Sheriff's Department had done any such tests, there was no mention of them in the documents Cheri had found.

Darryl was waiting for me at the airport in LA. The plan was to go to a gun shop, and then have lunch. On the way there I told him what I'd been thinking about the size of the powder tattooing on Eileen's chest, which seemed odd to me. If she wanted to die, wouldn't she have pressed the gun against her body?

"I noticed that myself when I was looking over the reports this morning," Darryl said. "How big did it say the circle of spittle was?"

"Eleven centimeters. About four and a half inches. Slightly smaller than a CD."

"That's unusual. Most suicides are contact wounds. People don't want to look down the barrel and they don't want to miss."

The gun that killed Eileen was a Colt Trooper .357 Magnum with a four-inch barrel. The clerk in the gun shop said he didn't have any in stock. Colt had stopped making the model years ago, and now it was illegal to sell them in California. The clerk didn't know why.

"Regulations," he said, rolling his eyes. "If they're fifty years old I can sell them as antiques." He took a Smith & Wesson revolver from the display case and said it was basically the same as the Trooper.

I held it in my hand. It weighed at least two pounds.

"Big gun for a little girl," Darryl said, reading my mind.

At lunch Darryl started talking about the California gun laws—specifically, about how overly restrictive he felt they were. Later when we stopped at his apartment in Santa Monica, I noticed a small flat pistol in plain sight on the bookshelf in his living room. I asked him if it was loaded.

"Absolutely. This isn't the greatest neighborhood in town." He got out his two revolvers—one had a chamber for five bullets; the other for seven. Neither was loaded. Much as I disliked guns, I picked up the larger revolver and found myself admiring the workmanship—the smooth slate-gray metal, the precision tooling, the lethal efficiency. Darryl showed me how to open the cylinder and check to make sure it was empty. I held the gun in the normal fashion with my index finger on the trigger; then I turned the revolver around and pointed it at my chest. The muzzle was only a few inches away. Was that far enough to create a four-and-a-half-inch circle of powder tattooing?

"The only way Eileen could have shot herself and made a wound like the one she had was to hold the gun backward with both hands and use her thumb on the trigger," Darryl said.

I shifted the gun in my hands and held it the way he had just described. The muzzle was about ten to twelve inches from my chest. Feeling the resistance, I squeezed the trigger slowly with my thumb until the hammer made a sharp click.

"Jesus Christ!" Darryl said, grabbing the gun from my hand. "Don't ever do that again."

In a phone call with Cheri, a gun owner herself, we talked about the pros and cons of keeping a gun in the house.

"You're flirting with disaster, especially if the gun is loaded," she said. "But a gun *can* help a woman protect herself."

"Until the guy takes it away from her," I said.

"Well, there's that too. I think that may be what happened with Eileen."

"What? That Vic tried to take the gun away from her?"

"Yeah, I keep thinking about that time he beat her up and tore her clothes off," Cheri said. "I can't help but wonder if he raped her too. He said she got the gun because she wanted to kill herself, but how do we know that? Maybe she got the gun to shoot *him*."

Of course, I thought, astounded once again by my naivete. In my mind my sister was still the sunny high school majorette, the starry-eyed teenage bride. Up to that point I had never considered that she might have been raped, that she might have grabbed that gun to defend herself. But Eileen *had* died a violent death, and if I were ever going to discover the truth about how it had happened, then I was going to have to admit to the possibility of just how violent her life might have been.

18

Elizabeth came through the doorway in her white flannel pajamas, one eye squinched against the light. I was sitting at the kitchen table writing in my journal, stacks of papers and file folders spread from one end to the other.

"Please, come to bed," she said. "Try to get some sleep."

"In a little while."

I finished the sentence I was writing and laid my pen on the open journal. Elizabeth sat down and took a sip from my glass of Diet Coke. It was three o'clock in the morning. I hadn't slept more than a few hours a night since I'd come home from California the week before.

"Pretty color," she said, picking up the pen. The ink was bright turquoise. "Is there a system?"

I shrugged. "There *used* to be." I had seven pens in different-color inks. The original idea had been to use a particular color for each aspect of the case, but I had lost track. Now I changed colors every time my mind caromed from one idea to another.

I was looking over some pages about powder tattooing I had photocopied from a book called *Gunshot Wounds* by Vincent J. M. Di-Maio. Elizabeth glanced at a page I had highlighted, then winced and averted her eyes. Above the text I'd just marked was a black-and-white photograph of a man with a gaping wound shaped like a starfish in his right temple. I turned the page over.

"Sorry. No reason why you should have to look at stuff like this."

"Tell me again why *you* have to," she said with an edge to her voice.

My hackles went up. "What am I *supposed* to do, pretend like none of this ever happened?" I needed her support, not admonishments.

"I don't know. I'm just worried about you." She put her arms around me, knowing I was already gone, tumbling headlong into a dark hole with perils and consequences no one could predict. "Are you sorry you started all this?"

"No, not at all."

"It's becoming an obsession, Jim."

"Obsession, mission, quest. It doesn't matter what you call it, I don't feel like I have a *choice*."

It had long been my impression that women rarely killed themselves with firearms. Occasionally, when I would talk with someone about Eileen's death, that person would express a similar point of view. Guns were a guy thing, we'd agree; women took pills or stuck their heads in the oven. The research I'd done since returning from California showed that this presumption was flawed.

While it was true that men killed themselves with firearms at a much higher rate, women were not averse to using guns. According to *Gunshot Wounds*, 30 percent of all suicides by women in 1970 were caused by firearms, while nearly half (48 percent) were the result of drug overdoses; by 1990, gunshot wounds had become the leading cause of female suicide, a trend that continued throughout the decade and beyond. Women, DiMaio wrote, shot themselves in the chest or abdomen 28 percent of the time, while men did so 16.5 percent of the time. He stated that suicide victims "commonly . . . will hold a handgun with the fingers wrapped around the back of the butt, using the thumb to depress the trigger."

In light of all this information, Eileen's suicide was not as rare as I had thought. What seemed to make it questionable was the powder tattooing.

Most suicides with firearms, DiMaio said, are classified as contact wounds—ones in which the muzzle of the gun is held directly against the body—and a "small (1 to 3%) but significant number are of intermediate range." Details like this had begun to captivate me. The eleven centimeters of stippling around Eileen's wound put her in that tiny minority. But how far had the muzzle been from her chest? In order to determine the distance a ballistics expert would need the actual gun (not just the same make and model), bullets from the same manufacturer's lot as the bullet that had been fired, and a photograph of the powder tattooing with a ruler next to the wound to be certain they got the measurements right. Without these three elements, an accurate assessment would not be possible. Tattooing is often called "powder burns," but DiMaio explained that this is a misnomer. The markings are actually tiny bruises or abrasions that are produced by the spittle striking the skin while the victim is still alive. If someone were to shoot a corpse, the tattooing would have "a moist gray or yellow appearance," and it would be easy to tell the difference.

When I wasn't reading police reports and books about gunshot wounds and criminal investigation procedures, I was searching through file cabinets and boxes of old papers stored in my garage, hoping to find more traces of Eileen. One day, in a box of financial records, I discovered a letter my father had written to Connie and me. It was dated October 12, 1974—one month and one day after Eileen's death.

"Mom has had a difficult time adjusting and accepting our loss," my father said. "Fortunately, many people have helped." Mrs. Z called at least once a day, and Aunt Pauline and Cousin Mary had been extremely supportive. A few paragraphs later, he mentioned how glad he was that Vic had come to see him and my mother twice before returning to California. He said Mom had visited Vic's aunt Helen several times, and Helen, who "sometimes drinks too much and says foolish things," had chided her for being so upset. Reading this letter so many years later, I was bewildered. I had always pictured myself as the good son—the *anti-Keith*—helping to sustain my mother and father, my sober, steady life a bulwark in a world turned upside down. But from the things my father was telling me, it appeared that I hadn't spoken or written to my parents in the three and a half weeks since I'd returned to Philadelphia. I reread the letter several times, hoping to find some mitigating evidence, something to explain away my thoughtlessness, but there was none. Why hadn't I reached out to my parents in their grief? Any word from me would have been a comfort, to say nothing of the solace I might have felt by talking to them. But I had chosen to deal with Eileen's suicide by pretending that it was over and done with. As if it were a sad but simple fact of life.

In the letter, my father said that Keith had become "a MUCH better man since he returned from Pittsburgh," cutting down on his drinking, staying home at night, doing some work around the house. Then he added, "I hope Keith continues to behave." It's curious, that word "behave"—a word adults use for children—an indication, perhaps, that my father's expectations were minimal. Throughout the letter his tone toward me was sweet and loving, without a hint of reproach or any sense that he had been hurt by my neglect. In those brokenhearted days it may have been enough for him to know that his sons were alive and well. That we were *behaving*. Any filial kindness from Keith or me would have been an unexpected bonus.

Dad went on to say that Vic had gone back to the house he and Eileen had lived in but was planning to find a smaller place. Then he wrote, "I am very glad that you, Jim, talked to him. Mom helped Vic a lot. Vic's mother and brothers helped Vic too." In my father's eyes, it seems as though the talk I'd had with Vic was not a matter of my finding out more about the circumstances surrounding Eileen's death but a way for me to give Vic comfort and support. I had never viewed my conversation with him in that light, but my father's words revealed the depth of his sympathy for Vic—compassion without blame for a man whose loss he perceived to be at least as great as his own. Reading between the lines, I began to wonder if my mother had suggested that I question Vic about Eileen's death simply because she thought it was something *I* needed to do in order to be at peace. At the end of the letter Dad said he was glad he had begun to accept Eileen's death. "I have convinced myself that she has gone away," he wrote. "I HOPE I do not remember that she is NOT coming back." He continued, "I am sorry I wrote that because my eyes were so full of tears that I stopped writing for several minutes. Maybe I do not have as much self-control as I think I have."

Self-control. That seems to have been the operative word in my family when it came to dealing with Eileen's death. There were no crying jags, no one raged and shook his fist at the sky. We put on our stoical faces and grieved silently—and alone. I remember my parents slogging through those days immediately after Eileen's death in a kind of zombielike stupor, a perpetual state of lethargy and disbelief, with little affect except for an occasional smile for Meg. Most likely my father was talking about this persistent melancholy when he says that "Mom has had a difficult time adjusting and accepting our loss." The way people grieve is, in large measure, defined by culture and family. In some societies people keen or ululate or beat their breasts. In my family the expression of grief—or seeming *lack* of expression—was rooted in the notion that every death is a part of the life cycle, something you have to accept and see your way through.

Perhaps the familiarity with death required it. Both my mother and father had three siblings who died before the age of thirteen. Mom's brother Frank killed himself at twenty-three. My dad's two-year-old brother Melvin passed away in the influenza epidemic of 1918. That experience had been particularly traumatizing for my father. He was eleven at the time, and he and his mother were the only ones in the family who did not get sick. As was the custom, they had the wake in the living room of their home. My grandfather, who was upstairs in bed with a high fever, kept fading in and out of consciousness; then, in a moment of lucidity, he asked my grandmother about the toddler. Fearing that the news of the boy's death would break his will to live, Mum told him the baby was fine. But my grandfather insisted on seeing him, so Mum went downstairs and lifted the child from the coffin and took him upstairs. "He's sleeping," she said. "Don't wake him." Every time my dad told that story, he'd get tears in his eyes and pause a few times to keep himself from losing control.

Reading the letter from my father, I wondered if my own need for self-control in dealing with Eileen's death had stifled not only my tears but my common sense. There was so much that needed to be done for my parents—to say nothing about what I might have done to dig deeper in discovering the truth about Eileen's death—but I turned my back on all of it, everything neatly stowed away in a dark corner of my mind. When I thought about Eileen's passing, I relegated it to the shit-happens category—one of life's aberrations, tragic but unpreventable. No use dwelling on it; that would only lead to despair.

In the long run, it was my father rather than my mother who had the most difficulty dealing with Eileen's death. Three months after she died, Dad was diagnosed with colon cancer. I went to Pittsburgh to be with him and my mother while he underwent surgery. Obviously, the cancer wasn't caused by a broken heart; still, I've never been able to shake the feeling that the two were related. Other family members have always accepted this as a given. Cousin Mary said to me once, "Your dad started dying the moment he heard about Eileen." In that same conversation, Mary told me that my mother had gone through a terrible spell for the first few weeks after Eileen's death, barely able to sleep, wondering what she could have done to prevent it. Then one night Eileen came to my mother in a dream and said, "Mom, I'm all

right. Just let me go." No doubt my mother considered that dream as
an unassailable sign—comfort and wisdom from beyond the grave. Ultimately, she let go of Eileen, but my father couldn't.

At the center of Dad's grief was the feeling that if he had listened
more carefully, he would have been able to help her. Shaking his head
in guilt and dismay, he would say, "She kept trying to tell me but I
didn't *listen*." For months, he seemed obsessed by this notion. "But,
Dad," I'd say, "Eileen didn't tell you what the *problem* was. She couldn't
tell anyone she was having an affair, not even the marriage counselor.
If someone goes to a doctor complaining about the pain in his knee
when it's really in his elbow, how is the doctor supposed to help him?"
My father would nod, mollified for the moment. Then, the next time I
spoke with him, he'd tell me he should have listened better.

In time, Dad stopped blaming himself for Eileen's death, and when
he did, he stopped talking about her entirely. He asked my mother to
take down all the photographs of Eileen in the house; he said that every
time he looked at one it made him upset. The rest of the family was
careful not to talk about her in his presence, not even to reminisce
about the good times. What good would it do? we seemed to tell ourselves. Every story, no matter how cheerful or funny, would always end
with the same unspoken sentence: *But then she killed herself.*

By the summer of 1979, the cancer had spread throughout my father's body and it was clear he wouldn't live much longer. I flew to
Pittsburgh to see him from my home in Atlanta. Once a large, muscular
man, he was now pitifully frail, his bones poking at his flesh, as if his
skeleton couldn't wait to shed its skin. With his legs no longer able to
support him, my mother had made a permanent place for him on the
couch, moving him back and forth between sitting up and lying down.
Although he was often in terrible pain, he refused to take any pills.
"They make me too groggy," he told me. "I don't have much time left. I
want to be *awake* for as long as I can." The pain came in waves, making
him cry out with fierce, gut-wrenching groans. When this happened,

he would ask us to leave the room, and Mom and I would go to the kitchen at the far end of the apartment, closing the doors behind us, so we couldn't hear him. Moved by his courage and resolve, I said to my mother, "He's putting up a good fight. He wants to savor every minute." She nodded without agreeing and smoked her cigarettes.

At one point in my last visit with my father, I asked him if Mum had been to see him. He rolled his eyes and gave his head a single shake. My grandmother was ninety-four and still going strong. She lived about a mile away, but she had been to our apartment on Chestnut Street only a few times since we'd moved there nearly two decades ago. At least twice a week she passed our house in a taxi on her way to the Lutheran church or the beauty parlor, but she never stopped to see her dying son. When he was healthy my father was devoted to her, but she seemed to see him as a failure. I despised the woman, but tried my best not to openly disparage her to him.

"What do you think it is with Mum?" I said to my father. "She's outlived two husbands. When you die, she will have outlived five of her six children. Don't you think that's kind of *strange*?"

"Jim," he said with a mischievous grin, "the good Lord and Satan are having an argument over which one will take her. And till one of them *loses*, she'll be here."

The next day I packed my bag, kissed my father's stubbled cheek, and told him I loved him. We both knew that we would never see each other again. In the three days we'd spent together we never mentioned Eileen's name.

19

Over time I began to tell my extended family about my investigation into Eileen's death, how I'd hired Darryl and gone out to California and uncovered the police reports. Aunt Pauline didn't seem surprised.

"I always thought there was more to it," she said matter-of-factly. "We all did."

"*What?*" I was astounded. "You mean you were suspicious of Vic?"

"Oh, sure. I had a lot of questions but I didn't want to stick my nose in." (The same expression my mother used when talking about Eileen's separation.) "If your mom wanted to talk about it, she would have told me. Otherwise, that was nobody's business but her own."

"So, you thought there might have been some foul play."

"Yes, and then we heard you and Keith went out to California and talked to the police, so I figured you worked things out."

"*No*, we didn't go out to there." I was confused; I'd never heard anyone say that before. "Neither one of us did."

"Oh, I thought yinz did." It was a simple statement, with no hint of disappointment in her voice. But I felt a sting, as if I'd failed to do something I was expected to do. Why *hadn't* Keith and I gone? The

belief in the family that he and I had ventured out to California af-
forded us a level of devotion to our sister—duty, concern, curiosity,
love—that we did not deserve. But Keith wasn't part of the decision to
do nothing. That was all on me.

A few days later Aunt Pauline called me back. She had spoken to
Maria, an old friend of my mother's, who had told her a police offi-
cer had accompanied Vic from California to Pittsburgh for the funeral.
This revelation was even more unsettling than the misconception that
Keith and I had gone to California. I called Maria immediately to verify
what she'd told Aunt Pauline.

"Oh, yes, there was a policeman," Maria said in her strong Italian
accent, "but he wasn't wearing no uniform. Your mother, she pointed
him out to me at the funeral home."

"Was Mom suspicious?"

"Well, sure. Like maybe the police sent somebody to keep an eye
on Vic."

"Did Mom think that Vic might have murdered Eileen?"

"A little bit, maybe. But she felt like she couldn't do nothing about
it, so she just let it go. Your mother always said, 'Live for the living; it
don't do no good to worry about the past.' I think that's why she was
always so strong and happy."

I couldn't understand why my parents hadn't mentioned this police officer to me. I wondered whether he was a friend of Vic's from the
San Bernardino Police offering support, or an investigator sent from
the sheriff's department to monitor Vic's behavior and see if he acted
suspiciously. Perhaps my parents thought I'd known about him, which
is why they hadn't said anything. Or maybe they'd been afraid I'd ask
too many questions and drive a wedge between them and Vic's mother.
This seemed unlikely—surely my parents weren't so concerned about
causing a scene that they suppressed any notion that their child
may have been murdered—but what bewildered me more than their

reaction was my own. How could I have been so oblivious to an out-of-state policeman's presence at my sister's funeral? How could I have missed something like that?

"It's almost like I didn't *want* to know," I told Elizabeth, still reeling from the revelation. "I just stuck my fucking head in the sand."

"Don't be so hard on yourself," she said. "You were young; you were distraught. You did the best you could."

"What? Talking to Vic for an hour? I should have gone to San Bernardino and started asking questions."

"Vic was a *cop*, Jim. The police wouldn't have told you anything."

"But I didn't even go through the motions. I could have done so much more."

"Okay, let's say that Vic *was* guilty. Aside from his going to prison—and I doubt that he would have been convicted of anything more than manslaughter—what difference would it have made?"

"That's a pretty big difference all by itself," I said bitterly. Reading those police reports had quashed any long-held rationalization that Vic, even if he were a killer, had already paid a fair price by living with his guilt. "And I wouldn't have been pissed off at my sister all these years for killing herself. But the *real* difference would've been for my dad. If Eileen was murdered, he wouldn't have blamed himself."

"Sure he would," Elizabeth said. "Murder or suicide—either way, your father would have punished himself for not saving her."

I started to object, then stopped in mid-sentence. Maybe she had a point. A parent is supposed to protect his child no matter what.

Her eyes slid past me then and she bit her lip. I knew what she was thinking.

Six years before we'd met, she had been driving slowly across the campus of a college in Maine on her way to meet her then husband, who was playing in an adult-league lacrosse game. It was a warm day in early July, and her younger son, David, a few weeks shy of his fourth birthday, was standing on the front seat with his hands on the dashboard.

This was a time before parents learned to strap their children in with seat belts. "Look for Daddy," Elizabeth said. "Help me find Daddy." She had never been on this campus before. The air was hazy and dappled with sunlight. As she went through an intersection, another car struck her on the driver's side. The impact rolled her car over, and David was thrown out the window. Elizabeth was unhurt, but David was dead on arrival at the hospital. Later, she discovered that there should have been a stop sign facing her direction at the intersection, but a week or two before, some teenagers had removed it as a high school graduation prank.

"When I think about David," Elizabeth said, trying to keep her voice steady, "I can get angry at the kids who took down the stop sign, or I can get angry at the people who didn't put it back up, or I can get angry at myself for not having David in a seat belt. But in the end, he's still dead. The loss I feel doesn't change no matter who's to blame."

"So you think this whole thing with Eileen is a waste of time?"

"I didn't say that."

"But that's what you think."

"What I think is, you've lost your whole family, Jim. In some way, maybe you're just starting to grieve."

Maybe she was right.

One by one they had passed away—Eileen, Dad, Keith. By the time Mom went in the spring of 1992, I was forty-six years old and practiced at dealing with death. I had her body brought back from upstate New York to Pittsburgh to be buried, back to Brady Funeral Home on Cedar Avenue, where we'd had the wakes for Eileen and Dad. Mom had been such a powerful presence in my life. She taught me to be kind, to work hard and be independent, to "take the good with the bad" and never complain. Now, in her coffin, she looked tiny and content, as if she'd had enough of life. The night before the funeral I had stayed up late composing a eulogy filled with anecdotes and touches of humor—a way to bring my mother to life and try to keep my sorrow at bay. I read it at the service in a clear, steady voice. Under control, as always. A day or two later I was back at my desk, working hard on a short story.

Several months later my dead family came to me, all four of them standing at the foot of my bed. I have never quite settled this in my mind. I do not believe in ghosts, but I swear I wasn't asleep and wasn't dreaming. They were themselves, corporeal and entirely *whole*—with no bloody wounds or cancer, no missing teeth or limbs. I propped myself up on one elbow. I felt such joy at seeing them.

"Hello, James," my mother said. "I know you worry about us sometimes. We just wanted to tell you we're okay."

"You're all together," I said.

"It's great," Dad said. "We were hoping you would join us."

"Yeah, come on," Keith said.

I tensed but wasn't afraid. "No, I can't," I said. "There are things I still have to do."

Eileen smiled wistfully. They nodded in unison, seeming a bit saddened by my response, and left without saying goodbye. I got up out of bed immediately. If it *was* a dream, I thought it would fade away quickly. But it stayed with me, sweet and alarming and all too real. I didn't spend much time thinking about the simple explanation I had given them—that I still had things to do. It wasn't something I felt I had to justify. I wanted to go on living. Wasn't that enough?

20

"VIC WAS running with some bad cops," Cheri said on the phone. "They accused a woman of being a prostitute and ransacked her apartment, then they made her undress in front of them and stood around laughing."

The incident had taken place in the late seventies, a few years after Eileen died. Cheri had found out about it while combing through some San Bernardino court records, looking for references to Vic.

"Was he reprimanded?" I said, unfazed. I was long past being alarmed by ugly revelations about Vic. "Maybe that's why he left the police force before retirement age."

"I don't know. One of the cops in the gang was eventually dismissed for harassing a bunch of other women."

"Do you have the paperwork on this?"

"Right here in front of me. I'll send you copies."

I thanked her and told her she was my Erin Brockovich. Cheri laughed proudly, but I wasn't joking. All the work she had been doing for Darryl and me had been in her spare time. He had given her a few hundred dollars' compensation when she'd started, but as she'd gotten deeper into the case, something more than money had begun to spur her on. She'd told me that she had been adopted, and while she'd had a happy childhood, she always felt as if something was missing. After her adoptive parents died, she sought out her birth family and now had a good relationship with her birth mother.

"It's real important to me to reconnect with the past and fit all the missing pieces together," she said. "I think of Eileen as my lost aunt. It's almost like I remember her from when I was a little girl. The day she died is the same date as my oldest daughter's birthday. The minute Darryl first told me about it, something clicked. After I read the police reports, I felt even more connected to her. I know firsthand what it's like to be in a relationship where you're constantly threatened and belittled and the person needs to control you so much you're not even allowed to shut the friggin' door when you go to the bathroom! It helps me understand what Eileen was going through. Vic made her feel completely worthless. He was the one who put the gun in her hand, even if he didn't pull the trigger."

Her intensity amazed me. I loved how the case had pulled her in. She and Darryl and I had formed an unshakable bond, hell-bent on uncovering the truth.

I said, "I have dozens of photographs of Eileen. Would you like me to send you some?"

"Oh, yes! I'd really appreciate that."

A few days later I received the documents that Cheri had sent regarding the incident Vic had been involved in. It was a chilling story. Chet Lechler—a police officer who was dismissed from the department several years later for sexual harassment—got the idea that a woman named Joyce Maddox, who worked as a photographer's nude model to supplement her income, was a prostitute, and he began to stalk her. On the day of the incident, Lechler and another plainclothes officer confronted her in her town house, which she was in the process of decorating for her son Eli's sixth birthday party. According to the official account, Lechler opened a door roughly, striking the boy in the face. Seeing her son bleeding, Maddox became hysterical. At this point Vic and two other officers in plain clothes arrived on the scene—five cops marshaled to arrest one suspected hooker. The report, which had been filed in a California superior court, said:

> . . . *Zaccagnini, Fisher and Lechler began to ransack the apartment, including all of the Appellant and Eli's personal belongings. They broke Eli's balloons, tore down the birthday decorations and took all of Eli's pictures, report cards and papers and . . . dumped them on the floor. These officers then proceeded to pull all of the books down from the library and rummage through the cabinets and drawers in the apartment.*

While they continued to ransack the apartment, the officers kept trying to get Maddox to admit she was a prostitute, but she insisted she was innocent. (The documents did not say if the police had a warrant.) Finally, after forcing her to change clothes in their presence for no apparent reason, they handcuffed her and placed her under arrest. When she and Eli were brought outside, some of the guests had begun to arrive for the birthday party, and the officers continued to bully her and the boy, shouting "obscenities and vulgarities" at them. One of the neighbors attempted to intervene on behalf of Maddox and her son, and he, too, was arrested.

Later, the district attorney admitted to Maddox "that she was arrested for something she didn't do and that this 'sometimes happens.'" He asked her to sign a stipulation that she had been arrested for probable cause, but she refused and insisted on a court trial, at which she was acquitted. Six years later, having completed law school and passed the California bar, she accepted a cash settlement from the San Bernardino Police Department for herself and her son.

As I read through the details, I wondered what had led Vic to become an active participant in such a despicable incident. The conduct of the police officers had been blatantly abusive and misogynistic, with an utter lack of concern for the child. Had Vic always been so brutish? Or had he, the once-cuckolded husband, become angry and resentful toward all women because of what had happened with Eileen? Either way, his behavior was cruel and disgusting. But that didn't make him a killer.

21

ONE EVENING Darryl called and told me he'd found Betty Clay—and this time, he was sure it was the right one. She lived in Twentynine Palms, out in the high desert near the Joshua Tree National Park. He asked me how I wanted to go about contacting her. I'd come to think of Betty as a long-lost friend of the family, but I felt uncertain about calling her myself and asked Darryl if he would make the initial contact.

"Sure," he said. "I'll tell her I'm working for Eileen's brother and you want to get some closure on her death. That'll give her a chance to jog her memory and collect her thoughts before she talks to you."

When he spoke to Betty, she was quite friendly and said she was anxious to talk to me too. I phoned her immediately. Sounding much younger than her age, she told me that she and Eileen had worked in the same office for several years, until Eileen moved to a different office to work for Dr. Boring in the spring before she died. When I asked her if she was aware that Eileen had been having an affair with him, her initial answer was no, but with some caveats.

"I knew that Eileen was having problems that summer, but she was a very private person and I guess I am too," Betty said. "I knew she and Vic were separated, but I didn't know why. We spent a lot of time together. I was alone myself at the time, and Eileen would come over to my house and we'd cook together and sometimes she'd sleep overnight. We didn't talk about personal things very much. I guess that's my fault as much as hers. I know she was devastated when she lost her pregnancy. She miscarried once, I remember, and then she got pregnant again. I think she was about three months along when she lost the second one and it really tore her up."

I read Betty the letter Eileen had written to my parents on the day she died. Betty was skeptical when she heard that Eileen had quit her job abruptly without a formal resignation and two weeks' notice.

I said, "Maybe things are different if you've been fooling around with your boss."

"Yes, that Boring was something else," Betty said. "I never cared for him myself. When he was younger—I think this was eight or ten years before Eileen passed away—he was the principal of Cypress Elementary School in Highland and there was a rumor going around that he was having an affair with one of the teachers or the school secretary. That woman's husband shot and killed her."

"You're kidding?!" I nearly dropped the phone. "You're saying Boring could've been involved in *two* fatal love triangles?"

"Yes, he'd probably deny it. But if it's true, well . . ." She left the rest unsaid.

The police reports made it clear that Boring was a weaselly liar who had seduced Eileen when she was depressed and vulnerable, but the news of *another* dead wife was like the plot twist out of a bad soap opera.

I told Betty that Boring had suggested to the police that Eileen had been sleeping around.

"Anything's possible, I suppose," Betty said. "But I find that hard to believe. She wasn't that kind of girl."

I thanked her for the letter she had written to my parents and told her how my mother had cherished it. Then I asked the question I'd been avoiding—and the one I most needed to ask. "Did you ever think of Eileen as suicidal?"

"No, not at all."

"And you weren't suspicious when you heard?"

"No, I guess not. I got a call that day from the secretary who worked in the same office with Eileen and Hal Boring. Her name was Ginny." She paused for a second. "I can't remember her last name. She and Eileen had gotten real close. She knew I was Eileen's friend and she called me and said she had just talked to Eileen, and Eileen said she was going to shoot herself."

"She *did*?"

"Yes, Ginny was really upset. She asked me what she thought we should do, and I said I didn't know."

"Did you try to call Eileen?"

"No, someone else called a few minutes later—I don't remember who it was—and said that Eileen had been rushed to the hospital. A little while later I heard she was dead."

Betty told me that she had never been fond of Ginny. "The day after Eileen died, Vic asked Ginny and me if we wanted to come to the funeral home to see Eileen's body. The two of us went right after work. Eileen looked like she was sleeping. She had on this real pretty dress. Pink, I think. Ginny was real emotional—hugging Eileen, kissing her, stroking her hair. I couldn't do that. I just stood off to the side, crying softly to myself. When we got outside, Ginny got angry at me for not showing Eileen more affection. I was really hurt. I'm sure I felt just as bad as she did."

"I'm sorry. I can see why you were hurt. That was a nice gesture on Vic's part, though, inviting you to come to the funeral home."

"Yes, it was. He was there, but he was very distant. I think we shook hands or something."

"Did you ever talk to him after that?"

"No, never."

• • •

After my conversation with Betty, I wasn't sure what to think. Her version of events seemed to tip the scales toward the conclusion that Eileen had taken her own life, but her recollection of the time between the two calls she received—the one from Ginny, telling her that Eileen had said she was *going* to shoot herself, and the second call "a few minutes later," informing her that Eileen had been rushed to the hospital—didn't jibe. As I tried to reconstruct the timeline, I assumed that Eileen wouldn't have called Ginny just before she pulled the trigger. Most likely, she had made the call before the final argument with Vic. That meant there would have been a lapse of at least twenty minutes between the gunshot and the time when someone (Who? Surely not Vic, given his state of mind) phoned Betty Clay to say that Eileen had been taken to the hospital. It was easy to see why the time between those two phone calls might have gotten skewed in Betty's mind. All this had happened twenty-seven years ago. But in the end, what difference did it make? The most important point was that in the midst of the crisis Eileen had told Ginny she was going to take her own life.

"Eileen may have *threatened* to shoot herself," Cheri said when I told her about my call with Betty, "but that doesn't mean she went through with it. How do we know that Vic wasn't holding a gun to her head when she made that call to Ginny? It would've given him a perfect alibi."

Much as I valued Cheri's hard work and devotion to the case, at times her logic seemed to be skewed by her need to prove that Vic was a murderer. When I spoke to Darryl, he was more evenhanded. He saw Vic as "a twenty-six-year-old kid" who was deeply in love with Eileen and got "caught in a buzz saw of lies" and conflicting emotions. As for Vic's guilt or innocence, Darryl wasn't ready to come down on either side of the question.

To clear my head, I put the investigation aside for several weeks and tried to busy myself with other things. Since hearing that Eileen had openly mentioned suicide to Ginny, there seemed to be little reason for going forward. But Darryl was still trying to put all the pieces together. One day I got a rambling message from him on my answering machine, telling me he had been reviewing the police reports point by point and realized it would take him hours to write a cogent summary.

"I don't want to run up the clock on you, but this case is a complete rat's nest," he said, dejected. "I've never seen such choppy, slipshod, misdirected police reporting. Why didn't they talk to Ginny and Betty? Why didn't they interview the psychologist Vic and Eileen went to see? To allow the conclusion of this matter to be in the hands of these incompetent officers reflects so badly on the police department and the community that I fear for the people of San Bernardino. The people out there deserve—" The machine cut him off.

Darryl's message got me thinking about the psychologist. I hadn't given him any serious consideration, and it appeared that the police hadn't either. He had met with Vic and Eileen several times, including a session the evening before she died, but no one had spoken with him as part of the investigation. Now I wondered if he thought Eileen might have been suicidal. I contacted Cheri to see if she could locate him, and she quickly discovered that he was still practicing in San Bernardino. I considered calling him, then I realized that the laws governing client-therapist confidentiality might preclude him from giving me any information. My hunch was confirmed by one of my poker pals, a forensic psychiatrist. He said Vic, as Eileen's executor, could block access to the therapist's records, though the district attorney could subpoena them if he suspected that Vic was trying to cover up a felony. My friend encouraged me to go back to my research on the gunshot wound. He thought that was my best chance of getting some concrete evidence.

Wading back into the arcana of ballistics and tattooing, I tried to determine how far the muzzle might have been from Eileen's chest. I held my reading glasses like a pistol to try to approximate the distance. Then I found a movie gun for sixty-nine dollars on the Internet, a die-cast replica of the Colt Trooper with no moving parts, but when I mentioned it to Elizabeth, she said she didn't want a gun in the house, not even a fake one.

Time to consult a professional.

I called a ballistics expert named Ralph Higgins from the pay phone in the basement of the public library. After I introduced myself and explained my reasons for the call, Higgins asked me to tell him Eileen's story. I gave him a detailed account, dropping in a reference to *Gunshot Wounds* to assure him that I had done my homework. Higgins listened, not saying much, until I got to the coroner's report.

"According to the report," I said, "the stippling is eleven centimeters."

"You mean eleven millimeters."

"No, centimeters. I'm reading it right off the protocol. It says the gunshot wound is a cluster of red flattened markings eleven by eleven centimeters."

"That looks like a *homicide* to me," Higgins said emphatically.

I sagged against the wall next to the pay phone, relieved and appalled in the same instant. "How can you be sure?"

"The tattooing. People who commit suicide don't hold a gun that far from their body."

"According to DiMaio, one to three percent of all suicides are not contact wounds."

"Way less than that. Half of one percent *maybe*. People press the barrel of the gun against their bodies. But the other thing about your sister's case? Mamas don't shoot themselves in front of their babies. It just doesn't happen." Cheri had said the same thing, but when I reminded Higgins that it wasn't *her* child, he dismissed the notion out of hand. "Once that little boy came through the door, he was just like her own," he said, as if the crime had suddenly become personal to him. "I've never heard of a woman shooting herself with a child in the home. *Never*."

I asked him if he would do some muzzle distance tests with a Colt Trooper for me, but he refused. Unless we could get the exact gun and the same lot of bullets, he said, any other test would just be an approximation. "I've done thousands of distance tests and I can tell you with absolute certainty that that gun was between twelve and sixteen inches from your sister's chest. What you need to do is gather up every scrap of evidence you can find. Emergency room records, the coroner's notes, crime scene photographs. It won't be easy, but don't give up. This was *not* a suicide. Either your sister was murdered or the two of them got into a struggle and the gun went off."

22

The phone call with Higgins was like a shot of adrenaline. I'd been sleepwalking for weeks after my conversation with Betty Clay, all but certain that Eileen had committed suicide. The ballistics expert quickly dispelled that notion. He had encouraged me to track down every scrap of evidence I could find. But that evidence, if it still existed, was in the hands of the San Bernardino County Sheriff's Department, the same cops who seemed to have either botched the investigation through incompetence and indifference or had willfully covered up a crime to protect a fellow police officer. Contacting them did not appear to be an option.

Darryl agreed. He thought we should get an attorney to look at the case, someone with a strong background in criminal law. I called my friend Bruce Edmands, a defense attorney and former prosecutor, and he said he'd be happy to review the file.

It didn't take long for Bruce to get back to me. He said he'd gone over the documents and found them deeply troubling. He thought there was a strong possibility that this was a homicide. The problem, he said, was that there might not be enough physical evidence to obtain an indictment let alone a conviction; perhaps the best route might be to try to get the US Attorney's Office to look into the matter as a violation of Eileen's civil rights. But before we went any further, he wanted me to prepare a chronology for the case.

"Start with a list of people who are involved, like the cast of characters at the beginning of a play," he said. "You might even want to do an introduction with some background information—where Eileen and Vic were from, their birth dates, how long they'd been married, that sort of thing. Then do a chronology of events. A timeline, starting with the incident on the lover's front lawn. Make sure you explain where you got your information—lieutenant so-and-so's police report, Eileen's letter to her parents, et cetera. Once you have the chronology you can do an analysis where you point out all the discrepancies, all the things the police didn't do, the various inferences we can make."

We agreed that I would create a rough draft, then go over it in his office the following week.

I had read all the documents so many times I was sure I would be able to sit down one afternoon and write the chronology from memory, but in practice, it proved to be quite difficult and time-consuming. There were discrepancies I hadn't considered before, facts I'd overlooked. One of the most peculiar centered on the date of the initial contact between Hal Boring and Detective Delaney. In his main report Delaney stated that he first spoke with Boring on the phone at "0745, 9-11-74," a conversation during which Boring told the detective he had left town because of the death threats Vic had made against him. But this conversation was six hours *before* the shooting. Either this was a typo and the call actually occurred on September 12, or Boring's call had been routed to Delaney, who ended up being the lead homicide detective on Eileen's case. Was this a weird coincidence, or had Delaney gotten the date wrong? All I could do was speculate.

When I mentioned it to Bruce during our meeting, he thought it was unlikely that Delaney would have made a mistake about the date. "That's pretty basic," he said.

"Well, the cops seemed to have skipped a lot of the basics."

"No argument on that front. I don't know if it was laziness or a cover-up, but as far as Delaney was concerned, this was a suicide no matter what the evidence showed." He leafed through the documents. "Look at the first line of Delaney's report."

It read: "<u>Assignment</u>: 9-11-74 at 1410 hours Lt. Vaughn and Det. Delaney assigned to go to 6313 Dunblane in regards to an attempt [sic] suicide at location involving a police officer's wife."

"Attempted suicide," Bruce said. "Not a *shooting*, which is the most neutral way of looking at it. Not a *reported* or a *possible* suicide attempt. It's a basic tenet of good police work that every gunshot death is considered a homicide until you can prove otherwise. Delaney had his mind made up about this case before he ever left the police station."

"Do you think it was a cover-up?"

"I don't know, Jim. Bad police work is not a crime in and of itself. The question is, what is the link between the notion that Eileen did not commit suicide and the notion that this case was never adequately investigated? The worse the police work—and this is about the worst I've ever seen—the more it looks like a cover-up."

That evening I told Darryl what Bruce had said about Delaney having his mind made up before he left the station.

"Write this down," Darryl said. "'It is a capital mistake to theorize before one has data. Insensibly one begins to twist facts to suit theories, instead of theories to suit facts.' That's from Arthur Conan Doyle, 'A Scandal in Bohemia,' written over a hundred years ago. We've had a lot of scientific developments in the past century to help us figure out whodunit—fingerprints, blood typing, DNA—but the principles behind a good investigation haven't changed one bit."

I worked for days perfecting the chronology. It made me appreciate the care and precision a lawyer must take in preparing a case. I also began reading true-crime books. One was *My Dark Places* by James Ellroy, author of *L.A. Confidential* and other popular crime novels. In 1958, when

Ellroy was ten years old, his mother was raped and murdered in El Monte, California, a small town about fifteen miles east of Los Angeles. No one was ever charged with the crime. Thirty-eight years later, with the help of a retired LA police officer, Ellroy set out to find the killer. He was never able to solve the case, but it was not because of inadequate police work by the Los Angeles County Sheriff's Department. In a warehouse filled with evidence from old cases, the police still had the victim's clothes (including the stockings that had been used to strangle her), dust and fiber samples from the victim's automobile, samples of the victim's fingernails and pubic hair, verbatim transcripts of interviews with suspects. This crime had taken place sixteen years before Eileen's death in the adjacent county west of San Bernardino. When I criticized the police work in Eileen's case, occasionally someone would suggest that the sheriff's department might not have known about various investigative techniques back in 1974. Ellroy's mother's case belied that notion. Whatever the reason behind the shoddy police work by the San Bernardino County Sheriff's Department, it wasn't for lack of knowledge of how to conduct a thorough investigation.

I felt a deep kinship with Ellroy after reading his book. He wrote of his mother, "Dead people belong to the live people who claim them most obsessively. She was all mine."

He had his mother; I had Eileen. No way for either one of us to turn back.

23

My father died in August 1979. Connie was eight months pregnant with Kelly and unable to fly, so I went back to Pittsburgh alone. We used Brady Funeral Home, the same undertaker as we had for Eileen. I took my mother to the cemetery to pick out a burial plot and she left the funeral arrangements up to me. Through all of this Keith had been no help at all. He was drinking heavily again and would sneak away whenever he could. At times I would notice my mother's eyes scanning the funeral home, wanting him near.

As he and I were getting dressed the morning of the funeral, Keith held out his right arm and said, "Will you button my shirt cuff?"

"Sure," I said, doing so quickly. "But why can't you button it yourself?"

"I don't know. I think I got a pinched nerve or something. I'm having trouble manipulating my fingers." He flapped his left hand rapidly as if it were asleep.

When we got to the funeral home, I realized I had forgotten to arrange for a minister to come and hold the service. Dismayed by my mistake, I locked myself in the bathroom and began to weep, my face buried in my hands. I thought I was crying because I had screwed up my dad's funeral; then I realized I was crying simply because he was gone and I would never be able to talk to him again.

My cousin Don and I borrowed a Bible from the funeral director and performed an impromptu service. Mum, as one would expect, was not pleased. But my mother told me the funeral was exactly what Dad would have wanted.

A few hours later Keith drove me to the airport. In the five years since Eileen's death, we'd had a guarded rapprochement; now I was disgusted with him again. He had come home to see our father in the hospital, knowing Dad had only few days left. Dad died around two in the morning, and the hospital called and asked my mother if she wanted to come see the body. She did, but Keith was out drinking, so Mom called Vic's brother Paul to come pick her up and take her to the hospital. This, along with the fact that Keith had left all of the funeral arrangements up to me, had left me deeply resentful.

When we got out of the car at the airport, he shook my hand, smiled, and said, "So long, big brother."

I didn't know if he was needling me or simply acknowledging the abdication of his birthright. Tension knotted the muscles at the back of my neck as I walked down the airport corridor toward my gate. My sister was dead, my father was dead, and I didn't care when I saw my brother again.

The estrangement I'd felt from Keith after Dad's funeral lasted only a few weeks. The reason he had not been able to button the cuff of his shirt was not a pinched nerve in his elbow. The doctors told him he had multiple sclerosis. Shaken by the diagnosis, Keith called me, and I told him I would help in any way I could. Over the next few months I spoke with him and Alide regularly, getting updates on his condition.

On Thanksgiving, a few days before Keith's thirty-eighth birthday, the pain in his left foot became intolerable. Alide took him to the emergency room and an internist quickly determined that Keith did not have MS; the loss of motor skills in his left hand were the result of a stroke. Now blood clots had formed behind his left knee, cutting off circulation to his lower leg. Doctors quickly transferred him from the small hospital in Kingston to Mount Sinai in New York City, where a prominent cardiovascular surgeon performed an arterial bypass to try to replenish the blood supply to Keith's lower leg. But the surgery was unsuccessful, and a week later his leg was amputated a few inches below the knee. I went to New York City to visit him, and he was in agony, his pain so intense he was barely compos mentis. A few weeks later, unable to save the knee joint, doctors had to amputate another eight inches off his leg.

While Keith was still in the hospital recovering, I contacted a medical malpractice attorney in Boston on his behalf. Seven years later the case went to court. In the trial, Keith's attorney was able to prove that the last, and most crucial, page of Keith's medical records from the neurologist had gone missing. When an expert witness for the opposing counsel made a statement on the stand that seemed to implicate the hospital in wrongdoing, the defense asked for a recess and made a settlement offer which Keith and his lawyer accepted.

The ordeal had left my brother with a crippled left hand and a severe limp on his prosthetic leg. But it also made him stop drinking and brought the two of us close together again.

When Elizabeth and I got married in June 1990, we thought it would be good luck to get married on her birthday. Good luck, indeed. But I sometimes wonder why I, and I alone, among my siblings seem to have *all* the luck.

Three weeks before the wedding, Keith was diagnosed with lung cancer. Tests showed that the cancer had already spread to his lymph nodes, his stomach, and his brain. I drove to Kingston and spent two days visiting him. At times we were able to have a normal conversation;

then the various drugs and painkillers would take hold and he would slip into a troubled sleep, his body writhing as he kicked off the sheets with his one good leg, his fingers groping for a phantom cigarette, which he would bring to his lips and take a deep drag on. He had been a two-pack-a-day man for thirty years. I had tears in my eyes, my fists clenched, thinking, *You stupid fuck! How could you have done this to yourself? Please don't die. Don't leave me. Don't make me have to tell our mother she's lost another child.*

He began his radiation treatments on a Monday morning. Alide said he was in good spirits, talking about how he was going to beat the odds, but that same night he died. Diagnosis to death in six days. The medical examiner who performed the autopsy could find no immediate cause for his death. Months later a toxicology report came back from the lab in Albany, stating that Keith had died of an overdose of morphine. When I learned this, I felt no outrage. Without a doubt, that overdose saved him from months of suffering. Perhaps it was the result of some nurse's carelessness or a faulty regulator on the morphine drip; then again, it seemed just as likely that Keith may have found a way to override the safety mechanism on the IV or charmed some caregiver into assisting him with a swift and painless exit. The circumstances of Keith's death are completely different from Eileen's, but each has an element of mystery, and the notion that my brother and sister both may have committed suicide leaves me dumbstruck with sorrow and disbelief.

Writing these words, I want to roll back the tape, rewind it to one of those pillow fights with Keith and Eileen in the front room on Wettach Street. "*Stop! Wait!*" I want to tell them. "I know what happens. We have to find a way to change the endings."

24

WHEN I finished the chronology, Bruce Edmands sent it to an old friend of his, a criminal defense attorney in Los Angeles. We both thought it would be a good idea to get someone who was actively engaged in the justice system in California to look at the evidence and see if there were any grounds on which the case might be reopened. The lawyer responded quickly, agreeing that the police reports were "an embarrassment and lend themselves to skepticism," but that, ultimately, he couldn't "see the presumptive logic of why a sheriff's department would allow a bunch of low-ranking officers [to] 'cover' for another low-ranking officer from another department in a murder case." In the absence of forensic tests, the only way to find out what happened would be to speak with key witnesses who were never interviewed by the police—witnesses, he cautioned, "who have little incentive to get re-involved."

At least I was on the right track.

Based on the reports, the lawyer said, one could only speculate about the truth.

But one thing does jump out. Eileen was terribly unhappy and acting in ways that show little insight into her depression. She's separated, has at least one unsatisfying affair, reconciles, continues her unhappy affair within a few days after reconciling, then writes to her parents—on the first day she starts caring for a young child after years of pregnancy issues—about her "prize" of a husband and her desire to become a "homemaker." On that same day she allegedly calls a friend and says she's going to kill herself and, at the very least, ingests a large quantity of aspirin.

I reread his analysis several times. What did he mean about Eileen continuing her "unhappy affair a few days after reconciling" with Vic? I went back and looked at the chronology and reread the police reports. Alex Waering, with whom Vic had been living all summer, had said Vic told him "around 9/2" that he and Eileen had worked out their problems and Vic would be moving back with Eileen. September 2 had been a Monday, Labor Day. Eileen and Vic had gone to Las Vegas on Saturday, two days before, and agreed to reconcile. Four days later they had the confrontation on the Borings' front lawn. In the crime scene interview with Lieutenant Vaughn, Vic "stated that *last week* [my emphasis] his wife had spent all night with Dr. Boring and that she had told him of this yesterday and what had occurred between her and Dr. Boring."

This revelation dumbfounded me. Through countless readings, and my own full reconstruction of the timeline, I had missed this simple but critical fact: after going to Las Vegas with Vic and asking him to end their separation, Eileen had apparently come home and had one last fling with Boring at the campground.

Gloria Boring must have gotten wind of this—her husband having been away for the night on some flimsy excuse—and decided to initiate the showdown with Eileen and Vic. (Exactly when Eileen confessed to this tryst to Vic remains unclear. Vic told me that she didn't tell him anything until the morning of the day she died; he told the police that her confession came at the therapist's the night before.)

I had to give the lawyer credit for homing in on this detail, but I wasn't ready to buy into his notion that Eileen had "little insight into her depression."

I showed the lawyer's letter to Elizabeth. "He thinks she was delusional," I said bitterly. "Yeah, she was pretty mixed-up, not sure if she wanted to be with Vic or Boring. But what about all the stuff in the police reports where they say Vic beat her up and threatened her life? He never mentions any of that. She's the one who ended up dead, and Vic was a helluva lot more volatile than she was."

"Welcome to the male view of the world," Elizabeth said. "In that lawyer's eyes, Eileen was just another hysterical woman. The word comes from the Greek word for womb. Hysteria is a *female* condition, Jim. Try thinking about this story with the sexes reversed. What if Eileen was the cop and Vic was cheating on her? Substitute booze for aspirin. Do you think anybody would believe this story if the *man* supposedly committed suicide out of guilt for having a love affair?"

Elizabeth had a good point. Bruce thought so too, but he encouraged me to look at it from another angle. "What if Eileen had fallen in love with Boring? She leaves Vic, thinking she and Boring are going to sail off into the sunset together. Then his wife finds out, they have that big blowup on their front lawn, and he dumps Eileen so fast she feels like she's been hit by a truck. Boring tells her, Sorry, honey, but it's *over*. And, by the way, I think it might be better for everybody if you started looking for a new job. All of a sudden, Eileen feels like her whole world is falling apart. She's lost her lover, lost her job, she can't have kids, she's ruined her marriage. Maybe she felt like she didn't have anything left to live for."

I didn't say anything, but Bruce could see the dejection in my face.

"I'm not saying I *believe* that's what happened, Jim. Based on everything we know right now, if I had to come down on one side or the other, I'd say there was a pretty good chance Vic had something to do with Eileen's death. But you have to think about the alternatives.

That's what defense attorneys like me do: we get the jury to consider *all* the possibilities."

"What about the lies Vic told me in my parents' kitchen? He said he slapped Eileen *once* when he actually beat her up. He never mentioned the argument on Boring's front lawn. He didn't tell me about the little boy being there, or about throwing the adoption papers at her."

"Those are more omissions than lies. What if Vic watered everything down for *your* benefit? He knew you were hurting. He didn't want to look you in the eye and say, 'Your sister was so frigging crazy she shot herself in front of a two-year-old.'"

"You're saying Vic left that stuff out to protect *me*, not himself?"

Bruce shrugged. "It's a possibility."

But not one I wanted to accept.

25

THE INVESTIGATION consumed me. It was all I could talk about with family and friends. Sometimes I'd launch into the story with a stranger, someone I'd met at a party or the passenger beside me on an airplane. Elizabeth and I would go out to dinner with another couple and I'd sit there expounding on timelines and gunshot wounds, referring to Vic and Hal Boring and Detective Delaney like they were figures in a high-profile murder trial we all followed on the evening news. Most listeners were captivated. They'd grimace at the details, shake their heads in outrage, and ask a lot of questions, though sometimes I'd notice a person getting uncomfortable, as if he'd accidentally seen me naked. When the conversation moved on to other things, I tended to get gloomy and remote. Laughter seemed inappropriate, any joy undeserved. Friends gave me considerable latitude, but my moodiness had already caused a fair amount of tension between Elizabeth and me. It didn't matter what I was doing—riding my bike or reading true-crime books, playing solitaire or watching the Red Sox on TV— the case droned on in my head. I couldn't turn it off. I didn't want to.

One question trumped all others when someone heard the story— "Do *you* think Vic murdered Eileen?" I refused to give a definitive answer. I told them I had written hundreds of pages in my journal trying to sort it out and still couldn't say for certain. It surprised me how many people ventured an opinion of their own. The fact that most of them weighed in against Vic no doubt had something to do with the way I told the story—I *wanted* Vic to be guilty, but I wouldn't let myself say it out loud. Sometimes I'd end up in the unlikely position where I was the one offering facts and theories to mitigate the case against him, just as Bruce had done with me. It was the only way I knew how to try to keep searching for truth more than vengeance.

Along with the matter of Vic's probable guilt or innocence, there was another question that people asked often. "Why now?" they'd say. "What made you start looking into your sister's death after all this time?" I told them how I had been trying to find a topic for a new novel, and since most of my fiction had sprung from my personal history, Eileen's story seemed like a natural choice. Then I'd explain how one thing led to another and I ended up in the San Bernardino Public Library with Darryl and Cheri, reading the police reports, and that changed everything.

Happenstance. This was my answer to "Why now?" It was something I stumbled on. A few people close to me, like my daughter Meg, all grown up and living in London, suggested that sounded too facile, that there had to be more to it than that. I insisted that the motives that had led me back to Eileen didn't interest me. I didn't feel I needed to focus on *why* I had started my exploration. I was too engrossed in trying to find out *what* had happened in that bedroom in San Bernardino.

But it was strange, almost like my sister had begun prodding me after all those years of silence. I'd started writing about Eileen in early 2001, almost immediately after I had stopped writing the journals for my children.

The journals had been a crucial (but private) part of my life for nearly two decades. I had decided I would give to them to the children when Kelly, the youngest, turned twenty-one. I had written a final common entry. In it I said that each of their journals was unique, a letter written over a long period of time. I had not edited the journals in any way—about 275 pages each—but I made copies in case I ever wanted to read them. In closing, I said: "Be kind. Be honest, especially with yourself. Work hard. Try to be happy." Thirteen words. That seemed like enough.

I took them to dinner in a private room at a restaurant, gave them the journals, and explained their origin. They opened their volumes randomly and began to peruse them, encountering long-forgotten stories and sharing them aloud. We all had tears in our eyes. It was a wonderful night, one of the best of my life.

I would never stop being a father to my children, of course, but giving them the journals was a metaphor for letting them go. Within a week or two, another child started angling for my attention—a troubled girl out in California, younger then than Meg was now. She had been mostly silent for the past twenty-seven years; now it felt like there were things she needed to say. Or maybe she'd been saying them all along, and I was finally ready to listen. The impetus didn't come to me like a bolt out of the blue, but I was ready to set a new goal for myself. I needed to find out more about my sister.

Eileen had written faithfully to my parents from San Bernardino. She had also sent them hundreds of photographs, which I'd collected from Mom's apartment. When the New Year came in 2001 and Eileen began to rattle around in my head, I got out the photographs and looked through them—Vic and Eileen boogying in front of the stereo; Eileen and Mrs. Z standing under a giant horseshoe at a casino in Las Vegas; a silver-blue Mustang with "our pride and joy" written on the back; a small house with a carport that she called "our castle." Eileen enjoyed being in front of the camera, posing like a pinup in her bathing suit, clowning in a paint-splattered T-shirt with smudges on her hands and face. She looked so tiny standing next to Vic. Her hairstyles and hair color were in constant flux, pixie to beehive, platinum blond to her natural dark brown. I hadn't remembered that she dyed her hair so frequently or that she sometimes wore glasses. It made me smile to see how much she loved her dog.

When I returned from California with the police reports in hand, I went through all the photos again. This time I was looking for clues—a forced smile or a telling look, some hint that her life was not as cheery as Eileen had always tried to make it seem. Most of the photographs had a handwritten date on the back or the film developer's automatic month-year stamp on the border, so I was able to organize them in chronological order.

Elizabeth saw me going through the photos and came and looked over my shoulder. "Find anything interesting?" she said.

"Actually, I have. There isn't a single picture from 1974. Not one."

"Not even the new house they bought?"

"No, I guess she was too busy."

"Busy and depressed," Elizabeth said. "Sad people don't take pictures." She began looking through the snapshots. "I see what you mean about the resemblance to Meg. No wonder you keep getting their names mixed up."

I'd been saying Meg when I meant Eileen. Eileen when I meant Meg. "The way this case has taken over my life, I guess it's only natural."

"Yes," Elizabeth said, "maybe that's why you finally decided to start the investigation in first place. You're looking at her differently now."

"What do you mean?"

"It's like Eileen isn't just your sister anymore. Now you're seeing her through the eyes of a father."

26

Darryl had been spending time in Mexico and Honduras working on other cases. When he returned, he did some old-fashioned sleuthing and found out that Eileen's friend Ginny still worked for the San Bernardino School District. She'd gone by a different name back then and now went by Harmon, but he was certain he had the right person. We needed to talk to her about that last phone call with Eileen, but for reasons I couldn't explain, I had an instinctive mistrust of Ginny. Perhaps I was echoing the feelings of Betty Clay, who had been hurt by the way Ginny had scolded her when they'd gone to see Eileen's body at the mortuary, but most likely it was a case of shoot-the-messenger— a much-too-apt metaphor in this case. Ginny told Betty that Eileen had called her and said she was going to shoot herself, a piece of evidence that seemed to put the gun in Eileen's hand. I didn't agree with Cheri's notion that Vic had coerced Eileen into making that telephone call, but in my bouts of paranoia I wondered if Ginny, despite all her keening, had been somehow allied with him.

Darryl shared my mistrust of Ginny. He thought the best way to approach her would be to try to interview her in person without any forewarning, rather than contact her by telephone first as we'd done with Betty. One day he drove out to San Bernardino to see if he could catch her at work, but when he got to the school administration building, Ginny's coworkers said she was at the courthouse serving as a juror in a murder case, and he left without identifying himself. He explained to me that he didn't want to dredge up memories of Eileen while Ginny was preoccupied with thoughts about another murder case, so he figured it was best to wait.

I agreed. I had already begun to plan another trip to California, and I wanted to be included in the interview with Ginny if she was willing to see us. Darryl said it would be too intimidating if the two of just showed up at her workplace, so he figured he'd just call after she got off jury duty and see how she reacted. He managed to reach her a few weeks later.

In that initial call, he asked her if she remembered Eileen Zaccagnini, and Ginny said of course she did. When Darryl told her he represented Eileen's brother, she asked him if Mae, my mother, was still living. He told Ginny that Mae had died about ten years ago and I was the only one in the family left. Ginny seemed sad to hear the news; she said she and my mother had kept in touch for a few years after Eileen passed away, exchanging Christmas cards and an occasional letter. Darryl told her I was coming out to California and asked if the two of us could sit down and talk with her.

"She sounded a little hesitant before she said okay," Darryl told me on the phone. "There was a long pause like she might be having second thoughts, then she said, 'Does Jim have questions for me?' I told her yes, and she said, '*Good*. Tell him I have questions too.'"

Darryl picked me up at the Los Angeles Airport and we headed east for our appointment with Betty Clay. We drove into the Yucca Valley east of San Bernardino, a sun-scorched landscape with stubby, unnatural-looking hills—thousands of rounded red-brown boulders heaped into enormous piles like stores of ammunition for a race of rock-wielding giants. An occasional stand of tall white windmills sprang up from a barren ridge, their slender three-bladed arms turning in the breeze. As we drove, Darryl told me we were still in San Bernardino County, the largest county in the US outside of Alaska, extending another eighty miles to the Nevada border. "This is real outlaw country," he said. "People around here mind their own business," he said. "Sometimes an investigator or newspaper reporter will come out here and start poking around and they'll find his body in a ditch."

He told me stories about renegade arms dealers and maverick CIA agents, ritualistic killings with decapitated corpses. I never tired of listening to him talk.

Betty Clay's directions were perfect. We turned off the highway onto a dirt road and saw a hand-painted sign, "Ed & Betty—1.3 miles." Halfway down the road was a large sinkhole from a flash flood, a sinkhole that Betty had warned us to drive around. A papery cloud floated like a discarded napkin in the eastern sky, but it was hard to imagine a single drop of rain ever falling in this parched landscape.

Betty and her husband, Ed, were standing outside the house, waiting to greet us. Darryl and I got out of the car and we shook hands all around. Ed was a bald, wiry man, the kind of person who looked as if he liked to be busy. He told us he had homesteaded this land back in 1953. Five acres for $250. Betty smiled and said she'd fallen in love with the place the first time she saw it. The inflections in her voice reminded me of Cheri. With her short yellow-gray hair and bright blue eyes, she looked much younger than mid-seventies. Ed excused himself and Betty led us into the dining room to talk.

I had brought some photographs of Eileen—something I'd forgotten to do on my first trip to California—and showed them to Betty. She fixed her gaze on a picture of Eileen leaning against a car with her hands behind her back.

"*This* is the girl I remember," Betty said, her face lighting up. "She was so *tiny*. Always smiling. And she was such a good secretary, even though we gave her the worst job. She had to take notes at the meetings between the board and the labor union, and nobody else wanted to do it. There were only four of us in one small office, so we were together all the time. It was like a constant tea party, except we had to get the work done."

Then, in September 1973, Betty had had surgery and was out of work for five weeks. Eileen ran the office in her absence, but when Betty returned she noticed something had changed.

"She seemed so *down*. I could see it right away. That was right around the time she had a miscarriage and it really took something out of her. She wanted children so much."

I asked if Eileen ever mentioned adoption. Betty thought about it for a second, then said no, Eileen never did.

"She liked to go to the movies," Betty said. "She loved to cook, lots of Italian dishes, and of course she was crazy about that dog. She was always coming over to my place, but we never discussed our problems. I was alone myself at the time. I had just gone through a divorce, but we were both very private people. I wish I could have said something to her then. All the signs were there. I just never put them together."

"What kind of signs?"

"The depression, of course. I was talking about Eileen with Nina Coburn the other day—Nina worked in the same office—and she reminded me of the time Eileen came to work with her face all bruised. She tried to laugh it off by saying how clumsy she was—that she'd fallen off her bicycle into a big cement planter right in front of her house. But Nina remembered that Eileen admitted later that Vic had beaten her up."

Darryl and I were careful not to react. We knew about at least one beating from the police reports. I felt myself seething inside, wondering how many there had been.

Nina Coburn still lived in San Bernardino, and Betty gave me her telephone number.

"I don't think Eileen's reunion with Vic was a happy one," she said.

"I remember we took a drive to Palm Springs one day and she was so blue."

I asked her what Vic was like, and she said that none of them ever really knew him, that he wasn't a friendly person. "I think Eileen was alone a lot. After she died none of us ever saw him again."

I mentioned what Vic had told me about Eileen always wanting everything to be perfect, how she couldn't even confront a salesclerk who had given her the wrong change.

"No, she was *feisty*," Betty said. "I worked with her every day. She knew how to stand up to people."

I wondered if Vic had lied to me about Eileen, or if she simply acted differently when she was around him. It was a big swing from his characterization of her to Betty's, which coincided with mine.

I asked her to tell me more about Hal Boring.

"He had such a slimy charm," Betty said, her voice animated with indignation on Eileen's behalf. "I have no idea if it's true, but I heard he had flings with lots of secretaries."

Darryl, who had been almost completely silent up till then, said, "I think Eileen probably had real low self-esteem from her relationship with Vic. He sounds like he was one of those husbands who liked to keep his wife on a short string. Boring probably turned on the charm and caught her off guard."

Betty agreed. She told us about the other woman who he'd been suspected of having a relationship with—his secretary at Cypress Elementary.

"Her husband shot her seven times in the face. I'm not sure what happened to him. Someone told me he spent a few months in a mental hospital and then was released. I never put two and two together until now, but after Eileen died, Boring's behavior toward me got real odd. He became very solicitous and tried to hire me to work for him, which would have been a step down for me. I was going away on a trip to Europe and he sent me a bottle of champagne. I never really trusted him."

The conversation turned to the day that Betty and Ginny went to see Eileen's body at the funeral home. Betty said Eileen looked so pretty and peaceful, "like a girl on her way to Sunday school." She was still miffed at the way Ginny had scolded her afterward for a lack of emotion.

I said I believed that everyone grieved in his own way, and told her about Dad singing in the truck when his father died.

Darryl and I reviewed some of the disturbing things we'd found in the police reports. Betty said they were so sloppy they made her lose faith in *any* police department. We speculated about the veracity of Vic's story regarding Eileen's previous suicide attempt. Betty hadn't known Vic was in the house when the shot was fired. She said she thought that Ginny had told her Vic was outside in the yard. This seemed like a significant discrepancy. If Betty was mistaken about this, she also could have been mistaken about other things Ginny told her on the phone. What if Ginny had called her *after* the fact and said, "Eileen just shot herself," not that Eileen said she *wanted* to shoot herself? That would change the story entirely.

As the conversation wound down, Betty remembered a happy time with Eileen, a Christmas party at the superintendent's home where Eileen got tipsy and giggly and became the life of the party. I asked Betty if Vic was there. She couldn't remember, and I found myself thinking, if he was, he would have tried to squelch that gaiety in Eileen or berated her for it on the way home.

Darryl and I got rooms in a motel in San Bernardino. The next morning we met with Cheri in the library to tell her about our meeting with Betty and go through the new research Cheri had done. She had found that the other house owned by Eileen and Vic—the one they had lived in before they moved to Dunblane—had been occupied in September 1974 by a woman named "Ginny Ames." It might have been a coincidence, but Cheri had a theory that "Ginny Ames" was Ginny Harmon. Slowly but surely, the pieces of the puzzle were starting to fit together.

27

Ginny had agreed to meet with Darryl and me the next day on her lunch break at the educational building in the center of town. She had told Darryl she wanted to meet in a public place, but he didn't know why. When we found her, she was sitting at a desk in a large room with about thirty other office workers. Short and dark-eyed, with thin black-metal-rimmed glasses, she had wavy black hair that fell past her shoulders. When I introduced myself, she didn't smile. She led us silently to the cafeteria, where we picked out our lunches, then settled into a booth in back. She seemed reticent, as if she had agreed to meet with us against her better judgment, but when I got out the photographs of Eileen she began to relax. Her eyes went from the pictures to my face and back to the pictures again.

"You look like her," she said. "It's the eyes."

As I'd done with Betty, I asked Ginny if she wanted to keep a few pictures for herself. After some small talk, we arrived at the reason for our conversation. I told her about the conversation I'd had with Vic in my parents' kitchen and how we'd believed him entirely. Then Darryl gave her a quick outline of the police reports, which raised a host of suspicions about Vic and cast him in a much different light. Ginny listened intently, the way she must have listened to the proceedings as a juror in the recent homicide trial.

I said, "Did you know Eileen was having an affair with Hal Boring?"

"That's what I *heard*," she said, "but I never believed it."

I told her it was true, and she frowned.

"Did you talk to Eileen on the day she died?" I asked, trying to make the question sound as neutral and open-ended as possible. I wanted to hear Ginny's recollections in her own words before asking her about the call she'd made to Betty Clay.

"Yes, there were a number of phone calls that day. Actually, the first one was from Vic." She said Vic called the office and demanded to speak to Hal Boring. "I told him Hal wasn't in and Vic started yelling, 'Quit lying, Ginny. Stop covering for him.'"

"*Was* Boring in?"

Ginny shook her head. "He was at a conference in Escondido. Vic was ranting, screaming into the telephone. He called Eileen a slut, a whore. He said, 'You know the two of them are sleeping together.' I told him I didn't know anything about that. They were always completely professional in the office. I asked him to put Eileen on the phone but he refused."

"Did you know Vic?"

"A little. At the time I was renting a house that he and Eileen owned, the one they used to live in. Eileen gave me a good deal on the rent." That explained the tenant's name. Cheri had been spot-on.

Ginny said the next call came from Eileen. "She was crying and sobbing. 'Ginny, what am I going to do? Vic's going to leave me. He's all I have. I can't live without him.'"

"Did she say she was going to shoot herself?"

"No," Ginny said. "Absolutely not."

"Did you think she *might* be suicidal?"

"No, she was very emotional and kept saying she couldn't live without him, but I never thought she'd hurt herself."

I asked Ginny what time she'd gotten that call. She said she wasn't certain but she thought it was right after lunch.

"Actually, there were two calls. The first was just Eileen, but when she called back, Vic was on the line. They were both really upset, crying, talking at the same time, and I kept trying to get them to calm down. I told them they could work things out, that they just needed some time. I was the only one in the office and couldn't leave, but I told them I would come to their house as soon as I got off work and the three of us could talk things over. They seemed to like that idea, and I made them promise they'd wait for me."

Ginny sighed. I asked her again if Eileen had mentioned suicide in those desperate phone calls.

"No, but here's the scary part. A little while later the phone rang again and it was Vic. He said, 'Ginny, Eileen just killed herself.' Then there was a click. That was all. He just said it and hung up." She shuddered at the memory. "His voice was so cold, completely without emotion."

"Jesus." I had gotten inured to bizarre twists in the story, but this one was beyond the pale. "How long was this after the last call? The one with both of them on the line?"

"Ten or fifteen minutes. I called back right away and a man answered. It wasn't Vic. I asked to speak to Eileen and the man said that she couldn't come to the phone right now. I tried to get more information, but he wouldn't talk to me. Later, I'm not sure how much longer, I got a call from a man who asked me if I was the one who called the Zaccagnini house looking for Eileen. There wasn't any caller ID back then, so I don't know how he knew it was me. When I told him yes, that was me who called, he asked me why I wanted to talk to her. I said, 'She's my friend. I'm worried about her. Is she all right?' And he told me, 'No, I'm sorry, she's dead.'"

None of us spoke for a moment, the horrific news delivered once again.

I found myself thinking that Vic didn't know Eileen was dead until the call came from the hospital approximately an hour and a half after the shot was fired—meaning he couldn't have telephoned Ginny to report Eileen's death ten or fifteen minutes after the call with him and Eileen on the line. Then again, if Vic shot Eileen and feared she was going to die, he might have called Ginny and informed her of Eileen's "suicide" in an attempt to cover up his crime. But if that were the case, then who was the man who answered the phone when Ginny called back a few minutes later? Surely not Deputy Larkin, the first officer on the scene. He was frantically administering CPR to Eileen, trying to save her life. I could only surmise that the events of that day had gotten skewed in Ginny's memory, just as they had with Betty—the various calls being compressed into a much tighter time frame.

Darryl asked Ginny if the person she'd spoken to was a police officer. Ginny said she didn't know; he'd hung up without identifying himself.

Darryl said, "Do you remember calling Betty Clay in Dr. Dwyer's office?"

Ginny nodded. "I think it was after I got that scary call from Vic, saying Eileen just killed herself." Right, I thought, *after* the shot was fired, not before. "His call had me so spooked I tried to call him back right away, but nobody picked up. Then I called Betty a minute or two later."

The day after Eileen's death, Ginny said she began getting phone calls from Vic threatening Boring. There were so many of them that she moved to Dr. Dwyer's office for the day to get her work done. She did not see Boring again until he came to work the following Monday. At some point she asked Vic about the funeral arrangements, and he said angrily, "Nobody's going to see her." Then in a subsequent call, he told her she could come to the funeral home. To my surprise, Ginny said she didn't remember Betty being there too.

I took notes while Ginny talked, trying to get as much as I could down on paper.

"I spoke to Gloria Boring a lot in the days after Eileen's death," Ginny said. "Gloria said Eileen and Hal were having an affair, and I told her I didn't know anything about that. Eileen didn't talk with me about her personal life, and she and Hal were always completely professional when they were in the office. I told her, 'Look, Gloria, Eileen is dead; there's nothing we can do about that. Do you love Hal? Can you forgive him? If you can, then you have to try and move forward; otherwise, your marriage is over.' When Hal came back to work on Monday, I told him I didn't know if he was having an affair with Eileen or not, and I didn't *want* to know. Then I gave him the same advice I'd given Gloria. Forget the past and try to keep going."

Darryl told Ginny she sounded like a well-grounded person, some-one that was good to have around in a crisis. She pursed her lips and gave a self-deprecating shrug.

I turned the conversation to the cloud of suspicion hanging over Boring's resignation. She bristled and said there was no such thing—a woman in the school department had gone to jail around that time over a "revolving cash fund," but Boring had nothing to do with it.

The conversation returned to the case, Darryl filling in more of the details. One thing we hadn't mentioned up to that point was the presence of Freddy Waering, the boy Eileen had been babysitting. I was curious to know if Ginny had been aware of the child being present in the house and whether she thought it made any difference.

Darryl leaned forward and said, "Do you think Eileen would have killed herself with a two-year-old in the house?"

"I don't think Eileen would have killed herself, *period*." Ginny thrust her chin out. "I went home and told my husband—he was still my boyfriend at the time—Eileen did *not* commit suicide. I thought the police would come around and investigate. I waited and waited, but nobody ever did. I *always* thought Vic did it."

I could tell by the look on her face that Ginny had wanted to say that for a long, long time.

"My husband's dead now," Ginny said, "but I'm real close to his brother, and he's the one I confide in. The other day I told him, I know why Eileen's brother and that private detective want to talk to me. They think Eileen was murdered. He warned me not to say anything. He said I could wind up getting sued for slander. But . . ." She lifted her shoulders in a defiant shrug.

I thanked her, then asked if she had had much contact with Vic after Eileen's death. No, she said. Virtually none. She had mailed him the rent for the house on 46th Street every month and moved out of that house in December 1976.

As we moved through various remaining threads and questions, Boring's name came up again. I told her how that man held a special place in the dark part of my heart.

"Hal is a friend of mine," Ginny said, ready to defend him.

For me, Vic wasn't the only villain in this story, and I wanted her to see what a rotter Boring had been. I took a copy of Delaney's interview with Boring from my briefcase and read her a few sentences in which Boring said Eileen had "gone with" other men. She asked if she could see it, and after she read the statement, she had a disgusted look on her face.

"This is upsetting," she said. "It really pisses me off." She blushed and apologized for her language. "Eileen wasn't like that. She didn't run around."

I liked hearing her say that, but there was a lingering thought that if Ginny and Betty, Eileen's closest friends, didn't know about the affair with Boring, they wouldn't have known about any other lovers either. I didn't want to believe Eileen was promiscuous any more than Ginny did, but I could not dismiss the possibility out of hand. In the end, it didn't matter to me how many other men Eileen had been with; what I hated was the idea of Boring smearing her reputation at the same time he denied his own involvement.

I told Ginny that I wanted to be honest with her—Darryl and I were going to try to get the DA to reopen the case. "I can't make you any promises," I said, "but there's a good chance the police will want to talk to you and you might have to testify in court."

Ginny nodded. Then she told us about the recent trial, five weeks and one day, in which Ginny had served as jury foreman: two members of the Mexican Mafia, the shooter and driver, were convicted of first-degree murder. The police still make a lot of mistakes, she told us, like not checking the hands of the suspects for gunshot residue. Her biggest frustration as a juror was not being able to ask questions in the courtroom. When it came to Eileen's case, she assured us she would help in any way she could.

The interview was over. As we left the cafeteria, I thanked Ginny for all her help and put out my hand to shake.

"Uh-uh," she said, opening her arms. "I need a hug."

28

Darryl and i met Cheri outside the San Bernardino educational building and gave her a rundown of our meeting with Ginny. We told her it had been immensely reassuring to learn that Ginny had never believed Eileen committed suicide. Still, as productive as the conversation had been, it opened us up to more questions. First and foremost was the timeline of the telephone calls. Even with the new information Ginny had provided, we couldn't make them fit. It simply wasn't possible for Vic to have called Ginny and said that Eileen had just killed herself ten or fifteen minutes after Ginny had been talking to both of them.

"Not if *he* already shot her," Cheri said. "He was probably trying to establish an alibi."

"Yes, I thought of that," I said. "But Ginny seemed so *certain*. I mean, why would Vic be so cold? Wouldn't he act like he was completely distraught and try and get her to be sympathetic?" Besides, I reasoned, Eileen was alive for more than an hour after they took her to the hospital. Even if he had shot her, he wouldn't have known she was going to die.

We went round and round, trying to make sense of who said what to whom, and when. But we were dealing with vagaries of time and memory, to say nothing of the unconscionable inadequacy of the police reports. Exhausted, we tried to work out the question of Boring's whereabouts. Detective Delaney's report had said that he had first talked to Boring about Vic's death threats at "0745, 9-11-74," six hours before the shooting. Ginny told us Boring wasn't in the office that day and had gone to a conference in Escondido, which is near San Diego. That jibed with the information in Delaney's report, but it didn't explain why Boring's call to the sheriff's department had been routed to Delaney, who hadn't yet been assigned to the case. Was it sheer coincidence that he spoke to the detective who would become the lead investigator five hours later? Boring was out of the office for the rest of the week, so our best guess was that Boring had remained at the conference, and called Delaney the day *after* the shooting, and the detective had gotten the date wrong in his report.

Moving beyond the interview with Ginny, we went back to questions about the shooting itself. Vic had told Vaughn that he had rushed into the bedroom after hearing the gunshot and found Eileen "kneeling on the floor and leaning against the bed" with a black spot on her blouse.

I said, "The first time I read that description I was a little confused, wondering how Vic could have seen the blood spot if Eileen was leaning face-first against the bed. Then I realized she must have been slumped over sideways with her shoulder against the bed."

It was unclear how blood had gotten on the carpet. There were no photos of the crime scene, just a drawing with a squiggly circle of indeterminate size indicating blood. Either Eileen had fallen forward and gotten blood on the carpet before Vic turned her over and began administering CPR or blood had seeped out of the wound and trickled along her rib cage while she was on her back.

"The autopsy report said the bleeding was *internal*," Cheri said. "I think she fell forward and got blood on the carpet after Vic shot her."

Darryl said, "Look, if Eileen didn't kill herself, it probably happened one of two ways. Either it was an accident, the two of them struggling over the gun, or else it was total impulse. They're in this bitter argument and the gun's sitting on top of the dresser, not in the closet where Vic claimed it was. All of a sudden, he grabs it and BOOM! He shoots her before he has time to think. Here's the thing: when people lie, *most* of the story is usually true; they just add a few details or change them around. Vic said Eileen was kneeling. What if that was right *before* the gun went off? Vic shoots her while she's on her knees." Darryl pointed an imaginary gun about belly high. "That explains the bullet angle. *Then* he sees the dark spot on her blouse."

I'd tried to imagine various scenarios in that bedroom dozens of times. Darryl's telling vividly brought one possibility to light. The house was only a mile or two away. On my previous trip to San Bernardino I hadn't wanted to linger there, but now my feelings had changed.

I said, "You think we might get a better idea of what might have happened if we could see the inside of that room?"

Darryl's eyebrows went up. "It wouldn't hurt."

That evening I called Betty Clay from my motel room and told her about the interview with Ginny.

"Oh, no wonder she was so emotional at the funeral home," Betty said, letting go of her old grudge. "She was right in the middle of it."

29

THE NEXT DAY Darryl and I went to see a lawyer named Evan Radford in Fontana, about ten miles west of San Bernardino. Radford had been recommended by a friend of a friend, who said he was an excellent defense attorney. In anticipation of the meeting, I had sent him the chronology and the police reports. I wanted to get his point of view on the case and see if he could help me find some official in San Bernardino County who could help reopen it. When we got to Radford's office, he told us he had asked a private investigator, Maura Buchanan, to join us. Her office was directly across the hall from his in an old building in downtown Fontana.

A soft-spoken man in his forties, Radford had a congenial smile and a small tuft of hair under his lower lip. Maura was a handsome woman, about fifty, with pale, freckled skin and a firm handshake. We dispensed with formalities and moved directly to the case. Maura hadn't read the chronology, and I gave her a thumbnail sketch. At times it was almost funny the way her face would scrunch up in disbelief as she heard some new fact. She and Radford both agreed the police work was abominable. How could there be no detailed description of Eileen's clothes? Why hadn't the police checked Eileen's and Vic's hands for gunshot residue or done any ballistics tests? This was exactly the response I had been hoping for, but what surprised me most was the depth of their outrage over the date on Vic's marriage license to Yvonne. Maura called it "the product of a sick mind."

"You couldn't use it against him in court," Radford said. "His attorney would make sure the jury never heard that particular piece of information, but this was one incredibly bitter, angry man." He gave a little shiver.

United in our suspicion of Vic and our contempt for the police, we began to discuss strategy. I said I thought we needed to find some young hotshot in the San Bernardino County Sheriff's Department who felt like he could make a name for himself by reopening and solving a cold case. Radford agreed, but Maura shook her head.

"I know cops," she said. Her father, two brothers, and ex-husband of seventeen years were all policemen. "All it would take is one guy in the sheriff's office—not necessarily somebody who knew Vic, just someone making sure no one tries to pin something on a fellow officer—and all the records in this case would be *gone* in a heartbeat."

Darryl nodded. "You got that right."

"What about somebody in the DA's office?" I asked.

Radford leaned back in his chair. "Maybe the Department of Justice. What you have to understand about the DOJ is, they like to take cases they're ninety percent sure they can win. We need something concrete we can show them, and I think the best piece of evidence we have is the gunshot wound. That ballistics expert in Colorado said he thought it was a homicide, but we need a detailed report. Maura and I know this fellow who works here in California. Troy Merriweather. He did the ballistics on the Symbionese Liberation Army case back in the seventies and has a great reputation. If Merriweather says this case looks inconsistent with suicide, I think we might be able to get the DOJ involved. If we get those guys interested in the case, the people in the sheriff's office will make sure none of the evidence goes missing. They don't want any trouble from the Feds."

Maura added her endorsement of Merriweather, and asked me if I wanted to go ahead and hire him.

"Yes, absolutely," I said.

From Radford's office, Darryl and I drove back to San Bernardino, where we had a late-afternoon appointment with Nina Coburn, the secretary who had worked in the superintendent's office with Eileen and Betty. Like Betty, she was now retired.

When I had phoned and introduced myself the day before, Nina said brusquely, "I don't know anything about Eileen's death."

"I'm sure you don't," I said, caught off guard by her tone. "I just . . ." It took me a moment to regain my composure. I hadn't expected her to be so off-putting. "I was hoping you could tell me something about Eileen's *life*. Simple stuff. The kind of things she liked to do. What made her laugh."

"That was a *long, long* time ago."

"Yes, it was."

I told her I'd gone to see Betty, and Nina said she knew that. She clearly did not want to talk to me, but I pressed on, trying to inject a little cheer into my voice, and she reluctantly agreed to see Darryl and me.

Her house was less than a mile from 6313 Dunblane. She invited us into her living room and offered us cold drinks. A fireplace made of flat fieldstones dominated the room. When Darryl complimented it, she told us that her husband, a retired plumber, had built the house with Betty's husband, Ed; the two men had also built the house in Twenty-nine Palms. Nina was about the same age as Betty but the polar opposite in personality—glum, nervous, suspicious. She told us her mother had lived with her and had passed away just a few months ago, and she was still quite shaken by the loss. I listened as she reminisced about her mother for a few minutes, then tried to steer the conversation to Eileen.

"Oh, I don't remember much," Nina said. "It's terrible the way your memory goes when you get older. I forget where I put something and I'll start looking for it, and then I can't remember what the heck I'm looking for."

Darryl smiled and said, "Happens to me all the time."

She didn't return his smile.

I showed her the photographs of Eileen, hoping they would jog her memory.

"She was such a breath of sunshine," Nina said. "When it came to work, she really wanted to better herself. She'd stay late, take on new projects. The rest of us were happy to let her do it. Everybody liked her. Never had a bad word for anyone. She was such a little thing and she was always dieting. Nothing but a piece of fruit or a small salad for lunch. One time, she looked so thin I said, 'Eileen, you better stop dieting. You're starting to lose your *figure*.'"

The photographs, which were still on the coffee table, confirmed what Nina had just said. A busty majorette in high school, Eileen appeared pixie-like in the last few years of her life.

"We took golfing lessons together," Nina said. "Eileen and Vic and me and my husband. We went after work every Friday for six weeks. I was terrible, but Eileen enjoyed it."

"What was Vic like?" I asked.

She thought about that for a moment. "You know, I *know* he was there. Sometimes we'd all go out to eat after the lesson, but I don't remember anything about him. I can't even recall what he looked like."

It was a remarkable echo of our prior interviews. To all three of Eileen's friends—Nina, Betty, and Ginny—Vic was a cypher. Surely one of these women would have remembered him if he had been opinionated or bullying, handsome or flirtatious or funny. It was, I suppose, the perfect profile for an undercover cop, someone you hardly noticed. But I wasn't getting any closer to understanding what Eileen had seen in this man, her "prize" as she called him in the letter she wrote a few hours before she died. Perhaps it was as simple as this—she was in love, and love is not given to answers or reasons. Neither is falling out of love, I suppose, although by the time that happens, most of us have lists of complaints and grievances, litanies we can recite to family and friends and divorce lawyers to justify why it's all gone wrong.

"Do you remember Eileen coming to work with bruises on her face?"

"Yes, she said she fell off her bike into a big planter in front of her house."

"But she admitted later that Vic had done it?"

"Oh, no, I don't remember her saying anything like *that*."

I stared at her, puzzled. Was Nina being evasive or had her memory failed her for the moment? According to Betty, it had been Nina who reminded her that Eileen eventually told her friends she'd been beaten. I didn't feel that I was in a position to probe and ask her about the discrepancy—unlike Ginny, she clearly did not want to walk us through it, and had no interest in testifying in a courtroom if we somehow managed to get the authorities to reopen this case. Darryl and I thanked her for her time, and she seemed relieved to see us go.

30

S COTT TWICHELL, who currently lived with his family at 6313 Dunblane, returned Darryl's phone call on Saturday morning and said we could come by that afternoon. Darryl hadn't told him much about the case, only that Eileen had died in the house back in 1974 and we were investigating the circumstances.

The front door opened onto the living room. As Darryl and I introduced ourselves, my eyes were already sliding across the room to the hallway that led to the rooms in back—my curiosity exceeded only by my apprehension, unsure how I'd react when I saw the bedroom where the shot was fired. We sat down in the living room and Twichell asked us about the case. Darryl explained at the outset that we needed to keep the investigation somewhat confidential because we didn't want Vic to hear about it. After we'd talked for about twenty minutes, Twichell looked at me and said, "You ready?"

The hallway was about five feet wide, the master bedroom halfway down on the left. There were two bedrooms on the right side of the hall—either could have been the one Vic called "the den," the place where he said he'd gone to look up my parents' telephone number. The door to the master bedroom opened inward at the corner of the room. Bright and neat and tastefully decorated in pastel shades, it was much smaller than it had been in my imagination. The head of the bed had been beneath the windows on the east wall of the house when Eileen and Vic lived there; now the bed was turned ninety degrees with the head against the north wall. With Twichell's permission, Darryl began taking photographs. I looked in the closet where Vic said the gun had been stored on the shelf, then stared at the carpet where the spot of blood had been, trying to conjure up the anger and turmoil of that day. But there was no aura of tragedy in that lovely space, no smell of death.

"How do you feel, being here like this?" Twichell asked.

"I'm fine," I said. "It's a beautiful room. You and your wife have chased all the bad vibes away."

He smiled, pleased, and I realized how generous it was for him to let me into his home, how uneasy it might have made him if I had stepped into his bedroom and broken down in tears.

I showed him the police drawing of the room. In it, the bed was askew, the head pushed away from the wall. Twichell got a tape measure so we could check the dimensions against the drawing. The width along the north wall was nine feet, six inches—nine inches narrower than the measurements taken by the police, another mistake on their part, as there was no way the dimensions of the room could have been altered. All the other dimensions were accurate. The police drawing indicated that the spot of blood was eleven feet, eleven inches from the doorway into the bedroom. By my measurement, it was another twenty-four feet from the doorway of the master bedroom to the front door. When Engel, the second officer on the scene, entered the front door and yelled for Deputy Larkin, he would have had a complete view of the empty rooms in the front of the house—living room, dining room, and kitchen. The hallway leading back to the bedrooms would have been directly in front of him, his voice carrying down the hall. It still troubled me that neither Larkin nor Vic responded when Engel first called out to them; the two men were about thirty feet away and the bedroom door would almost certainly have been open since they were expecting the ambulance. In addition, it seemed odd that Engel left the house and searched the grounds outside instead of proceeding down the hall to look for Larkin and the victim of a reported suicide attempt.

When we finished our tour of the inside of the house, Darryl and I thanked Twichell and went outside and took more photographs. Then we went next door to the house directly opposite the bedroom windows. The current residents, Dolores and Clarence Nichol, had lived there since the 1960s. Neither remembered Vic and Eileen, though Dolores remembered the police coming to the house the day of the shooting. The next day, she said, the dogs were left unattended in the backyard, hungry and thirsty. She'd put a hose through the fence to give them water, then called the police. I asked her what kind of dogs they were. "Very big," she said. "And fierce." I'm not sure about the dog Eileen called Topi, but her beloved Cal was a friendly little Cairn terrier.

Riding back to LA in the car with Darryl, I read over the police reports again, hoping to find something new now that we had been inside the house. Detective Delaney had written in his report that the "[C]rime scene is very neat . . . and . . . showed no evidence of physical violence or a struggle." Why had he failed to mention the "wrinkled papers" that Lieutenant Vaughn saw on the bed, papers that Vic admitted having thrown at Eileen? If there was no sign of a struggle, why was the bed askew? (Also, he described the bed as "king size," which had to be incorrect, given the dimensions, or the blood spot would have been under the bed.) It was hard to see how any of this might have been part of a cover-up, but each omission and inaccurate detail reaffirmed the slipshod nature of the investigation. Cheri was right that first day in the library—the police were never interested in finding out *exactly* what had happened in that room.

As I was leafing through my notes that evening, I came across a quote from Vernon J. Geberth's *Practical Homicide Investigation*—"The investigation of a murder necessitates a certain tenacity and perseverance that transcends the ordinary investigative pursuit. Homicides are solved because the detective cares."

31

Shortly after coming home from California, I went to Pittsburgh to see Aunt Pauline and attend the Constant family reunion. (Neither my grandfather Konstanty Konstantynovich nor my grandmother ever learned to speak English; the family Americanized their names when my mother, Maelena, was a young girl.) Aunt Pauline was the only one of my mother's eight siblings still living. I loved how she worried about me and prayed for me and made me laugh. The day after the reunion, she and I sat on her back porch, teasing each other and telling stories.

I asked her about the time my mother left my father and took Keith and Eileen to stay with her family at Babush's—four adults and four children sardined into a tiny two-bedroom house. I was three or four then, and had gone to my Mum's house, where I slept on two side-by-side chairs propped up next to my Aunt Mil and Uncle Norb's bed.

"Oh, Mae had it rough when your dad was drinking," Aunt Pauline said. "She came on the last bus from the North Side. It must have been midnight when she got here. She had all her stuff in two shopping bags, and sticking out of one of the bags was a big, framed picture of you. When I saw that, I had to laugh. Oh, Mae, I told her. At least we won't have trouble finding room for Jimmy."

I laughed and rolled my eyes. "Lotta drunks in this family, Aunt Pauline. What was it about you Constant sisters? You, Mom, Aunt Vaudie, every one of you married a drunk. And Aunt Mary? She married *two* drunks. You ladies didn't have very good judgment, did you?"

"No, I guess not." She chuckled, a hint of mischief in her eyes. "Unless we drove them to it."

As the conversation turned to Eileen, I asked her to tell me about Frank's suicide, wondering if there might be something in his story that would help me understand our family's reaction to Eileen's death.

Aunt Pauline explained that it wasn't a holdup like they said in the newspaper. Frank was just trying to get his friend's gun back from the owner of the gas station. There was a scuffle and Frank was shot in his upper arm. He drove to the home of the family physician, who bandaged his arm and then called the police to report the gunshot wound as required by law. Frank's injury was serious enough that they thought his arm would have to be amputated and he spent nearly two months in the hospital. When it was time for him to be released, his bail was set at five thousand dollars.

"I went down to the courthouse and talked to the DA and he reduced it to fifteen hundred," Aunt Pauline said. "The bail bondsman charged us five hundred. That was *big* money back then, and Frank had to go to jail for a few days while we were trying to scrape it together. After he came home, he had trouble sleeping. The doctor gave him some pills and they made him real angry. He thought he was going crazy. He told me he had dreams about killing people. I found a penknife under his pillow. Another time I found a rope with a noose hanging down in the cellar. The pills were capsules. One day I dumped them all out and filled them with cracker meal and Frank slept like a baby after that."

"So, why do you think he killed himself?"

"He didn't want to go to jail, Jim. I think something happened to him those two or three days he was in there after he got out of the hospital. Pete went to pick him up and he said this one fellow looked at

Frank and mumbled something, and Frank got real agitated. Pete asked him what the fellow said, but Frank didn't want to talk about it."

"Mom told me Babush used to say 'for shame' to Frank in Polish. She thought he couldn't live with the disgrace he'd brought on the family."

Aunt Pauline shrugged. "Maybe. I don't remember that."

Nothing in her reply suggested that she believed my mother was wrong, only that Mae had one way of looking at Frank's suicide and Pauline had another. Still, in my mind, the difference was significant. Both versions had the same moral tenor—be careful not to get into trouble; you might not be able to handle the consequences. Aunt Pauline believed Frank took his life because he didn't want to go to prison. In my mother's version, the one Eileen and I heard growing up, it had been Frank's *conscience*—the shame he felt for disgracing his family— that drove him to his death. The irony, of course, was that Vic ascribed this same motive to Eileen's suicide, attributing it to her remorse and shame over the love affair she'd had with her boss. Which may be why we were predisposed to believe him. I don't remember anyone in the family making this comparison between Frank and Eileen, but to me the parallels were obvious. My mother didn't *blame* Babush for Frank's suicide, but when she told the story there was a second, equally impor- tant lesson that stood alongside the first—be compassionate in your judgment of others; your righteous condemnation could be devastat- ing, maybe even fatal. If Eileen had been able to tell my parents about her shortcomings—her *sins*—they would not have reproached her. They would have offered her love and understanding, and tried to help her work things out. Why couldn't she see that?

I took Aunt Pauline for a drive. She showed me the service station where Frank's troubles began, then we went to the cemetery to see his grave as well as those of my grandparents and Uncle Pete. I didn't like visiting cemeteries, but it seemed important to Aunt Pauline, and I thought it would be good practice for what I had to do next.

The following morning I went alone to the Christ Our Redeemer Catholic Cemetery. When I arrived, the attendant in the office gave me directions to Eileen's grave along with photocopies of the papers in a thin file—internment invoice, burial permit, order for the headstone. As I remembered, the grave was near the top of a hill overlooking a valley of tombstones and tall, broad-leafed trees. In that section of the cemetery all the grave markers were flush to the ground—Eileen's was a rectangle of pale coral-colored granite inscribed with a cross and praying hands:

EILEEN LAVERNE

ZACCAGNINI

FEB. 4, 1947
SEPT. 11, 1974
Wife

There were artificial flowers next to the marker—bright red roses, white carnations, and a single pink daisy, glycerin dewdrops glistening on the petals. They hadn't faded in the weather yet, and couldn't have been more than a month or two old. I assumed that Vic's mother had placed them on the grave, and I felt a touch of guilt that I hadn't brought any flowers myself.

I pulled up some large tufts of crabgrass around the edges of Eileen's headstone and threw them in the bushes. I took several photographs of the headstone, then sat on the ground, waiting for an epiphany, some message from the grave.

The sun was hot and I started to get a headache. I got up and wandered down the hill, looking at the other markers. When I walked back to Eileen's grave, I stood on the burned-out grass and said out loud, "You have to help me, Eileen. *Please!* I don't know what to do next." I was shouting now, my eyes filled with tears. "Do you want me to quit? Is that it? Am I being a fool?"

Nothing.

I knelt on the grave and bent forward as if I were praying. It was a hot, muggy day, but the gravestone felt cool against my forehead. I closed my eyes and tried to let go of everything—sorrow, anger, vengeance, doubt. I can't say if I was prostrate for two minutes or ten, but a sense of calm slowly came over me. A plane droned overhead; the wind rustled the leaves in the trees. A bird chirped, its last note rising like a question, but Eileen had nothing to say.

I rose to my feet and took one last look at her name.

"It's okay," I said. "You rest. I need to keep going till I know the truth."

I drove to the Highwood Cemetery on the other end of the North Side to see my parents' grave. I had been there only two times, once at each of their funerals. The office wasn't open and I had to drive around looking for the headstone. I knew that it was on a gentle slope in the shade of a sycamore tree. I made several slow loops around the cemetery, parked, then got out and saw a tombstone that said "Thomson," black letters on gray granite. I sat on the grave. I wanted to talk to them, to tell them everything I had discovered about Eileen and Vic, but I was tapped out. I picked up a smooth pebble and placed it on top of the tombstone, the way people do in Jewish cemeteries, to let them know that I'd been there.

I told Aunt Pauline about the artificial flowers on Eileen's grave.

"I guess Mrs. Z put them there," I said. "She was devoted to Eileen. So was Vic's brother Paul. It makes me feel kind of strange. If I can get the district attorney in San Bernardino to reopen the case and start questioning Vic, his mother will be crushed."

"You just keep doing what you're doing, Jim," Aunt Pauline said. "You can't worry about her or anybody else." She set her jaw, a touch of anger in her voice. "Tell the truth, I never liked the way Bea talked about Vic. With her it was always poor Vic this and poor Vic that, like *he* was the victim and couldn't get over it. It just made your parents feel worse. Some of us gave your mother money at the funeral to help out with expenses and she gave it all to Vic. Then he went back to California and never called them. Never wrote. Not even a Christmas card."

Keith's widow, Alide, made a similar comment on the telephone a few weeks later with a touch of bitterness I hadn't heard in her before. Was it guilt or indifference that made Vic so neglectful? Even the smallest gesture of kindness or compassion would have meant so much to my parents.

That night at Aunt Pauline's, sleeping in the comforting drone of a fan, I dreamed about Eileen for the first time since I had begun my quest. In the dream, I was in a room talking to a woman I didn't recognize, though I somehow knew that she was a therapist. She and I were sitting in armchairs while Eileen, dead, was lying on a bed next to the wall on the far side of the room. The therapist gazed at Eileen from across the room and back at me.

"We really looked alike as children," I said.

Eileen seemed to hear us. She lifted her head and her eyes fluttered open.

"Oh, yes, it's the brown eyes," the therapist said. "I see what you mean."

For a moment I thought Eileen would say something, but she put her head down and went back to being dead.

I woke up immediately and lay awake for a long time.

I don't put much stock in dreams, but that one kept coming back to me. When I mentioned it to Darryl, I said, "You'd think the dream would've given me the creeps but it was kind of nice to see her again, even for just a few moments. That's what's so frustrating about all this. I keep reaching out for Eileen, but she's not there."

"Give it time," Darryl said. "She's getting closer."

•   •   •

A few weeks after my trip to Pittsburgh, my friend Peter called and I told him about the dream.

"Have you considered consulting a psychic?" he said.

"Not really."

"Maybe you should consider thinking outside the box. I was telling a friend at work about your sister's case the other day, and he said his wife had started having psychic experiences a few years ago, and he thought she might be able to help."

Peter's suggestion didn't surprise me. He'd recently been on a Vision Quest retreat somewhere out West that featured a solo, three-day fast. That sort of thing seemed like so much mumbo jumbo to me. I prided myself on being pragmatic—a hard-core realist. I never checked my horoscope, never worried about black cats or broken mirrors. But I took down the psychic's name and number, and a few days later I gave her a call and told her about Eileen.

When she got back to me about a week later, her "connections" were uselessly generic—a brick schoolhouse, a cardigan sweater, a short-haired dog, a doughy ex-cop with a guilty conscience, possible clues in Eileen's high school yearbook. She said Eileen seemed perfectly at peace, which was how the dead always came to her.

"What a crock of horseshit," I told Peter. "Go look in Eileen's high school yearbook? For two hundred and seventy-five bucks, I wanted her to tell me who was holding the *gun!*"

Discouraged as I was by the experience with the psychic, I willed myself to keep thinking outside the box as Peter had suggested, and scheduled an appointment with a hypnotist. Being a bit of a control freak, I wasn't sure if I could actually be hypnotized, but I figured it was worth a try. The hypnotist asked me if I had a specific goal in mind, and I told him I was hoping to find out more about the relationship I'd had with Eileen when we were younger, before she got married.

The hypnotist had no trouble putting me under, and he recorded our conversation on a cassette tape. What the session revealed was both welcome and disappointing—welcome because it showed that Eileen and I genuinely loved each other and got along well; disappointing because there were no revelations and no touching stories that could bring her back to me. Everything I'd said had obviously come from my own subconscious mind. But that was the problem—I seemed to have a streak of amnesia when it came to Eileen.

32

IN MID-AUGUST Cheri tracked down the information about Melissa Pratt, the woman with whom Hal Boring had allegedly been having an affair in 1966, eight years before Eileen's death. She was thirty-eight years old when she was murdered and had worked as a secretary at Cypress Elementary School. Her estranged husband, Gregory, shot her seven times with a .22-caliber pistol four days after Christmas. According to the newspaper account, police arrived at a house on North Sepulveda Avenue shortly after one o'clock in the afternoon and found her slumped in a chair in the living room. Gregory Pratt, a serviceman for the gas company, "was sitting across the room from the victim on the couch." The gun was on the floor. The article reported that Melissa Pratt was a "well-known semi-professional singer" who had once been the featured performer in the 1955 production of *Carousel* by the San Bernardino Civic Light Opera and was described by neighbors as "very lovely and very happy." Melissa and Gregory had recently been granted a divorce but still saw each other regularly. They had two teenage children.

There was no way to prove that Hal Boring had been having an affair with Melissa Pratt, and in some ways it didn't matter. Her death had nothing to do with Eileen's, but the twist in the story felt too bizarre to let go, and I was still seething from the insinuations that Boring had made about Eileen to the police. In my journal, I referred to him as a "scumbag." Never mind that I, too, had been an adulterer, stealing off with a married woman one afternoon only to greet her husband on the street a few days later with a smile and a handshake. It's easy to feel morally superior when one's own affair has produced nothing more than a gut-wrenching divorce and a small fortune in legal fees and alimony. To my mind, Melissa Pratt's violent death should have taught Hal Boring a very important lesson—*Don't fuck around with another man's wife. She might wind up in the mortuary.*

After the murder, Gregory Pratt pled guilty to voluntary manslaughter and was incarcerated at the California Institution for Men in Chino. Twenty-nine months later, in May 1969, he sent a handwritten letter to his lawyer regarding his status in prison and the possibility of his being released on probation. In it, he detailed various self-help programs he had participated in and the "emotional stability . . . and positive mental attitude" they had given him. Pratt said that he didn't want to discount the seriousness of his crime, but he felt he had been rehabilitated and had been incarcerated long enough. The letter continued: "If a person looks at it strictly from a punitive standpoint, it is hard to argue with the 'time' factor. [But] I feel that too much 'time' has the power to destroy, and in my particular case additional time would serve no purpose except as punishment."

The letter made me stop and think about justice. How much *time* should a man spend in prison for taking someone's life? It's a debt, one might argue, that can never be fully repaid—but we put a price on it anyway. Punishments are prescribed by law, with considerable leeway for juries to consider the difference between one killing and another, which is why we have terms like *first-* and *second-degree murder* and *manslaughter*. Gregory Pratt had not tried to deny or mitigate his culpability, but he felt that he had served enough time for his crime. The parole board disagreed. He spent another nineteen months in prison before he was released in December 1970.

My friends were appalled when I told them the story. "Four years?" one said. "That's less than one year per bullet."

Personally, I didn't care about Gregory Pratt one way or the other. No doubt I would have felt differently if Melissa had been my sister, but what really stuck in my craw was the fact that Hal Boring had seemingly been the catalyst in the death of *two* women and had managed to slip away with no apparent personal consequences whatsoever.

The days trickled by. I was depressed and angry, fit company for no one. Darryl was my usual sounding board. He'd listen patiently to all my carping and try to calm me down.

One day he said, "Listen, Jim, *anger* is just one letter away from *danger*. All that anger you're feeling toward Vic and Boring is eating you up inside. As soon as we start judging people, we're chained to them. You have to find a way to let all that bad stuff go. Try to think like a samurai. He respects his enemy but doesn't *judge* him."

"I'm sorry, Darryl, but I don't get that logic. A samurai respects his enemy, then cuts his head off? That's seems pretty fucking *judgmental* to me."

Darryl tried to explain, but I was in no mood to be mollified. I understood what he was trying to say—all that anger and bitterness was clearly taking its toll on me—yet, on some visceral level, I *needed* it. It was my raison d'être. I told people I was looking for truth, but I had become an avenging angel, unwilling—or unable—to forgive or forget.

Elizabeth and I had a house near the beach in eastern Long Island that we rented out every summer, then spent a month there just after Labor Day. The change of scenery had a calming effect on me. We would ride our bikes or take a long walk on the beach in the morning; then I'd go to the public library and write. Since my first trip to California, I had read the police reports dozen of times and filled an entire composition book with facts and quotations and endless speculation, but I hadn't tried to organize the material into a coherent narrative. Now I wanted to get back to work on the book that had led me to Darryl and triggered the investigation.

My journal was a jumble of entries documenting the contradictions and inconsistencies in the case, all of which needed to be marshaled into a consistent narrative. The chronology I'd created with my friend Bruce helped keep me focused, and I began to see the book as a journey—a chance to reflect on my life and think about all the people I had lost. I loved remembering my family, even when it made me cry. As always, the words came slowly, but I was not in a rush. Tuesday of my second week back at the desk would be the twenty-seventh anniversary of Eileen's death. Soon she would be dead as long as she had been alive.

Elizabeth and I woke that morning to bright sunshine and a warm breeze. We rode our bicycles over to Lazy Point in hope of seeing some windsurfers. I didn't mention the significance of the date to Elizabeth on our ride, though she knew, of course. I was looking forward to the afternoon in my carrel at the library. It seemed like a good way to honor Eileen and feel close to her for the whole day.

When we got home from our ride, Elizabeth left her bike by the fence and crossed the street to say hello to our neighbor. A few minutes later, she rushed back into the house and told me to turn on the television—a plane had just crashed into the World Trade Center.

My day of private remembrance had suddenly become a day of horror for the entire nation.

As I listened to the many heartbreaking stories over the next few days, I found myself thinking, *What difference does Eileen's story make in the face of such unspeakable loss?* It didn't matter if Vic murdered my sister; my own loss paled beside that of others. There was enough pain and outrage and irony buried in the smoking rubble in Lower Manhattan to fill a million bookshelves. I found myself doubting the importance of my investigation, my writing, my need for a sense of justice or closure. At times I wondered if I would ever find the energy or purpose to go back to work. But one day led to another as the sun in its indifferent glory kept rising out of the sea, and much sooner than I could have hoped, I started to write again, stitching my life and Eileen's death together, one word at a time.

PART THREE

33

IN THE DAYS after September 11, I wrote assiduously in my journal and on my laptop, thoughts about our national tragedy intertwined with Eileen's story. I couldn't pretend to understand the beliefs that had driven the hijackers to sacrifice their own lives and kill so many innocent people, but I knew how obsession can take over your life until it's hard to think about anything else. "Obsessions are dangerous," I wrote in my journal, "because they leave you completely exposed. People know what you want, what *means* something to you . . . what you might die for. Then of course there is the danger that you might not find the holy grail of truth or wealth or revenge you are seeking. You might fail . . . and everyone will know it."

One feature of my obsession was that my energy seemed boundless. I slept fitfully, but I didn't mind. Some of my best ideas seemed to come in the middle of the night. I was making excellent progress on Eileen's story, keeping track of the number of words I wrote each day. In the evening, Elizabeth and I would talk about my work, and she would often read what I had written. When I got to the part where Keith and I were discussing my questions about Eileen's suicide and my plan to interview Vic, Elizabeth said, "You know, it's odd. All the times I've heard you tell this story, I never heard you mention that Keith offered to talk to Vic with you."

"Well, he *did*. I just thought it'd be better to do it myself."

"Is this book going to be fact or fiction, Jim?"

"*Fact*," I said defensively.

"Fine, I'm not trying to back you into a corner. It's only natural to be unsure about something that happened so long ago. Details are bound to get confused. But have you ever thought about how the need to know pushes you into the unknown? For twenty-seven years you had this story down pat. That's the way you deal with things that are deeply emotional: you make a *story* out of them. It's the way you keep your feelings under control. You create a story and you're just another one of the characters in it." She held her palms out in front of her, as if she were holding the world at bay. "But once you started writing Eileen's story—the *real* story, the one you uncovered after you got the police reports—I think you started having doubts. Doubts about Vic, Keith, yourself. Doubts about everything. What you had for all those years was a nice, tight story. Now things are getting messy, and it's scary not having that pat story to fall back on."

I knew what she meant. I had taken a giant step into the unknown. Now all I could do was follow the facts I had found, write the truth as I remembered it, and hope that I wasn't creating fiction.

As for the investigation, the key to moving forward was to find out what, if any, physical evidence existed beyond the reports and the single photo of Eileen that Cheri had uncovered—photos of the crime scene, photos of Eileen's wounds and her clothing, the spent bullet, results of various forensic tests. Maura Buchanan, the private investigator from Fontana, feared this evidence would go missing if someone in the San Bernardino Sheriff's Department realized we were looking into the case again—someone who had known Vic was a cop and wanted to make sure that the cover-up was never revealed. Darryl agreed, and said that Maura, given her proximity to San Bernardino and her contacts within the bureaucracy, was in the best position to get the information as quietly as possible and obtain any additional reports.

A few weeks after September 11, Maura called to tell me she'd spoken with Troy Merriweather, the ballistics expert she'd hired to look at the case. Merriweather told her that the gunshot wound seemed "consistent with suicide" while other facts pointed toward foul play. If Eileen had held the gun backward and pulled the trigger with her thumb(s)—the only possible way she could have held it without producing a contact wound—the trigger pull would have caused a downward jerking of the gun barrel, which would explain the bullet's trajectory down into her abdomen. Without more evidence Merriweather could not determine how far the muzzle had been from her chest. As for the police work, he agreed with Maura and me that it was an abomination. There were numerous unexplained factors pointing to the possibility of foul play, but the sheriff's department had not followed up on any of them. He told Maura he wanted to wait and see if she uncovered any more physical evidence before submitting his final, written analysis.

In her search for Eileen's file within the police department, Maura discovered that it had been sealed years ago and sent to the archives in Los Angeles. The sheriff's department did that sometimes with a suicide, she explained, or when a cop was involved in order to protect him—that way they could red-flag the file if someone came in and started poking around. If Darryl or I made the request to see the paperwork, she said, it could raise alarm bells, but she felt she could get her hands on it without too much disruption.

I said, "But how can you see it if it's sealed?"

"That's my *job*, Jim. I won't have any trouble."

She was being cagey, but I got the message—she had no qualms about obtaining this information on the sly, and neither did I. We couldn't trust the San Bernardino Sheriff's Department, so the normal rules didn't apply.

When I told Darryl about my conversation with Maura, he was skeptical. He didn't say he thought she was lying, but he didn't believe Maura could "waltz" into the archives in LA—*his* territory—and gain access to a sealed file. A clerk could lose his job in a heartbeat allowing her to do something like that, he said. I had no way of knowing if Darryl's mistrust of Maura was legitimate or simply a matter of professional competition between one private investigator and another. In the end it probably didn't matter; I'd just have to wait and see.

Evan Radford, the lawyer in Fontana, had told me the Department of Justice (DOJ) might be interested in looking into Eileen's case as a civil rights violation.

I liked the idea of getting the DOJ involved, but I didn't want to approach them prematurely; if I did, chances were they would give me the runaround or dismiss me out of hand. I explained my dilemma to an old friend, and he said he knew a lawyer named Dick Landry, a former US attorney, who might be able to help. My friend thought it would be worth the time and money to hire Landry and find out if he could tell me if the DOJ would be interested in Eileen's case. Landry received my phone call warmly and agreed to review the documents.

After reading the file, Landry and his law partner in Seattle both came to the conclusion that Eileen had committed suicide. They felt that the significant quantity of aspirin in Eileen's stomach, as reported in the autopsy protocol, and the open aspirin bottle found in the bathroom at the crime scene corroborated Vic's story. With no hard evidence and no witnesses, Landry said he didn't think that *any* jurisdiction would take on the case, and certainly not the DOJ.

"But what about the horrible police work?" I asked him. "Isn't that enough to make them take a second look?"

"It's sloppy but not egregious," he said. "Actually, it's fairly typical of the kind of stuff you see from local sheriff's offices."

That characterization flabbergasted me. If this police work wasn't egregious, what was?

"It's a zigzag course with almost every case," Landry said. "You're kind of plodding your way to the truth. Cops leave things out, misquote people, make all kinds of mistakes. The discrepancies of fact get explained away as you move toward trial."

I asked Landry if the boy who was in the house at the time of the shooting might be of some value to the case, but he said a two-year-old child would not be considered a credible witness, even if he had been interviewed at the time.

As he continued to outline the realities of the criminal justice system, I offered no counterarguments. He was the expert; I wasn't paying him to tell me what I *wanted* to hear. Still, I could feel myself getting more and more disappointed and dismayed. To me, the facts of the case clearly incriminated Vic. I couldn't understand how *anyone* could see it differently. Landry sensed my frustration and encouraged me to continue to pursue the case through the San Bernardino district attorney, saying that the DA might find inconsistencies where he did not. When I asked him how I could find someone I could trust in the San Bernardino County District Attorney's Office, he said my concerns were legitimate and told me he'd think it over. In the meantime, as a gesture of professional courtesy, he offered to send the file to a friend in the King County (Seattle) prosecutor's office and ask her to look it over, gratis. I thanked him for the offer but asked him to wait. Landry was the second seasoned attorney—along with Bruce's friend who felt Eileen had "little insight into her depression"—who had looked at the case and concluded that she had taken her own life. The only thing that might change their minds was more evidence. I wanted to see if Maura Buchanan could get a copy of the official file before I had another attorney review the case.

34

IN DECEMBER 2001, Maura called to say she'd sent a request to the San Bernardino Sheriff's Department on my behalf, asking for Eileen's file through the Freedom of Information Act. I was curious why she felt this file, which she'd previously told me had been sealed, would now be released, but I didn't press her for an explanation. A few months before, her sister was diagnosed with terminal cancer, and Maura had immediately suspended all her investigations so she could help the family. Now, with her sister's passing, she was back on the case.

It took several weeks, but Maura got the documents from the sheriff's department and sent them along to me. The packet included two reports I had not seen before. One was written by Deputy Ken Larkin, the first sheriff's deputy to respond to the dispatcher's call about the shooting at 6313 Dunblane. According to the *Criminal Investigation Handbook*, the actions and observations of "the first officer on the scene" are vital to any homicide investigation. I had no idea why Larkin's report was not included in the packet of documents that Cheri had obtained from the coroner's office. The report written by Deputy Engel (Vic's friend and the *second* officer to arrive on the scene), which I had read numerous times, had included Larkin's name and badge number at the bottom, leading me to conclude that his report was meant to cover the actions of both men. Now I could compare Larkin's version of events with Engel's.

In the first line of his report Larkin said he was "dispatched via sheriff's radio to an alleged female shooting herself in the chest." The use of the qualifying adjective *alleged* immediately caught my eye, seeming to indicate a more cautious and professional approach to the nature of the shooting.

Larkin next noted that, upon his arrival at the scene, he had observed a man, whom he later identified as Vic, "dressed in blue Levis with no shirt and no shoes." Vic was "waving frantically from the front of residence . . . [saying] 'Hurry up, she's in the bedroom, she needs help bad.'" Larkin proceeded to the bedroom, where he found Eileen on the floor. He began mouth-to-mouth resuscitation while Vic administered CPR, then the two switched places. There was, he noted, "a blue steel revolver, Colt 357 Magnum trooper" lying on the floor approximately three feet from the bedroom entrance.

After Engel arrived on the scene the ambulance came and took Eileen away. Larkin's report said Vic appeared to be "despondent and very emotionally disturbed," and "was noted to undergo fits of extreme depression and fits of violent nature and, in general, was acting in an irrational and erratic manner." As Vic was leaving the bedroom, he attempted to pick up the revolver from the floor, but Engel interceded and "retrieved the firearm for safekeeping." That explained why the gun had been moved from the floor. While Vic and Engel were walking toward the living room, Larkin heard Vic say to Engel, "I'll kill him, I'm going to kill him . . . she's going to be alright, she's not going to die." When Larkin asked Vic who he was referring to, Vic said, "No one, never mind, forget it. I'm not going to kill anyone." A few minutes later, Vic went to a closet, saying he wanted to get a handkerchief. Larkin saw two guns on the closet shelf; he wrote that Vic "made an attempt to reach for one of these firearms," but once again the deputies stopped him. At this point Engel unloaded the Colt revolver, which, according to Larkin's report, contained four complete cartridges and one expended round.

A single line near the end of the report referred to the third person who had been in the house. "Upon initial entry to the residence," Larkin said, "R/O noted the presence of WMJ, approx. 3 yrs., known only as [name blacked out] to be in and around the residence during the entire proceedings."

Reading the stark shorthand of that sentence made me blanch. "WMJ" is a white male juvenile; "R/O" is the reporting officer, Larkin. The deputy's cold bureaucratic words gave no indication of the turmoil the child may have witnessed—the screaming and arguing, the loud gunshot, sirens wailing, police running in and out of the house, Eileen receiving CPR with a loaded gun on the floor. Perhaps the deputies were trained to leave their feelings out of the reports, but I found myself seething, wondering how long it took before some compassionate person came on the scene, someone with a heart as well a gun, who would take the boy in his arms and try to comfort him.

When the homicide detectives arrived, Larkin was dispatched to the hospital to check on Eileen:

> At approx. 1510 hrs., R/O was informed by Dr. Moersch that the victim had at approx. 1508 hours . . . succumbed to her wounds. Dr. Moersch related that the victim never gained consciousness. Dr. Moersch related that the projectile entered the victim's body at the lower end of the breast bone, upon entering did extensive damage to the liver, aorta, and extensive damage to the spine. Dr. Moersch listed the cause of death as exsanguination [bled to death].

Having noted these details, the deputy said he took custody of Eileen's clothing and accompanied her body to the morgue. At that point a criminalist from the sheriff's department arrived "for chemical tests of the victim's body."

I sat back, absorbing what I had just read. In spite of the stilted language, there was something that made me trust Larkin's account and think he was a good, honest cop. I appreciated his attempts to save Eileen's life. His account filled in a few of the gaps in the story, but it did not tilt the scales one way or the other regarding Vic's culpability. It seemed to me that Larkin's report showed at least *one* officer from the sheriff's department acting in a professional and competent manner.

But when I told Darryl about the report, he saw it differently.

"This was a fundamental breakdown of procedure," he said. "You're the *police*. You're in charge. As soon as Vic went after the gun on the floor, they should have handcuffed him to a chair in the middle of the room. These guys were total amateurs. We don't know why Vic was trying to get those guns, but if he was emotionally disturbed, they should have cuffed him and secured the crime scene."

Elizabeth had her doubts as well. She didn't see how the police could have witnessed Vic's violent behavior and concluded so readily that Eileen had committed suicide.

"I'm not saying Vic's guilty," she said. "But here you have this guy who threatened to kill Eileen, who's threatening to kill Boring. He's raging around trying to get his hands on a gun, but the police just say the *wife* shot herself. Poor woman must have been out of her head."

The other report in the FOIA file was from the crime laboratory of the sheriff's department—"Report on the Examination of Physical Evidence." The gun that apparently killed Eileen had been fired in the lab, but the bullet was never matched against the bullet that took her life. There was no record of the manufacturer or lot number of the fatal bullet, which was essential for accurate ballistics tests. "Nitric acid swabs" had been taken of Eileen's hands at the hospital to check for traces of gunshot residue, but there was no record of the swabs having been tested.

There was also no description of Eileen's clothing or the blood-stains on them, no mention of any crime scene photographs, and no photographs of her wounds, which are absolutely vital for comparison when performing a ballistics test. (According to the "Report on the Examination of Physical Evidence," the gun was released to a sheriff's deputy within a few weeks, presumably to be returned to Vic.) A statement at the bottom of the report dated February 11, 1976, said, "Items . . . will be kept on file for an additional thirty days, after which they will be destroyed unless the Laboratory is otherwise notified." The date was exactly seventeen months after Eileen's death. I assumed this was all standard operating procedure, and the crime lab routinely held on to evidence for eighteen months, then got rid of it unless some authority told them not to.

The report devastated me. All the physical evidence had been destroyed twenty-six years ago—the case was closed and forgotten.

In the various documents I had obtained through the Freedom of Information Act, most of the personal names had been blacked out—not the names of the investigating officers, but those of Betty Clay, Hal Boring, and the little boy and his father. Perhaps it was standard policy to cross out names on the reports that were released to family members, but I began to have misgivings when I compared these documents with the ones I'd gotten from Cheri. Not only had the sheriff's department crossed out the names, but several reports were missing entirely—specifically, the two interoffice memorandums describing the incident on the Borings' front lawn a week before Eileen's death. In these reports, Vic told a cop to come back in a half hour and "pick her up off the lawn and . . . take me to jail." These documents provided the most incriminating evidence against Vic, yet someone had chosen to exclude them from the file that had been sent to me. My paranoia shifted into overdrive. The evidence was all gone, but even now the sheriff's department seemed to have something to hide.

35

I FORWARDED the sheriff's department reports that Maura had obtained to the ballistics expert Troy Merriweather. His final analysis was a litany of things the police could have done and did not do, all the mistakes they had made. When Vic had told me his story, he said that Eileen had loaded the gun while he was out of the room trying to find the phone number for my mother. The reports made no mention of this, only that the gun had been moved from its usual place on the nightstand to a high shelf in the closet to keep it out of reach of the child. If Eileen had to load the gun, how many bullets were in the chamber? Deputy Larkin said five, Detective Delaney said four, leaving this basic forensic detail open to question. Merriweather wrote at length about this discrepancy and said that it was peculiar that a handgun that had been kept in the house for protection was not fully loaded. In the end, with no additional physical evidence available, he concluded that the gunshot wound seemed to be consistent with suicide but little else did.

Maura had gone over the packet of reports before she sent them to me and one day we began to discuss them on the telephone. She said Larkin's report had cleared up some of the earlier questions about the

police work, namely how and why Engel had picked up the gun from
the floor after the shooting.

"It makes sense that the deputy wanted to keep it out of Vic's
hands," she said. "He could have unloaded it without compromising
the fingerprints. Officers are taught to do that. The *real* mistake was
not checking it for fingerprints afterward."

"Why do you think Vic was trying to get the gun in the first place?"

"That's impossible to say. This was after they'd taken Eileen off
to the hospital. Maybe he just didn't want the gun lying on the floor,
especially with the little boy still in the house."

"Wouldn't that be disturbing the crime scene?"

"Vic wasn't thinking like a cop at that moment. It's one thing not to
want a gun lying on the bedroom floor. But trying to get the *other* gun
out of the closet, that's a different ballgame."

I asked her what she thought he was doing.

"God only knows. Go to shoot Boring? Shoot himself? We're not
talking about a rational situation here."

I was sitting at my desk at a rental house in Puerto Rico. A soft gust
of wind lifted a sheet of paper, held it suspended for a moment, and set
it back down again.

"Given what we have, and you had to make the call," I said, "what
would it be? Murder or suicide?"

"Do you want the truth?"

"Of course."

"I think it was suicide."

"Really?" I couldn't hide the disappointment in my voice.

"For months and months, I felt certain that Vic had done it. Then
a few weeks ago I changed my mind. One day I was all alone and I just
thought, *I want out, I don't want to do this anymore.* It was real scary,
Jim. This was right after my sister's funeral and it was just a dark, dark
time." She told me the last straw was when her ex-husband showed
up at her sister's funeral with his new wife totally by surprise. "I came

home in the late afternoon, made myself a drink, and pulled down all the shades in the living room. I must have been in a trance. I'm not sure how long it lasted—it could have been two minutes or ten or fifteen. All I know is, when I finally snapped out of it, I was sitting there with an empty glass in one hand and a gun in the other."

"Jesus!" I shuddered. I had an image of her in a darkened room— heavy Spanish-style furniture with wooden arms and brocade upholstery, a black jacket tossed carelessly on the sofa—with a whiskey glass in one hand and a small, flat gun like the one I saw in Darryl's apartment in the other.

"When I came out of it," she went on, "I started thinking about Eileen, and I got this spooky feeling like she had been in the same place I was . . . only she went through with it."

"That's what happens when people have guns around the house," I said angrily, a mantra I had repeated a hundred times before. "They usually end up shooting themselves or someone they love."

"I'm licensed to carry. I've had a gun on my person most of my adult life, but when I come home, I put it away. *Really* away. That's what made this whole thing so scary. I had time to think about it before I got the gun out. But here's the strange part: if I *had* done something, everyone would have suspected my ex. We had a real rocky relationship. He was a cop, a drinker. He got violent with me. Nobody would have believed I was capable of hurting myself. You can see the parallels with Eileen."

I did. I had met Maura in person only once for about an hour, but we'd talked on the phone many times and I felt a strong connection with her, as she must have felt with me.

"The thing is," she said, "Vic may not have pulled the trigger, but he's still very much to *blame*."

She wasn't the first person who had said this, but it gave me no consolation. "So how do I deal with that?"

"Yeah, that's the hard part."

"I feel like I may have to forgive him for something he didn't actually do."

"Oh, fuck that, Jim, he did *enough*."

A week or two later, Cheri—who, on most days, was ready to send Vic to jail for life—recounted an episode similar to Maura's. "When you have someone telling you over and over again that you're a worthless piece of shit," she said, "you start to believe it. The thought that I had no say in my own life and no power to stop the abuse was completely overwhelming. One night I started looking for a gun that I had hidden in a safe in the closet. Thank God I couldn't remember the four-digit code for the lock."

I began to wonder if situations like Maura's and Cheri's were much more common than I had ever known. Women live different lives than men; they have different rules, different fears. They are more vulnerable than men in the most fundamental ways. It's a simple truth my mother tried to teach me—like the times she sent me to walk Eileen home from a friend's house after dark, worried she might be accosted on the street. Or the way she cautioned me that "no means no, even if the girl is naked." It's embarrassing to admit how long it took me to understand this fact and appreciate how a woman's view of the world is radically different from my own.

When I told Elizabeth about my conversation with Maura, she asked me once again if I thought it was murder or suicide.

"I'm not ready to say."

"What about innocent until proven guilty?"

She was right, of course, but I pushed back immediately. "Yeah, okay, but that's not the way the cops are supposed to look at it. They're supposed to gather enough evidence to convince themselves there *wasn't* a crime. They seemed so anxious to close the case and protect Vic they didn't bother to match the bullets, didn't confirm how close the muzzle was to Eileen's chest, didn't interview key witnesses, didn't test Eileen's hands for gunshot residue. You know whose hands they should have tested? Vic's. If his hands were clean, then he wasn't holding the gun." The logic of this statement was such a fundamental part of good police work, that it seemed absurd that I was the one who was making it. "But here's the irony. The incompetence of the sheriff's department cuts both ways. They destroyed all the evidence that could have implicated Vic, but that evidence could have exonerated him too. He benefited from the lousy investigation back then. Now it's the other way around. He can't *prove* he's innocent."

"Do you think you can live with not knowing for certain?"

"No. I need it to be one way or the other."

36

FROM THE START I had said that I was searching for the *truth*—nothing else mattered. Now I found it had become nearly impossible for me to maintain my objectivity. I wanted to prove that Vic was guilty, and it disappointed me when anyone suggested otherwise, especially someone like Maura, who had taken such a close look at the case. I didn't need a psychoanalyst to understand why. Suicide was old truth—the truth I had lived with for nearly three decades. If Eileen was murdered, it would remove the sting of her suicide and let me forgive her entirely. Any anger that I had felt toward her for killing herself could now be heaped onto Vic Zaccagnini. Tricked by his doleful eyes and muted, self-serving story in my parents' kitchen, I had let him slip away. Now I could be an avenging angel and bring him to justice. But I knew it was more than Vic's evasiveness that had thrown me off the first time around: it was my hubris and eagerness to get on with my life. Proving Eileen had been murdered wouldn't just bring Vic to justice; it would let me redeem myself.

This tug between trying to be objective and the need for redemption—my own as well as Eileen's—was complicated by another factor, one that is evident in the very first entry of the journal I started when I went to California to work on Eileen's case. I was sitting in a restaurant just off the freeway, waiting for Darryl to arrive.

This was several hours before I would meet Cheri and see those appalling police reports, but my suspicions about Vic had already been piqued. In the journal I wrote:

> . . . *On 9/11/75, one year to the day after Eileen's death, Vic applied for a marriage license to Yvonne Marie Burdette. That felt like a punch in the stomach . . . Me, Jim, the man wants to see him* [Vic] *to go over it all one more time. To ask him point blank—Did you kill her? The writer in me worries that Vic can squelch this whole thing and keep me from publishing the best book I'll ever write.*

We want a verdict in cases like this, truth sealed with an imprimatur of a court of law. Television shows like *Dateline, Cold Case Files,* and *Forensic Files,* which have aired hundreds of episodes, are invariably about cases in which the perpetrators have been caught, tried, convicted, and sentenced. Occasionally there will be a story about some innocent person who has been wrongfully accused and convicted, but the point of the episode is to show how this individual was subsequently exonerated. Virtually all of these cases are about murder. The producers of these TV programs know their audience. Viewers don't want ambiguity; they want stories about cases that have been *solved* and reaffirm their belief that there is order in the universe, that justice will win out. This is what I wanted for Eileen—and for me—order, justice, redemption, resolution. *Certainty.*

Dick Landry, the former US attorney I had hired to review Eileen's case, passed a complete set of documents on to his friend in the King County, Washington, prosecutor's office. When I read her opinion, my heart sank. She did *not* think the case, as it stood, could be brought to trial, though she said that getting statements from Vic would be beneficial, as they would open the door to interviews with others in case he had ever mentioned to them that he had killed someone.

The only real hope to change the classification of this case is through state-ments of the husband. An investigator could interview people the husband has had relationships with since this incident to see if he ever made refer-ence to it in a manner inconsistent with the original story. If, for hypo-thetical instance, there were incidents of domestic violence in subsequent relationships, it is possible that he could have mentioned that he killed before.

This line of thinking echoed a front-page murder case that was currently about to go to trial. Michael Skakel, a cousin of Robert Ken-nedy's children, was accused of murdering Martha Moxley, his fifteen-year-old neighbor, who was bludgeoned to death with a golf club. The crime occurred in tony Greenwich, Connecticut, in 1975, but no one was charged at the time and the case went cold. In the late 1990s the case began to garner publicity and Mark Fuhrman, the infamous police detective from the O. J. Simpson trial, wrote a book suggesting that Michael Skakel was the murderer. Although the golf club used in the crime came from the Skakel household, there was no forensic evidence linking Michael Skakel directly to the murder. But two men who had attended a private school with him a few years after the crime came forward and said that Skakel had admitted killing the girl when he was a student and bragged about getting away with it. This wasn't exactly a smoking gun, but it was the key that allowed the prosecution to reopen the case. Skakel was convicted of the crime, but the conviction was ultimately overturned on appeal when the court determined that his trial lawyer had "rendered ineffective assistance," and the prosecution chose not to retry the case.

The possibility of a similar sort of "confession" by Vic in Eileen's case put my focus squarely on Vic's second wife, Yvonne. But, as Dar-ryl and I had discussed, I couldn't approach her without the risk of alerting Vic. Yvonne might call Vic herself and tell him about the in-vestigation or relay the information through their grown daughter. If

Yvonne was bitterly angry with Vic, she might be inclined to get inventive and tell us what we wanted to hear—a malicious but effective way to bring trouble into his life. But if *the police* interviewed Yvonne, her words would be part of a verifiable public record, and she would be much more apt to tell the truth. Ironically, the same institution that had botched, if not covered up, the case back in 1974—the San Bernardino Sheriff's Department, which might *still* be trying to keep me from finding out the truth about the original investigation—seemed to be the only vehicle to see it through to the end. I needed to find a way to get them involved.

37

I SPENT COUNTLESS HOURS trying to devise a strategy to compel the authorities in San Bernardino to take an unbiased and comprehensive look at Eileen's case. One scheme I seriously began to consider was to enlist the support of an investigative reporter. Perhaps someone at the *San Bernardino Sun* or the *Los Angeles Times*. The story contained all the elements a newspaper would want for a front-page exposé—sex, violent death, police corruption, rumors about a trusted school official using his position to prey upon women. I was fairly certain that when the story broke in the paper, the sheriff's department would rush to defend itself and hasten to assure the public that this case would be thoroughly *re*investigated, which was precisely what I wanted. But I was a writer; this was *my* story, and I wasn't ready to hand it over to someone else.

When I reviewed my notes on the case, I still chafed at Dick Landry's characterization of the police work as "sloppy but not egregious." But Dick had taken a personal interest in the case and he seemed determined to help me find a way to move it to the next level. One day he called to say he had bumped into an old friend who now lived in San Bernardino and worked for a community outreach program for the county government. Dick told his friend about Eileen's case. The friend said he knew the chief investigator—a person he was sure I could trust—for the San Bernardino district attorney and offered to give me his name or call him on my behalf. I chose to speak to the chief investigator directly. That man referred me to one of his assistants, Herb Winter. When I called him, Winter started to ask probing questions and wanted to hear all the details.

"Given what you've told me, I think there's a strong possibility of foul play on the part of your ex-brother-in-law," Winter said, "but I can't see the sheriff's deputies covering up a homicide. I just don't think they would have done that, not even in the bad old days. Maybe they'd cover for a cop who had shot an unarmed suspect, throwing down a weapon to make it look like it was self-defense, but not a blatant homicide. I think it was more a case of giving a fellow officer the benefit of the doubt. They just *assumed* it was a suicide and never took all the necessary steps to make sure they got it right."

Winter worked for the DA, but he told me he would speak with a friend in the sheriff's department, a man of impeccable integrity, and ask his advice. Soon after, Winter was directed to Lieutenant Sean Wallace in the homicide division of the sheriff's department, who told Winter I should send him the file.

"I think you can trust Wallace," Winter said. "He has a reputation as a great cop. When I spoke to him, I only told him two things—that Vic threatened Eileen's life a week before she died and that the stippling around the gunshot wound made it look suspicious. I figured I'd let him read the file and draw his own conclusions."

I agreed with the approach. I was well aware that the police might see me as a conspiracy theorist or simply as a guy with a grudge against his ex-brother-in-law. I had already given up on the idea of getting the newspapers involved to try to put pressure on the sheriff's department to reopen the case. Now it seemed like my best chance was to get the department to assess the discrepancies themselves and draw their own conclusions.

Lieutenant Wallace turned the case over to Sergeant Toby Kazarian, who, in turn, assigned it to one of his detectives, Logan Jarrow.
Kazarian and Jarrow were six steps removed from Dick Landry, but
I had *finally* found some officials from the sheriff's department who
were willing to take a look at the case.

A cursory reading of the file convinced Kazarian and Jarrow that
there were serious flaws in the original investigation, and they ordered
copies of all the records and test results from the crime lab. I spoke to
Kazarian on the phone, and he told me he felt confident that he would
find more evidence. He also said he was trying to locate the gun that
killed Eileen. He promised he wouldn't let me down.

Thrilled as I was to have the sergeant's attention, three months
later nothing had been done and I was deeply frustrated by the lack of
progress. I couldn't *demand* the sheriff's department take action, but
I figured if I sat down face-to-face with the detectives, they'd be more
inclined to move forward.

In early November 2002, nineteen months after I first contacted
Darryl, I was back in San Bernardino. Before meeting with the detectives, I took the time to stop by Herb Winter's office to thank him for
his help. In our conversation I told him that Merriweather, the ballistics expert, had said the gunshot wound *did* seem consistent with
suicide.

"Hmm," Winter said. "What else did he say?"

"He was really focused on the number of bullets in the gun. One
report says four, the other says five. He said it seemed odd that the
weapon wasn't fully loaded."

"Cowboys only kept five bullets in their gun. The chamber under
the hammer was empty to prevent accidental firings. Modern guns
don't have this problem. You could throw a Colt Trooper down on a
concrete floor with all your might and the thing wouldn't go off."

I asked him to tell me about a "half-jacketed" .38 bullet, which, according to the coroner's report, was the type that killed Eileen. Winter explained that there were basically three types of bullets—full metal jacket for maximum penetration; hollow point, which mushroom upon impact; and half-jacketed, which are a combination of the two. He retrieved a box of miscellaneous cartridges from his desk and gave me one. I felt a touch of nausea as I held that tiny wad of metal in my hand, thinking of it tearing through my sister's flesh.

Winter and I talked for about an hour. His attentiveness and concern buoyed my spirits. If the men over at the San Bernardino Sheriff's Department were half as simpatico, I'd be in good shape.

I left Winter's office and drove north toward the sheriff's headquarters, where I had a scheduled appointment with Toby Kazarian. The billboards advertising bail bondsmen along Waterman Avenue let me know I was in the right neighborhood. The sheriff's headquarters was a low buff-colored building on a wide street. I waited in the lobby for about fifteen minutes before a young woman came out and told me that Sergeant Kazarian had been out on a case all night and would be able to see me the *following* morning. I didn't mind the delay. I was ready to come back the next day or the day after that and pitch a tent in the parking lot if necessary.

The next morning Logan Jarrow came out to the lobby of the sheriff's headquarters to greet me. He was a short, barrel-chested man in his late thirties with a thick mustache, a country twang, and a full head of brown hair combed up in a longish flattop. He led me through a doorway and past a row of cubicles to Sergeant Kazarian's office. In his mid-to-late forties, Kazarian looked like a TV cop—six feet, handsome, steel-gray hair, starched white shirt with a perfectly knotted tie. An autographed Wayne Gretzky hockey jersey was tacked to the wall behind his desk.

The three of us got past the preliminaries quickly and began to discuss the case. The bad news was that all the physical evidence had indeed been destroyed except for the gun, which they had managed to track down but said there was no reason to retrieve it at this time. I felt a sense of relief, knowing they had made some progress, and it seemed remarkable that they were able to locate the weapon so many years later, a tribute to California gun laws. But the best news for me was when Kazarian looked me in the eye and said he thought the 1974 investigation was "shoddy, an embarrassment, one of the worst I've ever seen." He didn't try to defend the original investigators or mitigate the mistakes and omissions of 1974, but he did point out that this had been the 413th case the two teams in the homicide division had investigated that year, so the detectives were tremendously overworked. He said Bill Delaney, the lead detective in Eileen's case, had died a few years ago; Eric Vaughn, the other detective, had retired.

"I'll contact Vaughn and see what he remembers," Kazarian said, "but he's a private investigator now, working for defense attorneys, so he's sorta gone over to the other side. Delaney had a reputation as a brilliant detective. He and Vaughn saw this as a run-of-the-mill suicide and got complacent."

"What about Vic and Engel being friends? Does that raise any suspicions?"

"It was a smaller world back in those days. The city cops and our department worked together much more closely, and the guys hung out with one another. But there was no collusion here. It was not a cover-up, just sloppy police work. Unfortunately, they stopped following through."

Pressing him, I brought up the department's failure to follow through with the gunshot residue (GSR) test on Eileen's hands, a point the ballistics expert had commented on extensively.

"GSR tests are notoriously unreliable," Kazarian said. "We've had cases where the suspect *admitted* to the crime and the GSR came back as inconclusive." Then he leaned forward in his chair. "I'll tell you what I'd like to do. After we've done all our homework, I'd like to get your guy Vic to take a polygraph." There was a gleam in his eye. "He probably wouldn't agree to it, just tell us to go pound sand, but I'd love to put him in that position."

"Do you find polygraphs are pretty accurate?"

"*Very* accurate."

His confidence surprised me. I had no intention of disputing his claim, but I'd recently read a book by a forensic psychologist that asserted that psychopaths had no trouble passing a lie detector test while giving false answers.

As we continued to review the case, I steered the detectives to Vic's description of Eileen's first suicide attempt. "Here's what bothers me," I said. "Vic tells Vaughn that he and Eileen had a fight and she took a bunch of aspirin and he stopped her, then he went to call his mother back in Pittsburgh and Eileen got the gun case and he took it away from her. That's the same story he told when she died. The only difference is, in the second story, he goes to call *my* mother instead of his. It sounds too pat."

Both officers concurred. Kazarian asked if Vic had benefited financially from Eileen's death, and I said no, except for inheriting her share of the two houses.

"One thing comes through loud and clear," he said, making no attempt to hide his disdain for Vic. "He wanted Eileen out of the picture. He may not have pulled the trigger, but he wanted her *gone*." Almost exactly the same conclusion Maura had reached.

The sergeant told me police work had changed enormously in the past three decades. "I'm not trying to offer this as any consolation," he said, "but there is no way the sheriff's department could get away with an investigation like that today. If it looks like an officer is involved in a crime, we have to be super careful to dot our *i*'s and cross our *t*'s. We had a case eighteen months ago where a deputy's wife committed suicide and we *know* there was absolutely no foul play, but we're still getting questions from the DA's office."

"Actually, it *is* kind of a consolation," I said. "Makes me think the world's getting to be a better place."

Sergeant Kazarian considered that for a half second and shrugged— the idea of a better world seemed dubious from his perspective. "Thanks for coming in," he said. "This case may be thirty years old, but it's still important to us. We'll do our best. I give you my word."

Detective Jarrow led me past the warren of cubicles to an interrogation room. I asked him what he'd thought of the police reports when he first read them.

His upper lip curled with scorn. "We write them in plain English now," he said, thinking I meant the stilted, third-person prose.

"What I meant was, what was your gut feeling about the case?"

"I'm not convinced. I was reading along and I kept seeing all these red flags and I'm thinking, Okay, they'll interview so-and-so and that will clear things up. Then I got to the end of the file and thought, Man, this can't be it. Of course, not everything that was said got written down back then. Now we tape all our interviews, which helps tremendously when people try to change their stories or the private dicks try to get witnesses to change their minds. But a police report is still a summary. Those investigators on Eileen's case might've seen things at the scene that suggested a suicide that didn't make it into their reports."

I gave him a copy of my chronology and a list of potential witnesses, which he seemed pleased to receive. He told me he'd do his best with the investigation, then paused and added a caution.

"I'm gonna be straight with you," he said. "Unless Vic confesses, this case is never going to reach a courtroom. Nowadays, even with our active cases, we need a mountain of evidence before we can go to trial. The DA never wants to lose, so . . ." He gave a little shrug. There was no frustration in voice; he was simply stating a fact. A little deflating for me, but I appreciated his honesty.

The conversation moved to family. He told me about his children, how he made sure to put his service revolver in a safe when he came home because he didn't want his kids growing up around guns. We had developed a good rapport. Meeting with him and Sergeant Kazarian made me feel validated.

As I passed through the lobby on my way out of the headquarters, I bought a black baseball cap with a gold star and "SBSD" in red letters embroidered on the front. There was a little spring in my step as I walked across the parking lot to my rental. The officers in the San Bernardino Sheriff's Department had become the good guys.

Darryl had driven out from LA to spend the day with me. We had lunch, then stopped by the education building to say hello to Ginny Harmon, Eileen's old office mate. Ginny's face lit up when she saw us. She came out from behind her desk and gave each of us a hug. Her daughter, about eighteen, was standing nearby and Ginny introduced us.

We went to the cafeteria, and I told her about my meeting with the sheriff's deputies. "I wanted to come by and give you a heads-up. I'm sure they'll call."

"Thank you," she said, clearly pleased. "I was wondering if anything would ever happen."

"My hopes aren't too high. All the evidence has been destroyed. They told me this will probably never go to trial."

"That's okay, as long as Vic knows we know." She gave me a look of determination and vengeful satisfaction.

"There was one thing I didn't ask you the last time. Did you ever think Eileen had been abused by Vic?"

"Oh, sure, she had some bruises, but she made excuses for them."

"On her face?"

"Her face, on her arms where he grabbed her." She clutched her upper arm to demonstrate. "Eileen would never admit it, but I knew. I had that, too. The same kind of bruises, the same excuses about walking into doors and tripping and falling."

I wore my SBSD cap on the plane home. The trip had been a marked success, much more than I had hoped for. What I did not know then was that I was still an apprentice in the art of waiting.

38

IT WAS February 4, 2003, Eileen's fifty-sixth birthday, nearly two years since I'd begun my strange and seemingly never-ending journey. Elizabeth and I were back in Rincón, a small town on the west coast of Puerto Rico, our refuge from the New England winter. It had been three months since I had met with Kazarian and Jarrow in San Bernardino. I'd had a few telephone conversations with Jarrow, but I knew he still hadn't started the investigation. Hoping to nudge him along, I wrote him an email:

Dear Logan,

I woke up feeling very down this morning and it took me almost an hour to realize why. Today is my sister Eileen's 56th birthday. This has never been a good day for me. Oddly, I feel much more nostalgic and/or depressed on this date than on the anniversary of her death.

I told the detective that I understood that ongoing cases must be his first priority and that he couldn't work twenty-four hours a day, but I was hoping he could find a way to get Eileen's case back on his radar screen. I suggested that he begin by interviewing Ginny Harmon. A conversation with her, I promised, would intrigue him and make him want to dig deeper into the case. Switching tactics, I said I was considering asking Darryl to move forward with a parallel investigation, but I had some reservations about it.

> *Frankly, I'm nervous about the idea of a p.i. talking with key witnesses such as Hal Boring and Vic's ex-wife Yvonne (neither of whom know that this case is under consideration again) because I think that it could give them time to prepare their stories before talking to you. Also, I don't want anything I do to put Vic on the alert and let him know that I have been investigating this matter.*

It was shameless baiting on my part, hoping to get a response. I had absolutely no intention of siccing Darryl on these witnesses—he and I had already agreed that it was not a good idea—but if Jarrow thought we were getting impatient and were about to encroach on *his* investigation, maybe he'd take ownership and actually begin to do the work himself. I agonized over each word, hoping to say something that would move Eileen's file to the top of the stack. I'd spent a sizable chunk of my life as a salesman, crafting letters like this to send to prospective clients, trying to "incentivize" them as we said in the corporate world. In closing, I wrote:

> *Bottom line is, I realize that the Sheriff's Department has no compelling reason to reopen this case. Still, I've been hoping to find some closure on Eileen's death for a long time and I'm hoping you can find a small window of opportunity to give it a nudge toward some final "truth." Ultimately, I know that I'm asking a huge favor from you and the department and I do so with the utmost humility and gratitude.*

Fearing all else might fail, I had resorted to the oldest sales strategy in a salesman's book—groveling. Anything to get Detective Jarrow to start the investigation.

After writing the email, I called my friend Kim Prince at his home in Naples, Florida. February 4 was Kim's birthday too, and this year marked his fifty-eighth. Kim and I were classmates at Harvard, but I hadn't gotten to know him until 1992, when I cajoled him into participating in a symposium on the Vietnam War at our twenty-fifth reunion. Kim had done a tour of duty in Vietnam's Central Highlands, serving as an adviser to a team of South Vietnamese army rangers, one of only a handful of men in our Harvard class who actually saw any combat. In the years that followed our twenty-fifth reunion, Kim and I became close friends. We rode our bicycles and played golf together, traveled to England to visit my daughter Meg, who was producing her first feature film, went hiking in the New Hampshire mountains where he had grown up. Now semiretired, he had worked as a commentator for TV sports and once hosted a daytime newsmagazine show on a local channel in Boston.

He was six four and movie-star handsome with a deep voice and a smile that could make a nun reconsider her vows. The one chink in Kim's seemingly invincible armor was an endless list of physical ailments. He had a bad back, his spine bolted and fused together in numerous surgeries—fourteen and counting—that were on the cutting edge of medical know-how. He'd also had rotator cuff surgery about a month before his birthday. When he grew impatient with his recovery and tried to play tennis, he tore up his shoulder again. He told me on the telephone that he was in terrible pain and couldn't find a comfortable position to sleep.

Kim was scheduled to have another back surgery the day after his birthday, but he told me he had decided to call it off. He sounded despondent, uncertain whether he had made the right decision. I tried to make him laugh, tried get him to promise me that he and his girlfriend Lane would visit Elizabeth and me in Puerto Rico. But his voice was full of pain and despair, and he all but begged to be let off the phone.

"Well, okay," I said before I hung up. "Happy birthday, man. I love you."

"I love you too," he said. Words that came easily to both of us.

The conversation with Kim unsettled me and I began to write about it in my journal. It was frustrating to watch him suffer and not be able to help. As close as we were, I could not understand if his affliction was physical or psychological. This was a guy who could still play an extremely competitive game of tennis and outstrip me hill for hill when we rode our bikes. Sometimes it seemed to me that the goal of his surgeries was not so much about relieving his physical pain as it was about the hope that he would awaken from the anesthesia and magically be twenty-nine years old again, his spine as supple as an alley cat's with a libido to match.

It was the dead of winter back in Boston, a big storm predicted for the weekend, while I sat at my desk in Puerto Rico in shorts and a T-shirt. From my window I could see the sun, palm trees, the ballet of surfers on bright blue water, but I couldn't shake my funk.

"The one person I miss most today," I wrote in my journal, "is my mother."

No particular reason except the obvious. What better place to turn when you've got the blues? I missed Mom's love and simple, unencumbered goodness. She used to get a solicitation every year from the Harvard College Fund and she would send them a check for five dollars from her wages as a clerk at Murphy's five-and-dime. A sweetly naive (and often gullible) woman, she was completely without any subtext or hidden agenda, and she treated others as if they were the same. People who met her at work or in the laundromat told her their life stories, knowing she would not judge them. When I had called her to say I was getting divorced, she said, "Well, Jim, I'm sorry. I know you and I know how hard you must have tried to make it work. I hope you don't mind if I stay in touch with Connie." When Mom was alive, I always phoned her on Eileen's birthday, and I wished I could do that again. In my journal I wrote, "At one point [today], I was feeling so aggrieved I felt like calling our old phone number—FAirfax 2-7679—and seeing if anyone answered. Then I felt privately embarrassed, as if I were dreaming up some hokey plot device for a character in a short story."

Unable to write myself out of my depression, I spent the rest of the afternoon reading. Then, just before dinner, Kim's girlfriend Lane called and told me he had committed suicide.

I was desolate but not completely shocked. Perhaps this was the only possible ending for Kim. (He had told me once that if he ever found himself in too much pain he would take his own life.) But knowing a particular heartache is inevitable can't erase the sorrow when it finally comes.

I flew to Naples the next day to be with Kim's friends and family. He had a twin sister, Lawson. She was the last person he talked to on the phone before he pulled the trigger, though he didn't tell her what he was planning to do. I tried to assure her it was okay to be angry. After all, the day he killed himself was *her* birthday too. Kim shot himself with the same kind of gun that killed Eileen, a .357 Magnum revolver. It was a cruel irony, as if the gods were toying with me, turning this whole story into a farce.

39

As time went by, communications with Logan Jarrow at the SBSD remained friendly but completely unproductive, as nothing had been done on Eileen's case. In June 2003, I wrote an email to Sergeant Kazarian, gently reminding him that he had given me his word seven months ago; now I wanted him to keep it and give me "a clear-cut commitment" when this investigation would get underway. When he did not respond, I called the department trying to find him, but the administrative assistant said he was out of the office. Hearing the frustration in my voice, she asked for my number and said she would try to reach the sergeant.

A few minutes later Kazarian called me from his home, where he'd been for the past few weeks recovering from a sporting accident. We made small talk briefly, and then he told me about all the pressures in the sheriff's department—the caseloads, the budget cutbacks, a mandate prohibiting overtime. He also said Detective Jarrow was being transferred to the high-tech crimes division, which had contributed to the delay. I didn't have to prompt him to get to the obvious—all excuses aside, Eileen's case was still dormant. He said he would meet with his supervisor, Lieutenant Wallace, when he got back on the job and try to come up with a plan.

A week later he sent me an email saying he was going to take over the case himself rather than assign it to a new detective. It was three months more, October 2003, before Kazarian finally conducted his first interview. He spoke with Ginny Harmon.

Ginny told Sergeant Kazarian about the various phone calls Eileen and Vic made to her in Hal Boring's office the day of the shooting, while pointing out that she had not known about the affair between Eileen and Hal. The details she recounted about these conversations were pretty much the same as she had told Darryl and me, with one baffling exception—she said the call in which someone said, "Ginny, Eileen just killed herself," had come from an anonymous man, not from Vic. I hadn't told the sergeant anything about the conversation Darryl and I had had with Ginny, and I didn't want to interrupt him to mention the discrepancy, but I put a few giant exclamation points in the margin in my notes.

Ginny told Kazarian that she and Eileen had spent a great deal of time together, going to the movies and taking long lunches. She remarked on Eileen's bruises and the fact that her eyes were often red from crying and lack of sleep. Ginny said that she had met Vic only once, when she and her fiancé went out to dinner with him and Eileen. She described him as bossy and condescending with Eileen, a person who talked a lot about how much he liked being a cop and bragged about the kind of things police could get away with. Then Vic related a story about a buddy of his who handcuffed his wife to a bureau and beat her up.

I found it surprising that Ginny had told Kazarian about the dinner with Vic and Eileen but never mentioned it to Darryl and me. Perhaps she didn't recall it until she spoke with the sergeant. Whatever the reason, Kazarian clearly came away from the interview with newfound contempt for Vic.

Vic's second wife, Yvonne, was the next person Kazarian planned to interview, but he was having trouble locating her. She had been married three times since her divorce from Vic and now worked as a long-haul trucker. "I'm sure we'll find her," the sergeant said, "but the woman's moved more times over the last ten years than a traveling circus."

He said he had a bead on Deputy Engel, Vic's friend and the second cop on the scene that day. I suggested he also talk with Hal Boring, but the sergeant said he wanted to wait. Apparently, while Kazarian was interviewing Ginny in the cafeteria at the school administration building, Boring had walked into the room and she quietly pointed him out to the sergeant. "If he's still coming into the education building," Kazarian said, "he's probably still connected with the school department. I need to find out how much juice he has with local politicians. If I contact him now, I might get a call the next day from someone up the chain of command asking me why I'm digging into a thirty-year-old suicide case. I want to have a better handle on everything before I rattle his cage. Then if someone calls me on it, I'll be able to explain why it was necessary."

I appreciated his savvy. He seemed anxious to move ahead with the case and said he'd try to get back to me quickly. A year before I might have hung up the phone and pumped my fist and done a little jig, but delays and disappointment had become the norm for me. This was only one interview, nothing more.

As I reflected on Kazarian's interview with Ginny, I wasn't entirely sure what to make of it. I didn't want to call her and back her into a corner by asking her why the story about Vic had changed, but I found the discrepancy unnerving. Perhaps one could simply chalk it up to the vagaries of memory, zigzagging our way to truth. If Vic did not make that phone call saying Eileen had just killed herself, it made him seem less like a coldhearted monster. But if the story about the dinner with Eileen and Vic was accurate, he'd earned the title back again. I could not imagine her sitting next to him, proudly wearing her wedding ring while he boasted about a friend beating up his wife. Wouldn't she have been as appalled by Vic's boorishness as Ginny was? It was easy to see why Eileen might have wanted to escape. That may be why she fell for Hal Boring with his "slimy charm." Still, she must have known that Boring had remarried only a little over a year earlier. Was she so desperate to put Vic behind her that she convinced herself she could have a future with Boring, or was she simply relieved to be with a lover who didn't belittle her and act like a misogynistic jerk? No doubt a little of both. One thing seemed clear: she was deeply troubled and didn't know what she wanted. No wonder I was struggling to discover who she really was. She wasn't sure herself.

Meanwhile, Cheri continued to poke around and found another case in the San Bernardino County Court records involving Vic. This time, he had been sued by two men he'd arrested. The men claimed he had used excessive force against them, striking them in the face with his flashlight—one man had been admitted to the hospital for stitches due to the altercation—while Vic maintained that the men, who were both drunk, had attacked him, forcing him to act in self-defense. In a motion filed by the plaintiffs, their attorney claimed that Vic ". . . was several times accused of excessive use of force on citizens and that the [San Bernardino Police] department was negligent in failing to have discharged him for these actions." The motion cited three incidents where Vic had allegedly acted improperly—ramming a suspect's head through a garage door, beating up a man he had chased onto Norton Air Force Base, closing down a bar because they had refused to serve him the night before. I had no way of knowing if any of the allegations in the motion were true, but they certainly portrayed him as a man it was unwise to cross.

According to the motion, Vic resigned his position with the police force a few months after the encounter with the two men who said he beat them with his flashlight. He then reapplied within ninety days to get his old job back—supposedly a routine process—but his application was refused.

• • •

A few days after Kazarian's interview with Ginny Harmon in mid-October 2003, brush fires swept across the hills of Southern California. The fires raged for weeks, destroying thousands of homes and scorching tens of thousands of acres of land. San Bernardino County reeled as high winds carried embers over the firebreaks of culverts and highways and the flames kept spreading. The sheriff's department had to deploy its personnel to assist in firefighting efforts, evacuate people from endangered areas, and make sure that homes were not looted. On the phone, Cheri told me it was eerie: one home in a neighborhood might be fine while the houses on either side had been burned to the ground. Sergeant Kazarian sent me an email saying he had to evacuate his own home and couldn't get back to it for five days. Sixty county employees sustained total losses to their homes. Kazarian's email was written the day before Thanksgiving. It was hard to imagine the devastation those fires had wreaked on the county. I knew that he'd be working flat out for the rest of the year trying to catch up with routine police business. In my reply to his email, I wished him well and said I'd talk to him after New Year's.

In Pittsburgh, Aunt Pauline got a Christmas card from Vic's mother, as she did every year. In this year's card Mrs. Z enclosed pictures of her family, including one of Vic and his third wife, Laura. Worried that it might upset me, Aunt Pauline waited a few weeks before telling me about the photos; when she finally did, I asked her to send them to me. In one of them Vic was standing next to his little grandson, the child of Vic and Yvonne's daughter, Christina. Vic had a full mustache, and was bald on top of his head with graying hair by the temples, his torso thick but not fat. He and the boy, who was sitting on a tricycle, were looking up, perhaps at a passing airplane. In another photo, Laura, about fifty, was holding an infant, apparently another grandchild. As I studied the photo of her, I thought, *This is what Eileen would have looked like today.*

Not the same features but the same gentleness in her eyes, a soft pucker in her mouth to soothe the child. My aunt was right, the photographs rattled me. They transported Vic from that odious, shadowy past and gave him a face. A wife, a family. A life that would be completely turned upside down by the investigation I had set in motion. The photographs reminded me of the gravity of my endeavor, dredging up so many ugly things Vic surely wanted to forget—or hide.

40

I TRIED TO no avail to contact Sergeant Kazarian in January. Several close friends had been suggesting for months that I try another tactic and go to the San Bernardino district attorney—raise my voice, pound my fist on the table, and *demand* that someone take action—but I refused. I was convinced the sergeant *wanted* to do a thorough investigation, and I worried that he might turn against me if I went over his head. For me, it wasn't enough for him to *do* the investigation; I needed him to keep me informed, to apprise me of the various interviews and tell me what the witnesses said. Without that, I might end up getting a phone call from him telling me he had finished the investigation and had concluded that the original finding was valid. Case closed again, period. I felt like I had only one shot at getting this done; if I erred, I wanted it to be on the side of patience and caution.

Darryl agreed with me wholeheartedly. In spite of the delays, he said he felt the kind of cooperation I was now getting from the police was unique, especially their willingness to share information with me and follow my leads. Darryl had a saying he liked to tell his clients—"You're in the *legal* system, not the justice system." Meaning, the former is reality, clogged with technicalities and missteps and bureaucratic delays; the latter is a fantasy, thorough and forthright and eminently fair.

Those words of wisdom helped sustain me, but the waiting was taking its toll. I was silent and moody, a tangle of frustration and bitterness and depression. One day Elizabeth said, "Do you have any idea what a drag it is to live with you? You promised me that you'd be done with this by the middle of last year." I could only nod and apologize. At least she could escape sometimes; I was stuck with myself.

Only one witness had been interviewed in the year and half since I had contacted Lieutenant Wallace of the San Bernardino County Sheriff's Department: Ginny. By the middle of February I was so frustrated I decided to take another tack and wrote a letter to Lieutenant Wallace. My only previous contact with him had been a telephone conversation in the summer of 2002. I wasn't sure if he had ever read Eileen's case file, so I gave him a brief history and reminded him of the lack of progress made by his department.

It has been twenty months since I first contacted you, and I am very discouraged. I have been extremely patient and I have not made any undue demands on the Sheriff's Department, but my patience has been rewarded with nothing but delays. Whenever I have spoken to Sgt. Kazarian I have found him to be a sympathetic and highly professional police officer. I sincerely believe he wants to complete this investigation and is frustrated that he cannot find the time to do so. I have told Sgt. Kazarian that I am well aware that current criminal cases must be the Department's first concern. But crime is never going to disappear in San Bernardino County, and this case is never going to be investigated until someone decides to make it a priority and allocates the time and manpower to see it through.

As you can imagine, this whole matter has been very difficult for me and my family, and we need to get some closure on this issue . . . a thorough investigation is needed in order to discover the truth about what happened in that bedroom on 9/11/74. In my last email to Sgt. Kazarian I told him that given the passage of time I am concerned that there is "a

very real chance that some of the people who could be interviewed [in this
case] *will pass away and whatever information they may have will be
permanently lost."*

Before mailing the letter, I sent a copy of the draft to my pal Jack
to get his input and see if I'd gotten the right tone—firm but realistic
with a hint of desperation. Jack made a few changes, then suggested I
include an appendix highlighting the various issues and problems surrounding the original investigation. I did so, and sent it along.

A week later, I followed up the letter with a phone call to Lieutenant Wallace. The appendix proved to be a good idea—Wallace wanted
to discuss some of the details of the case, specifically the gunshot
wound. He thought the description of the stippling as eleven *centimeters* in diameter might be a mistake. When I told him this fact was corroborated by the coroner's report, he seemed stunned.

"Well, that's the fault of our department," he said. "Somebody
should have picked up on that." Meaning, someone in the sheriff's department thirty years ago.

He finally understood just how deeply flawed the original investigation had been. He had known—or *should have* known—that basic fact
twenty months before, when Herb Winter, my advocate from the District Attorney's Office, had told him about Eileen's case. But there was
no way for me to point this out to him. I was just grateful something
finally might get done.

Wallace used the same phrase to describe the case as Kazarian, calling it *an embarrassment,* but he offered no apology for the long delays that
had brought us to this point. He said he was going to take the sergeant
off the direct investigation of the case and assign it to one of his young
detectives, Brock Quinlan. He told me the detective would need a little
time to familiarize himself with the file before getting in touch with me.

"I want you to understand though," he warned, "we're very limited
in what we can do."

I thought he was referring to the time constraints on his men, but he went on to say that the lack of physical evidence seriously impeded any investigation.

"I've come to terms with that," I said. "I just want to find out as much as possible about what happened that day. When I talked to Detective Jarrow some time ago, he made it clear there was no chance Vic could ever be charged with a crime."

"Oh, I disagree," the lieutenant said. "If we come to believe the man is guilty, I would *expect* this case to lead to an indictment."

It seemed like an odd thing for him to say, given that all the physical evidence had been destroyed, but I was glad to hear him say it.

A few days after my conversation with Wallace, I got my first email from Detective Brock Quinlan. The subject of the email was "Case #327525-01"—Eileen's original case number—written proof that the San Bernardino Sheriff's Department had *officially* reopened the case. I stared at my computer, not sure whether to laugh or cry.

The first person Detective Quinlan interviewed was Betty Clay. In a follow-up email, Quinlan reported that Betty had told him the same basic facts she had told me and reaffirmed that she believed "Vic was physically abusive to Eileen."

Next, he spoke with Gloria Boring, Hal Boring's wife of thirty-one years. As Boring's secretary, Eileen had often talked with Gloria Boring on the telephone. Mrs. Boring told Quinlan that Eileen was usually "perky and upbeat," but on the call Gloria received the morning of September 11, her voice had been low and subdued. Gloria said they spoke for about twenty minutes and Eileen apologized several times for her affair with Hal. After Eileen died, Hal started getting death threats from Vic, so, out of caution, Gloria and Hal and Hal's daughter from his first marriage went to live for six or seven weeks with his sister in Redlands. Beyond that, she had little else to add.

Quinlan told me about this interview in a telephone conversation.

I was hoping he'd talk to me like a friend, exploring the subtleties of the interview, but his manner was dry and reserved. He answered my questions succinctly and made no attempt to further the conversation. I could not seem to build the same rapport with him that I'd established with Jarrow and Kazarian, and we often fell into uncomfortable silences. I asked him if he would send me copies of the transcripts of his interviews, but he demurred.

Soon after, Quinlan informed me via email that he would be getting a court order to obtain the session notes of Dr. MacLaren, the psychologist who had counseled Eileen and Vic the night before she died. Laws protecting therapist-patient confidentiality prevented MacLaren from discussing the case with the detective, but his notes were subject to review. Dr. MacLaren subsequently told Quinlan he remembered Eileen, but he couldn't find the notes among his old files. This was a disheartening setback. The notes could have described the course of Eileen's depression, helped uncover her lies or Vic's, and, more important, revealed whether or not Eileen had told Vic about the affair during that last session and what Vic's reaction had been.

Hal Boring, now in his late sixties, was next on Quinlan's list. After his wife had been interviewed, Boring obviously knew it was only a matter of time before the police contacted him too. He also knew—presumably from Ginny Harmon—that I was the person who had instigated the investigation. In the interview with Quinlan, Boring readily admitted to the affair. He said that Eileen had been a very upbeat person until she started having marital problems, and he didn't remember Eileen resigning from her position the day before she died.

What Quinlan gave me was a thumbnail sketch of the interview, but it was enough to rekindle all my resentment against Boring. Did he see the irony in his statement that Eileen had been a very upbeat until she started having marital problems? That would be like Vic saying, *She was in perfectly good health until I beat the shit out of her.* I decided not to press Quinlan for more information. I was planning to be in San

Bernardino the following week and would have a chance to talk to him in person.

In May 2004 I met with Detective Quinlan at the sheriff's department headquarters. He was a good-looking man in his mid-thirties with close-cropped hair and a military bearing, strong handshake, and easy smile—much friendlier face-to-face than he had been on the phone. We went into a conference room and talked for about forty-five minutes. Quinlan spoke about Vic with a distaste that mirrored that of Jarrow and Kazarian. "It's clear he had no character," the detective said. "He was physically abusive and probably even more so mentally."

He wanted me to know that the next people on his interview list were the former sheriff's deputies—Larkin, Engel, and Vaughn. I encouraged him to talk to Alex Waering as well. Waering was the friend Vic had lived with while he was separated from Eileen and the father of the two-year-old boy who had been in the house when she was shot.

I asked him to tell me more about his interview with Hal Boring. To my relief, Quinlan viewed him with the same contempt he had for Vic. He said Boring told him that when he heard Eileen was dead his first thought was that she was murdered by her husband.

"Of course he did," Quinlan said, sneering. "The same thing had happened with his *other* secretary."

"You mean Melissa Pratt?" I was surprised that Quinlan even knew about her. I had never told him or anyone else in the sheriff's department about the Pratt homicide because the story had no bearing on the case against Vic and I didn't want the detectives to think I was trying to smear Eileen's lover. "How did you know about that murder?"

"Boring told me. It came up when we were talking about how Eileen died. He said there had been a rumor that he was having an affair with Mrs. Pratt, but that absolutely wasn't true. He said he wasn't sure how it got started. Maybe when he went to her house one evening to drop off some papers from work. They were standing outside talking for a long time and someone must have driven by and seen them and gotten suspicious."

I snickered in disgust and so did Quinlan. In his interview with Detective Delaney in 1974, when Boring was still trying to deny his affair with Eileen, he said he "had occasion to go by her house when he went to pick up some papers in the nighttime hours," and when Vic came home, he tried to hide in the garage. Boring may have gotten long in the tooth, but he hadn't lost his capacity for deceit. Maybe he had even managed to deceive himself.

I said, "Eileen was his *second* dead lover, and that shithead couldn't even come up a new excuse." I told Quinlan he'd been married to Gloria for only about a year when he'd started the affair with Eileen.

"I know. I interviewed Mrs. Boring on their thirty-first wedding anniversary. She seemed so proud. I guess she felt like she won something."

The next day Cheri and I went to see Joyce Maddox, the woman who had been intimidated and falsely arrested by Vic and Officer Lechler back in the late seventies. Maddox, now about sixty—a sinewy, sunparched woman—was anxious to talk. Her story was long and sordid, and the humiliation she had endured back then still rankled her. She said her son, who was six at the time, was deeply traumatized by the incident and became withdrawn and fearful for several years afterward and would not go to school unless she walked him there.

"Lechler and Zaccagnini were the main instigators," she said. "They were both very profane. I had a friend, an assistant prosecutor, who was very incensed about my case. He knew what was going on over there at the police department. He really disliked Lechler and Zaccagnini and always used their names in the same breath."

She told us she had confronted Vic in the police station the day after the arrest. "He seemed to realize he had made a mistake," Maddox recalled. "He said, 'I guess Lechler really dumped on you.'"

She told us Lechler's eventual dismissal from the police for sexual harassment was front-page news in the early eighties. Her settlement from the Police Department, which came without any admission of wrongdoing, was seventeen thousand dollars.

"That was a lot of money back then," she said, with unsmiling satisfaction. "The settlement came without any admission of wrongdoing, but it still made me feel vindicated."

She told us she had once mentioned Lechler and Zaccagnini to a police officer she'd gotten to know through her work as an attorney, and he had confirmed what she already knew. "They were bad apples," he said. "We got rid of them."

I told Ms. Maddox briefly about my relationship to Vic and why I was doing this research. Nodding in acknowledgment, she said, "I think he could have done it," but she didn't ask me anything more about Eileen's case.

That evening, as I thought about the interview, I wondered how much of what Joyce had told Cheri and me about Vic was true. I didn't question the things she recounted about her own ordeal; that part was well-documented in the court records. But what about the rest of it? Years later she was still seething with justifiable indignation about what had been done to her and her son. Did she attest to Zaccagnini's vile behavior and link his name with Lechler's because she thought it was what I wanted to hear? I'm not suggesting this was something she would have done on a conscious level, just one of those little tricks the mind plays on itself to establish a bond with the person across the table and get him nodding in empathy. Of course, I was the one who had sought her out. I'd gone looking for dirt on Vic and found it. If I had tried, perhaps I could have found other people who would have told me he was a good cop and a stand-up guy.

Two and half months after my meeting with Detective Quinlan, the sheriff's department still had not found Yvonne. They had her Social

Security number and a dozen former addresses, but all the usual computer searches came up blank. Quinlan seemed to be shrugging his shoulders. No one in the sheriff's department acknowledged it openly, but I was the driving force behind this investigation. I had long ago given up on the TV version of the conscientious precinct captain who kept track of open cases on a corkboard and regularly asked his investigators for updates. The sheriff's detectives followed the leads I had given them and reported back to me when they got new information. Without my prodding, Eileen's reopened case would have been forgotten, lost in the pile along with dozens of other unresolved cases no one had the energy or obligation to see through to the end. For me, the goal was to keep the investigation moving forward without overstepping some invisible line of demand and control.

I assumed the child Vic and Yvonne had together would know where to find her mother, but I didn't suggest that to Quinlan. If I kept nudging him, he would find her one way or another.

From the court filings Cheri had uncovered we knew Yvonne was not Vic's biggest fan. They had had one daughter together, Vic's only child, and split up when the girl was seven or eight years old. In a child support suit against Vic in 1994, Yvonne claimed she had entered into the most recent agreement "only as a means of stopping the defendant's harassment and demanding and manipulative phone calls."

Sometimes, in my most hopeful and most vindictive fantasies, I would imagine an argument that had taken place between Vic and Yvonne—animosities and jealousies and broken promises spilling over until Vic grabs her by the arms, a look of hatred in his eyes. Yvonne tries to convince herself that he won't hurt her, not with their young daughter in the next room, but she is more frightened than she's ever been in her life, his angry face a few inches from hers, droplets of spit flying from his mouth. Don't push your luck, bitch, he says. You better learn to keep your fucking mouth shut or you're gonna end up like Eileen. Then he squeezes her arms a little harder before he throws her on the floor and goes into the next room to—what else?—call his mother.

• • •

Yvonne Marie Burdette Zaccagnini Winnick Smith Draper seemed to have had a rough ride since marrying Vic when she was a twenty-two-year-old sheriff's deputy. She had been married four times and relinquished custody of a young son to her second husband when she was unemployed in 1991, then went through a long court battle to get the boy back.

Cheri discovered a copy of a videotape of Yvonne's most recent divorce hearing. The taping had been installed by the California courts as a cost-saving measure to forego the use of a stenographer, and Cheri and I sat down in her living room to watch. I had my own preconceived bias of what Yvonne would be like—a little overweight, her face saggy and careworn, a strident edge to her voice—but I was wrong. She was trim and pretty with long dark hair, and dressed in a well-cut lime-green suit. She spoke softly and politely. It was easy to see how men would be attracted to her.

In August my patience with Quinlan finally paid off and I received the following email:

*I just spoke to Yvonne. She was a deputy with the Sheriff's
Department and had been seeing Vic while he and Eileen were
separated. The two split up when Vic and Eileen tried to reconcile.
Vic never said anything negative about Eileen and told Yvonne
that Eileen had shot herself with his gun. Yvonne said that Eileen
was depressed because she and Vic were unable to have children.
Yvonne and Vic were married for nine years and she did not
experience any domestic violence. She also said the San Bernardino
P.D. gave Vic a polygraph before allowing him to return to work.
I'll try to confirm that.*

I'll be talking to Vaughn today and Vic on Thursday.

41

I TRIED TO call Detective Quinlan as soon as I read his email telling me he had spoken to Yvonne, but I got his voicemail and wasn't able to reach him until the next day. He said she had been very matter-of-fact when she talked about Vic.

"She didn't have anything bad to say about him," Quinlan said with a touch of sarcasm. "Maybe after three other husbands he looks pretty good."

I couldn't hide my disappointment. "So there was no domestic abuse or anything like that?"

"Apparently not. I asked her about the court filings for back child support, and she said something like, Oh, we were always fighting about money."

"Did you ask her when they started their relationship?"

"Yes, apparently it was during that summer when Eileen and Vic were separated. He broke it off with Yvonne for a short while when he and Eileen tried to reconcile, then they got back together again after she died."

"How romantic," I said sarcastically. "And applied for a marriage license on the first anniversary of Eileen's death!"

It seems a bit absurd in retrospect, but up till the moment Quinlan told me about Vic and Yvonne, it had never occurred to me that Vic was also having an affair that summer. Did he fuck Yvonne, then go over to the house on Dunblane and beat up Eileen for being unfaithful? Had she gone to her grave thinking she was the only adulterer?

Quinlan said, "Yvonne said the police department made Vic take a lie detector test before he went back on the job after Eileen's funeral. I'll call over there and see if I can verify that."

"Sounds like you didn't get a whole lot out of her?"

"Not much. She wasn't being evasive. More like, Sorry, but that was a long time ago. She did mention one thing that caught my attention. She said Eileen shot herself with Vic's service revolver."

"Huh? That's not right. Not according to the police report."

"Yeah, that's one thing that's pretty clear. It was the gun they kept in the house for her protection."

I asked him about his interview with Vaughn, the homicide investigator who had accompanied the now-deceased Detective Delaney to the crime scene.

"He was pretty vague at first," Quinlan said. "Didn't remember being in the house until I showed him the police report and that jogged his memory. He got defensive and said he was sure the sheriff's department had done everything possible to eliminate Vic as a suspect. Their main concern after the incident was for Hal Boring's safety. I guess they took Vic's threats seriously."

"So all that's left is Vic."

"Yeah, I've got his phone number. I'll let you know when I get in touch with him."

I had hoped that someone from the sheriff's department would interview Vic in person—a phone call seemed too tenuous, too easily deflected—but Quinlan made it clear they had no money in the budget for that. Now, as I waited to hear back from him, I began to worry that a phone call from the detective would simply put Vic on high alert.

Quinlan couldn't compel him to answer any questions. Vic could "lawyer up," as they say in the TV shows, and hide behind his attorney. Once Vic adopted this stance, it seemed unlikely that he would ever talk to the detective, and he certainly wasn't going to talk to me.

With that last thought I came to a stark realization—something I had known intuitively since I got the police reports through the Freedom of Information Act two years before and discovered that all the physical evidence had been destroyed—this case was never going to be adjudicated in a court of law. Even if Vic agreed to talk to Quinlan, unless he broke down and confessed to pulling the trigger, whatever story the detective pried out of him would not be enough. I wanted *closure*. This whole thing had started with a conversation between Vic and me, and that was how I wanted it to end.

My instinct was to call Quinlan and ask him to back off. He'd told me he was being transferred out of the homicide division in the next month and promised he would finish the case before the transfer. But I knew he'd drop it if I asked him to, and no one in the sheriff's office would ever mention it again. I spoke with Elizabeth and several close friends, explaining that my first priority was to talk to Vic, and I didn't want the police investigation to jeopardize that possibility. They all thought I should ask Quinlan not to contact Vic, and I should find a way to get in touch with him myself. Only Darryl disagreed.

"Stop trying to micromanage this, Jim," he said. "Let the police finish the investigation. You can't predict how Vic is going to react when they contact him. He might break down and confess. You never know. What if you and I discover some new piece of information three months from now and want to take that to the sheriff's office? If you call this off now, I don't think you're ever going to be able to start it up again."

Quinlan did not call back the next day or the day after. When he finally did, he said he hadn't tried to reach Vic yet, but he had been in touch with the San Bernardino Police Department and they told him they had no record that Vic had been required to take a polygraph. He'd asked the department if he could get a copy of Vic's personnel file and they said it was unlikely records going back that far still existed.

"Chances are they're stonewalling me," Quinlan said, frustrated. "I'm not sure if I could get a copy of Vic's records even with a court order."

One week passed and then another with no further word from Quinlan. He did not return my phone calls or emails. The secretary in the homicide division said he had already gone to his new duty station. I got in touch with Sergeant Kazarian, who told me he had just made lieutenant and would soon be transferred himself, but he promised he'd get Quinlan to finish the investigation.

Three months later I had not heard from either Quinlan or Kazarian. No Vic, no resolution.

Finally, in the middle of January 2005, Quinlan called and said he'd been trying to reach Vic. He told me he had left repeated messages on an answering machine, but there'd been no response. He said Vic had probably learned from Yvonne or their daughter why the sheriff's department wanted to talk to him, and he did not intend to cooperate. Quinlan said that, if necessary, he would get in touch with the police department in the Seattle area where Vic lived and ask them to make contact with Vic personally. He sounded discouraged and so was I. No doubt Vic had built a wall around himself, making him virtually impossible to reach.

Then, a few days later, Quinlan called back and told me he'd spoken to Vic.

"He was real cagey at first," the detective said. "He said he'd gone over this a hundred times with the police thirty years ago, so why was this coming up again? I told him it was just routine, the sheriff's department occasionally reviewed old cases, and he started to relax. He kept telling me how he had taken two polygraphs—one for us and one for the police department. When I started asking him about Eileen, he didn't get angry or defensive. Actually, he was pretty emotional. He said the whole thing just brought up a lot of difficult memories and sometimes he felt responsible."

"Responsible how?"

"The way he was storming around the bedroom, trying to call your folks back in Pittsburgh. He kept saying, 'I should have waited. I should have waited.'"

I was taking notes as the detective spoke, my pulse racing. Quinlan said he asked Vic about his affair with Yvonne, and Vic told him Eileen knew about it, that they'd gone to see a counselor and gotten everything out on the table. I put three exclamation points in the margin next to this comment. It was hard to believe Vic was telling the truth. How could Eileen have been so distraught over her own affair with Boring when she knew about Vic and Yvonne? Did she think he was entitled to sleep with someone else because she was the one who had asked for the separation? Or was the so-called double standard fixed so firmly in her personal morality code that she could forgive Vic but not herself?

Quinlan said, "I asked him to talk about the day of the shooting, but it was like he has amnesia or something. He remembered telling Eileen he was going to call your mother, but the rest of it is kind of a blank slate. I asked him where the little boy was when the shot was fired, and he goes, 'What little boy?' He didn't remember the kid being there. Didn't remember it was his friend's kid, the guy he'd been living with all summer. I read him a few quotes from the police report. Then I asked him about the gun and he got real shaky. 'Yeah,' he goes, 'it was my service revolver.'"

"But that's not right."

"I know. I told him. But he was very confused. I almost wanted to say, *So what did it feel like when you got the gun back? Did you carry it around on your hip? The gun that killed your wife?*"

In the end, it was Vic's confusion that made Quinlan believe he was telling the truth.

"The thing with practiced liars," the detective said, "they usually get the basic facts straight, then they twist the truth in other ways. Find stuff that's hard to contradict. With Vic, his responses seemed credible. Completely unrehearsed."

Quinlan thought that Vic had erased the boy from his memory as a way of mitigating his guilt about his role in the melee. In other words, Vic didn't *want* to remember that a child had been there, a witness to all that mayhem as a shot rang out and police barged into the house and a loaded gun lay on the floor. This was pure speculation on the detective's part, but not an unreasonable deduction. That said, I found myself wondering if Vic had already managed to "forget" the boy by the time he came to Pittsburgh and told me his story, or if he left him out because he knew it would raise questions he didn't want to answer.

On the other side of the ledger, the detective thought Vic's belief that Eileen had shot herself with his service revolver was his way of accepting a measure of guilt for the shooting. Not that he pulled the trigger, but that he had gotten careless with his gun.

"When I told him it wasn't *his* gun, it was like he couldn't believe it. He kept muttering, 'Huh? What? No, I . . .'"

In Quinlan's mind, it was the two mistakes in Vic's memory—the missing boy and the wrong gun—that made his story sound true. These were basic facts, and Vic couldn't remember them. This wasn't lying; it was just befuddlement.

"From everything he told me," the detective said, "I'm inclined to believe his story. The simple fact that he talked to me without going to a lawyer, I mean, that's what most people would do. Most *guilty* people anyway. The way he's got these facts all jumbled up, I've interrogated a lot of suspects, and after a while you get a pretty good idea when someone is lying through their teeth. But with Vic, he didn't sound that way. More like he'd been through some real traumatic stuff and was trying his best to forget about it."

I wasn't surprised by Quinlan's conclusion, and, in an odd way, I wasn't upset by it. Either Vic had pulled off a masterful acting job or else he was telling the truth—the truth as he remembered it, anyway.

I said, "So, you're gonna close the case?"

"Yes, I don't think there's anything else we can do. I'll file a report internally saying that we found nothing to indicate this was a homicide, and that will be the end of it."

"From what I can see, there are only two things we can say for certain about this case. One is that Eileen and Vic were involved in an ugly domestic dispute that went terribly awry and left her dead. The other is that the sheriff's department did a really lousy job of investigating this case back in 1974."

"That pretty much sums it up," Quinlan said.

I hung up the phone. I was alone in the house, sitting at my desk. I began to write feverishly in my notebook, then found myself getting choked up. A moment later, I was weeping, my forehead on the edge of my desk, tears dripping onto the floor between my feet. It was pure release, as if a cramped muscle had finally loosened, freeing me from the pain. My quest was almost over. All that was left was to talk to Vic.

42

Elizabeth and i spent hours strategizing about when and how I should approach Vic. I told her I wanted to wait until I got a copy of Quinlan's final report along with the transcripts of the interviews, but she thought I should act quickly.

"Vic's got this little box where he's been hiding everything about Eileen for thirty years," she said. "Now the police forced him to open it. But it's not going to stay open very long. I *know*. I have a little box of my own." She was alluding to the automobile accident in which her son David was killed. "Sometimes something forces me to open it, but I close it up again as fast as I can. The same is probably true for Vic when it comes to Eileen. You should try to see him right away, Jim, the sooner the better. The longer you wait, the more likely it is he'll put you off."

Darryl agreed. I asked him to call Vic and try to arrange a meeting. He said he'd think about how to handle it and get back to me. Elizabeth asked me why I wanted to approach Vic through Darryl instead of calling him myself.

"I think I'd be too nervous," I said. "I don't want to talk to Vic on the phone. I want to meet him face-to-face. I'm afraid if I call him, he'll start asking me questions and I don't want to lie and make up some excuse about why I want to see him."

I not only wanted Darryl to call and make the arrangements; I wanted him to be with me when I met Vic. Early in this journey, when I first envisioned such an encounter, I thought I'd need Darryl as a bodyguard, someone to protect me from a man who might get violent, who might be a killer—but now I just wanted him as a moderator to help keep things on an even keel. I also wanted him as a witness, someone I could talk to and compare notes with afterward.

Elizabeth asked me what I was hoping to learn by meeting up with Vic.

"I want him to tell me everything he can remember. Maybe get him to reminisce about Eileen and make her come alive again. Talk about the good times, before everything fell apart."

"But what about everything you found out in the police reports? All the things Eileen's friends said he did? Do you really think he's gonna want to talk about stuff like that?"

"I hope so. I'm just gonna lay it all out for him. He can't sit there and pretend those things never happened."

"No, he'll just say, Sorry, conversation over. And walk out the door."

"Maybe. But if he agrees to the meeting, it probably means he needs something from me."

"Like what?"

"I don't know. I'm just guessing. But if he's ever going to make peace with all this, he needs to talk to someone who was close to Eileen, and I'm the only one left."

"I don't care about *his* peace. Just yours. The way he treated Eileen? I hope it haunts him for the rest of his life."

It took Darryl nearly a week to get Vic's unlisted phone number, a week in which I played a lot of solitaire and didn't get much sleep. The telephone number had been changed shortly after Vic was interviewed by Quinlan—a coincidence perhaps, but one that gave me pause. As Darryl and I discussed his strategy for the call, we came up with one small ruse—Darryl would tell Vic I would be coming to Seattle to see my son, Brett, and hoped I could meet with Vic while I was there. We figured if he thought I had a reason to be in town and wasn't simply coming there to confront him, he might feel a little more comfortable and agree to see us.

The following night my phone rang shortly past midnight. When I picked it up there was silence on the line. After a moment, I hung up. A few minutes later, the phone rang again. Silence. And again. The hairs on my arms went up, thinking that it might be Vic, harassing me. The fourth time the phone rang it was Darryl.

"Sorry for all the confusion," he said. "I've been having some trouble with my cell phone lately."

"Gremlins."

He chuckled. "Yeah, they're everywhere. Listen, I just got off the phone with Vic. When you hear what I have to tell you you're gonna sleep like a bear in hibernation tonight."

"Jeez, Darryl, that's great."

"Yeah, he was just so open and welcoming."

"Did you ask about the shooting?"

"Oh, sure, we got into it right away. He said he was surprised when the sheriff's department called and started asking about Eileen. He told me he had taken two polygraphs and he thought that cleared everything up. He said he couldn't understand why anyone would think he had something to do with Eileen's . . . Then he stopped and things seemed to shift a little. Like he couldn't say the word *death*. Almost like he was afraid he'd get too emotional if he did."

"Did he know I was the one who opened the case?"

"Yeah, he sorta figured it out. We started talking about your family, how his mother was so close to your folks. He said he knew Keith better than you. I told him you never suspected him of any wrongdoing. We just found a few gaps in the investigation the police did back then, and needed to clear them up."

"Really?" I said incredulously. "You said I never *suspected* him?"

"Well, you know, that you always kept an open mind. There's absolutely no animosity in him, Jim. He said he'd be happy to get together with you when you come to Seattle."

"Wow, that's fantastic! Does he know you'll be coming with me?"

"Yeah, I mentioned it and that threw him off a little, but I just slipped around it. I told him he should bring his wife along. He seemed to like that."

"So, we got a plan?"

"Yes, we do."

After I hung up, I had an odd reaction to Darryl's description of the conversation. The things he said made Vic seem like a good guy. Someone *likable*. I found myself trying to quash that feeling. I was looking forward to the meeting, but I wasn't ready to like Vic Zaccagnini.

Over the next week Darryl and I had several conversations about the upcoming meeting with Vic. The word Darryl kept using over and over was *healing*, telling me how this encounter would allow Vic and me to move to "a higher level of consciousness." He said, "The ultimate reality is spirit, and spirit is always good," which sounded like New Age psychobabble to me. At times his relentless optimism drove me to distraction, but he wouldn't let up.

"Just let things evolve naturally," he said. "Don't try to fit this story into a box. We don't know how it's gonna end, but I think it could surprise both of us."

43

Dᴀʀʀʏʟ ᴀɴᴅ ɪ agreed that we could not go into the meeting with Vic with a prescribed agenda. We felt it would be a mistake to have a long list of questions and grievances, then run down the list and start taking notes. The only way to do it was to go in empty-handed and see where the conversation took us.

Vic chose the meeting place—the 13 Coins restaurant near the Seattle-Tacoma Airport. He was standing in the waiting area near the hostess station when Darryl and I walked in. Short leather jacket, bushy salt-and-pepper mustache, a random sprinkling of hairs on top of his bald head. We shook hands and I introduced him to Darryl. A few moments later, Vic's wife, Laura, joined us. She was a pleasant-looking woman with stylish glasses and sandy brown hair.

We sat in a large booth with high-backed seats that gave us a nice feeling of privacy—Darryl on the inside across from Laura, Vic and I on the outside facing each other. Laura said she worked as a gemologist in a jewelry factory. She did not smile readily and seemed reserved, perhaps a little wary. Vic told us he was a loss-prevention manager for a large office-supply chain, twenty-three stores in his territory. The waiter came and Laura asked for a glass of red wine while the rest of us stuck with water. We made small talk as we looked at the menu and ordered our food. I asked about Vic's mother and brothers, and he got me to fill him in on my various careers. Vic and Laura said they spent most of their free time visiting Vic's daughter, who was married with three children and living in Las Vegas. He still had his Pittsburgh accent, which I pointed out. He laughed and said some people still noticed. As he must have done thirty years before, Vic called me Jimmy. Laura quickly picked it up as well. Some of my old college pals still call me Jimmy, but each time Vic or Laura said it, it jarred me, a little too familiar somehow.

I asked him casually why he had left the police force.

"That's a long story," he said, one corner of his mouth curling somewhere between a smile and disgust. "When you first become a cop, you think you're John Wayne and wanna put all the bad guys in jail. Then, after a couple of years, you realize you're doing it mostly for your buddies, the guys you work with every day. Just like the military. Finally, you get to the point where you're just putting in your time. It feels like you're fighting the criminals with one hand and the system with the other. I was doing okay. Made it to sergeant, but I was really getting burned out."

He continued—talking about the endless paperwork, the pettiness of superior officers who focused on things like checking on patrolmen to see if they were wearing their hats—and finished with a shrug. Though I was well aware of some ugly chapters in his career as a police officer, I had no intention of bringing them up and putting him on the defensive.

We started discussing our jobs. Laura told a story about a diamond that had gotten lost behind a copy machine at work. Darryl followed with an even longer tale about a thief who went into jewelry stores and slyly substituted fake stones for real ones. As they talked, I stared at my plate from time to time. I had ordered a Cobb salad but could not eat. Laura's presence had unexpectedly thrown me. She seemed like a confident, plainspoken woman—someone who would quickly come to the defense of her husband if things got ugly. How could I say the things I needed to say to Vic with her there? We had been seated for at least twenty minutes and no one had mentioned Eileen.

Laura finally turned to me and said, "Why did you want to see us, Jimmy?"

Unsure how to bring up the investigation, I told her I wanted to find out more about Eileen—the good times, what her life had been like with Vic in California. Laura asked if Eileen and I had been close. I muttered, embarrassed, "Not exactly."

Vic had little to add, only saying that he and Eileen had had "plans," and she wanted to finish college. We went off on one tangent and another, including the story about Keith's health problems and his death. Laura spoke less than anyone else at the table, yet she seemed to control the conversation. She had a way of fixing me with her eyes that made me uneasy, pausing slightly before she spoke, as if each sentence that followed—usually a question—was precise and well considered. *Why did you want to see us, Jimmy?* She had given me the perfect opening and I'd blown it.

As the conversation rambled on, Darryl and Vic started trading stories about the Air Force. Laura said she was an Air Force brat herself, from everywhere and nowhere. I was becoming increasingly agitated, rearranging the wedges of hard-boiled eggs in my salad. Then Laura gave me another opening.

"You seem troubled, Jimmy," she said. "How can we help you?"

"Well, I *am* troubled." I looked up at her, and in that moment I realized Vic hadn't given her any real sense of what this evening was about. Maybe he wasn't sure himself. "About four years ago I decided to try to find out more about Eileen's death. I wasn't suspicious about anything; I just wanted to get more details. That's when I met Darryl. We got copies of the police reports, the coroner's report, things like that, and when I started reading them . . ." I looked across the table at Vic. "They paint a real ugly picture of you, Vic."

Laura glared at me. "What're you *talking* about?"

I ignored her and kept my eyes locked on Vic's.

"Well, let's start with the little boy Eileen was babysitting. Freddy Waering, the two-year-old. The one you told the police you can't remember being there. The way the police report reads, it sounds like one minute Eileen is changing the kid's clothes, the next minute she *shoots herself*? From where I'm sitting, I find that hard to believe. Especially with a girl who really wanted to be a mother. You never mentioned the little boy when I talked to you in my parents' kitchen."

Vic did not respond. He looked apprehensive, trapped. I took a few minutes to tell Laura about the long talk I'd had with Vic thirty years before. She listened intently, then I turned back to Vic.

"Try to see it through my eyes," I said. "I thought I knew my sister. Everybody I've talked to says the same things about her—she was spunky, vivacious, terrific at her job. A real go-getter. Then one day, out of the blue, she commits suicide. I didn't even know you guys had been separated until after she was dead. She asked my parents not to tell anyone and they didn't. Anyway, that kid being there in the house really changed the picture for me. The boy's father, your old friend Alex Waering, said the police told him his son was in the living room. Okay, maybe the kid wasn't standing right there in the room *watching* the two of you tear each other apart. But still. Eileen was crazy about children. Couldn't wait to have her own. Everyone says how upset she was by the miscarriages. So the idea of her shooting herself while she's taking care of a child? You can see how that might make me wonder."

Laura asked how many miscarriages Eileen had had. I said two or three. Vic said firmly that it was two, and I was surprised by his certainty. Laura wanted to know how long it had been since Eileen's last one.

"About eight or nine months," Vic said.

Laura began trying to connect the two events, clearly thinking it might be significant.

"The miscarriage doesn't make any difference," I said, trying to regain control of the conversation. "It doesn't have anything to do with the boy being in the house."

Laura said the miscarriages mattered a lot, and the two of us began to bicker.

"Forget about the miscarriages, honey," Vic said, cutting her off. "That isn't the point he's trying to make."

It was a telling moment. Laura changed her posture and moved away from Vic into the corner of the booth. Darryl had already gone silent. A new order had been established. The issue at hand was between Vic and me. Darryl's and Laura's participation, while not verboten, would be minimal and unintrusive. Laura had backed away, but I knew if I stepped over some invisible line and attacked Vic viciously or underhandedly, she wouldn't hesitate to intercede and tell me that they'd heard enough and it was time to leave. But Laura's presence tempered my words and my demeanor, making me more measured. More formidable.

For the next fifteen or twenty minutes I built my case against Vic. I reminded him of the death threat he'd made on the Borings' front lawn, about the adoption papers he had thrown at Eileen, about the disturbing coincidences between the fatal suicide and the earlier suicide attempt he described to the police. As I laid out the evidence, he sat there perplexed, mystified, as if he remembered none of it. Occasionally he would question some detail, then shake his head, not quite able to believe what I was saying.

I explained how the stippling around the gunshot wound made it appear inconsistent with suicide, how Eileen would have had to hold the gun backward and pulled the trigger with her thumb. I avoided any mention of the ballistics experts I'd consulted or the discrepancy over the number of bullets in the gun. I didn't want to linger on the gunshot wound. The topic was fraught with questions, and I didn't want to drift off into a technical analysis of muzzle distance and powder tattooing. I reminded Vic that it was the spare gun they had kept in the house, *not* his service revolver, that Eileen had used. I offered to send him copies of the police reports so he could read all these details for himself, but he made no response.

I said, "Did you know Eileen wrote a letter to my parents the morning she died?"

Vic did not.

"It came on the day of her funeral."

I had a photocopy folded in my shirt pocket, the only document I'd brought into the restaurant with me. I took it out and handed it to him. I wanted him to read Eileen's words and see that she loved him. Or was *trying* to love him. I wanted him to read it and weep. He had to borrow Darryl's glasses to make out the handwriting in the soft light of the booth. Mouth taut, he read the letter, then held it out to Laura, but she wouldn't take it.

She looked at me. "Is she saying goodbye?"

I shook my head, realizing she didn't want to read a suicide note. "Just the opposite. It's very upbeat. She thinks the worst is over. Says what a prize she has in Vic."

Laura picked up the letter, read it without comment, and handed it back to me. I refolded it and left it sitting in the middle of the table, a reminder of wishes that had never come true.

"The thing that disturbs me most," I said, almost matter-of-factly, "is the abuse. You were jealous. Controlling. You made Eileen feel like dirt and you slapped her around."

"That's bullshit," Vic said. His voice was firm but not angry. "I only laid hands on her *once*, that one time when she tried to take a bunch of aspirin. I grabbed her by the arms. That's all." He reached out and clutched the empty air, his hands blameless of anything but the desire to keep Eileen from hurting herself.

"Actually, the police mention that incident in their report. Only their description is a little different. This is an exact quote." I paused to collect myself. "'. . . this was on an occasion when he tore her clothes off, smacked her and beat her and called her a whore.'"

"It wasn't like that," he said softly, his shoulders slumping as if he were getting smaller, shrinking in on himself.

"Those are *your* words, Vic. The police didn't make them up. They just wrote down what you told them."

He winced and stared off into the void. I couldn't tell if he was trying to recall the past or keep it at bay.

"It was more than *once*, Vic. I've talked to three different people who say you hit Eileen. They saw bruises on her arms and face. These are people she worked with. It's not like they got together and made up a story. So, you tell me—What's the truth?"

He put his elbows on the table and held his head in his hands.

I said, "When you hear me say all this, do you think, *No, this is wrong, there must be some mistake.* Or do you think you just repressed all those memories?"

Eyes haunted, he said, "I don't know."

Had this been a courtroom I would not have said another word, just turned my back and left him slumped on the witness stand looking confused and broken. Looking guilty.

A few moments later, he turned to Laura and said, "I'm sorry you had to hear all this."

She lifted her chin resolutely and gave him a wink that seemed to say, *I love you, I believe in you, we'll get through this together.* I was touched by the strength and intimacy of that gesture. I found myself thinking she was a good woman; Vic was lucky to have her by his side.

The waiter cleared away our dishes and asked if anyone wanted coffee or dessert. It was a welcome break in the tension, and for a moment everyone seemed to relax. But we all knew there was much more to say.

44

WE ORDERED coffee, tea for Laura. She leaned toward me, anxiety in her voice. "Why didn't you come to us sooner, Jimmy?"

Was she being naive or trying to trick me? *Because I didn't trust you. Because I thought Vic might have murdered my sister.*

"I had to wait for the police to finish their investigation."

I asked Vic if he knew that I had initiated the investigation. He said he'd figured it out after Quinlan called. Some friends in law enforcement had told him that a case like this would never be reopened unless someone came forward and started asking questions, and I was the only possible one.

We began to discuss his telephone interview with Quinlan.

"Everything is real fuzzy," Vic said. "When I talked to the detective, I thought Eileen killed herself the same day we talked to that lady on her front lawn." He was referring to Gloria Boring. "She called the house and we went over there. I thought it was going to be a simple conversation to clear things up, but she flew into a rage and came at Eileen." He clawed the air in front of his face. "She was all over her, so I just put Eileen in the truck and we got out of there."

Then you went home and beat the shit out of her. Selective memory.

We all have it to some degree. Maybe it's the only thing that lets us look in the mirror every morning.

"Do you remember what you said to the sheriff's deputy when he showed up at the Borings' house to diffuse the situation?"

Vic shrugged.

"You told him he could come back to your place in a half hour and pick up Eileen off the lawn and take you to jail. Does that ring any bells?"

He looked like he wanted to crawl under the table. I thought I caught a shift in Laura's eyes, a flicker of doubt about Vic's innocence.

I told him about Hal Boring's dalliance with Melissa Pratt and its deadly outcome. I said as far I could find, Eileen had not confided in anyone about the affair, not even her best friend, Betty Clay.

Laura scoffed. "I don't believe that," she said. "Women *talk*."

I let her comment go without rebuttal.

Vic couldn't remember Betty Clay. When he tried to recall the details of the day Eileen died, he remembered almost nothing. He said he knew he dialed the wrong number trying to call back to Pittsburgh, but he wasn't sure which room he was in. He grimaced as if he were dismayed by his amnesia. Once again, I offered to send him copies of the police reports, and once again he let the offer pass without comment.

I said, "Detective Quinlan told me you said you felt some responsibility for Eileen's death. What did you mean by that?"

He seemed to steady himself and become more reflective. "Well, not *directly*. It was my immaturity. I couldn't let things go and let them come out slowly. I kept pushing, saying we had to get everything out in the open. If only I hadn't tried to make that phone call to Mrs. T and had just let things cool off for a while . . ."

I waited for him to elaborate, but he had nothing more to add.

As we sat there in that heavy silence, I wanted to lean across the table, my finger puncturing the neutral zone between us, and say, *Come on, Vic. Get real. You've had thirty years to think about Eileen's death, and this is the guilt you live with? Your immaturity? A poor cuckolded young husband trying to call his wife's mother and tell her that her daughter had been a bad girl? Never mind that you'd spent the summer fucking Yvonne. You've convinced yourself that things would have turned out differently if you'd just waited a little longer before you picked up the phone. Which may be true. But the point is you've spent your entire life repressing every detail about that day until it's just a blur. You've forgotten which gun it was. Eliminated the little boy from the scene, the only possible witness. Excused yourself for all the times you battered Eileen and cursed her and threatened her. Now it's all lost in a haze. That's why you avert those hangdog eyes and say nothing when I offer to send you the police reports. You don't want to remember what you did. And you know what really pisses me off? It's the fact that you made Eileen taboo. Not just her death. Everything. You took every memory, every scrap of paper that reminded you of her, and stuck it in a file marked "Bad Shit." Then you put the file away where no one could find it, not even yourself. I'd lay odds that fair Laura here, steadfast Wife Number Three, has never even seen a picture of Wife Number One. I'll bet if someone asked her two weeks ago, she wouldn't have even known Eileen's name. Maybe you didn't kill my sister. Maybe you didn't grab a gun and pull the trigger. But you've erased her. Obliterated every trace of her existence along with all the terrible things you did to her. And in my mind, that's a monstrous fucking crime.*

I wanted to let those words pour out of me, as frank and unimpeachable as the chorus in a Greek tragedy. But I held myself in check. It isn't the best part of me—self-righteous, vulgar, dripping with sarcasm. Besides, if I had attacked him, what good would it have done? Vic's belief that he felt "responsible" for his role in Eileen's death was simply a disclaimer filled with myths and evasions. Nothing I said was going to dispel the story he had concocted in his mind. The only way he was ever going to discover the truth about his role in this tragedy was to climb into that dark hole and start digging through the muck.

I had managed to tamp down my indignation, but I was taken

aback by his feeble mea culpa. Eileen's final letter was still sitting in the middle of the table. I picked it up for a moment and put it down again.

"Vic, do you know the date Eileen died?"

"Yeah, it was September, uh . . ." He winced and shook his head.

"September eleventh, 1974. Do you know what you were doing on September eleventh, 1975, the first anniversary of her death?"

"Me? No, what?"

"You were taking out a marriage license with Yvonne."

There was confusion in Vic's eyes.

"That can't be true," Laura said.

I said, "I can show you a copy of the license if you'd like."

She looked at Vic in disbelief. "My God, honey, what were you *thinking*?"

"I didn't . . ." he said. "I'm not sure I even . . ." He lifted his empty hands.

". . . remembered what day it was," I said, finishing the sentence for him. "You know, for most people, the first anniversary of someone's death is a pretty big deal. It certainly was for me and my parents. Taking out that license on the anniversary doesn't make you guilty of anything. Maybe you'd just decided to move on, but it seemed to me like you were trying to make a point."

Vic dropped his gaze and offered no defense.

Thirty years later we had come full circle, Vic and I sitting across a table from each other as we had in my parents' kitchen, his face lined with sorrow and shame. Only this time I was the one with all the information. This time I had done my homework—combed through the police reports, studied the arcana of bullet trajectories and gunshot wounds, interviewed (or persuaded the sheriff's department to interview) every person who could help me understand what had happened. This time I was patient, watchful. Obsessed. Vic had lived the story, but I was the expert on what happened that day; he had forgotten almost everything. Perplexed and rattled by the things I'd told him, he had no explanation for the discrepancies of fact, no mitigating evidence to counter all the brutish and thoughtless things he had done. Once again, Vic sat there waiting for my judgment. Waiting to see if I believed him when he said that he was not responsible for Eileen's death. Not *directly*.

I was struck by the irony of the situation. There was no hard evidence to implicate Vic in Eileen's death. On the other hand, there was nothing to prove he was innocent, nothing beyond those missing polygraphs he claimed to have taken. But proof of innocence is not required in a court of law, only reasonable doubt, and I was the sole juror now. The big brother in me wanted Vic to be guilty because it would erase the stigma of Eileen's suicide and help me forgive myself for all the things I hadn't done thirty years before. The writer in me wanted Vic to be guilty because that's how these stories are supposed to end, with the violent and abusive husband finally getting punished for his crimes.

"Look, Vic," I said, "this is more or less over for me. The police have concluded that there's no reason to go ahead with a homicide investigation. There's a lot of circumstantial evidence against you, but nothing definitive. Nothing that puts the gun in your hand, so I'm gonna agree with the police and accept the idea that things happened pretty much the way you said they did. I'm certain there was no foul play."

Certain, that was the word I used. Even as I said it, I wasn't sure why.

Vic shook his head and said, "I don't know how you can be. *I* wouldn't."

Laura said, "There *are* no certainties."

Their reaction took me aback. Had I done such a good of a job laying out the case that they were ready to accept his guilt?

"Vic, thirty years ago you sat down with me in my parents' kitchen and told me what happened, and I believed you. You left out some things, changed some of the details, but maybe that's normal. When we had that talk, there were two things you said that made me think you were telling the truth. The first was, you said Eileen called out your name just before you heard the gunshot. I don't know why, but that one detail—the look on your face when you said it—made me think you weren't lying. The other was when I asked you about the gunshot wound and how long Eileen lived after they took her to the hospital. What you said was, 'Those guns are made to kill people.' To me, that didn't sound like the kind of thing a guilty person would say. It's too stark. Too close to the bone. You probably don't remember saying either of those things, but they've stuck with me all these years. I believed you once. I'm going to believe you again."

He looked stunned. Relieved. "Why?"

"Maybe it's because *I* need it. Me." I slapped my chest, my voice gaining strength along with my conviction. "There's a part of me that feels like I don't have any choice. I can't go through the rest of my life believing you're a murderer. How could I live with that?" It was the first time I had used the M-word, *murder*. He didn't flinch and neither did Laura. We sat in silence for a moment as the word resonated in the air.

"I'm not going to buy a gun and shoot you or hire some thugs to beat you senseless. I don't have it in me to do something like that." I shrugged. "I need to put this behind me and get on with my life."

Darryl jumped in and attempted to reassure Vic, explaining that I had always kept an open mind about the case and never tried to manipulate the facts to make Vic look guilty. He said this was rare in clients. Working side by side, Darryl said, we had become extremely close, "almost like brothers." Darryl's reassurances helped relieve the tension and let us all breathe a little easier.

Laura turned to me. "What's next then?"

"I don't know. I'm not sure what you mean?"

"Do you want us to be family?" It seemed like a genuine question.

"No," I said, recoiling in my seat. "I don't want that at all."

She was hurt by my abrupt response, and once more Darryl stepped in. Speaking directly to Laura, he told her how the investigation had developed—how we found Cheri, how we weren't sure if we could trust the people in the sheriff's department.

"You have to understand," he said, "Jim's been doing this for four years. Now everything has sort of come together all at once. I think the idea of being family caught him a little off guard. Maybe this meeting can help in the future. Make sure the lines of communication are open and we're not closing any doors."

"I apologize," Laura said to me. "I didn't mean it the way it came out. I just thought you might want to stay in touch."

"Maybe. I've said what I had to say. We can stay in touch if you want, but I'm not going to call Vic and keep asking him questions." I looked at him. "If you have things you want to talk about, fine, feel free. But me? I'm done. I'm not going to keep coming at you."

Vic breathed a sigh of relief, but Laura was puzzled.

She said, "Just this one conversation and it's all *finished*?"

I lifted my hand as if to say, *What else?*

"Okay, if that's what you guys want," she said. "But if this were two women, I know we'd have to talk about it more than once. This is something we'd have to keep coming back to again and again."

In another context I might have made a quip about the eternal differences between the sexes, but I let her remark go without comment. I wrote down my address, phone number, and email address on a slip of paper, and Laura did the same. As we were passing the slips across the table, I picked up the copy of Eileen's letter and handed it to Vic.

"Are you sure?" he said, as if it were something of untold value.

I was glad he wanted the letter, though maybe he felt like I had given him no choice. "Sure, I have the original, still in the same envelope."

The waiter came by and put the check on the table. I reached for it but Vic got there first. It seemed important to him that he pay, and I did not object.

"Look," he said to me earnestly. "I know I'm not perfect. I've made my share of mistakes like everybody else, but I've *learned* from them. I live my life the best I can. I don't lie and I don't cheat and I don't break the law. That's the kind of person I am."

I said nothing. Perhaps it was true, or mostly so.

Then he looked at me with sad eyes and said, "I'm sorry."

I wanted to say, Sorry for what? But I simply said, "I'm sorry too." By which I meant, I'm sorry Eileen is dead. I'm sorry you had to say you're sorry. I'm sorry we both had to live through this.

We all stood up and Vic and I gave each other a genuine hug. For me, the relief was palpable—and incomplete. Vic excused himself to go to the men's room. Darryl and Laura talked in the reception area while I paced, knowing I wasn't quite finished.

After a moment, I pulled Darryl aside. "Do you think I should tell him I'm writing a book?"

Darryl nodded, no discussion needed.

When Vic came out of the men's room, I told him I wanted to talk to him alone. We went through the foyer and stood outside the restaurant under the covered overhang. The air was chilly and heavy with mist, my shoulders hunched in my jacket.

I said, "Thanks for coming tonight, Vic. I've been waiting to talk to you about this stuff for a long, long time."

He nodded. "I can see why you needed to. The sheriff's department really made some bad mistakes. When that detective called me and I told him I'd taken a polygraph, he was like, 'You did?' And I'm thinking, *You're the detective, you oughta know*."

I was tempted to say it wasn't just the mistakes the police had made but the things they *did* find that made me suspect him, but I let it go.

"There's one more thing I have to tell you," I said. "This has been a great evening for me. Really cathartic. We had a lot of tough stuff to deal with, but we got through it and I feel a thousand times better. Back in the restaurant I put all my cards on the table. All except one—I've been writing a book about this. I have no idea what will come of it or if anyone will publish it. But I just wanted you to know."

His eyes narrowed as if he couldn't understand what I'd just said. Then he sighed, a hint of self-pity in his voice. "You're a better man than I am, Jim. I could never have done what you did."

Whatever response I might have anticipated—indignation or dismay, litigious threats or abject pleadings for me to keep the story a secret—Vic's words caught me completely off guard. I tried to speak, but for the first time that night I was too choked up.

I reached out and wrapped him in a bear hug, my cheek against his stubbled head. "This has been so fucking hard," I said. Then I turned and walked away.

45

Darryl joined me in the rental car. "Looks like those two are gonna have a lot to talk about on the ride home."

I shrugged. For all my avowed certainty, I'd been shrugging a lot that evening. Vic too.

"Did you tell him about the book?"

I said I had and recounted our brief conversation. "It was really strange, almost like he didn't hear me."

"Oh, he heard you. You did good, Jim. You gave him forgiveness. Vic just didn't know he needed it till you gave it to him."

"Maybe that's why he said I'm a better man than he is. I guess he felt he couldn't have forgiven me if the shoe were on the other foot."

"Not just that. It's the whole investigation, everything you did. Eileen's death was too painful for him. That's why he remembers so little about it. He's been living his life in denial and pretense and excuse."

"Yeah. In the restaurant I kept thinking, *How could he have forgotten so much?* Did you see how he ignored me when I offered to send him copies of the police reports? It's like there's this deep dark hole in his past, but he's afraid to crawl down in it."

"He doesn't even want to peek over the edge."

"Do you think he ever will?"

"Maybe. Do you *want* him to?"

"I honestly don't care, Darryl. It's over for me now. I feel a hundred pounds lighter."

Darryl put his big hand on my shoulder the way he often did, to keep me safe and grounded.

Back in his motel room, we talked about the evening with Vic and Laura, and I wrote copious notes, trying to get it all down on paper. Trying to get it right.

EPILOGUE

THE DAY AFTER I returned from Seattle, I told my friend Jack about my meeting with Vic and all that was said.

"I think you might be letting Vic off the hook too easily," he said. "And yourself too. Are you sure you want to let it end like this?"

"What else do you want me to do?" I said peevishly. "The police have closed the case again. I can't re-create the missing evidence out of thin air. It's *over*, man. I'm not going to keep pounding my head against a brick wall."

Jack let the subject drop, but his comment gnawed on me. That evening I asked Elizabeth if she thought I'd given up too soon.

"No," she said, alarmed at the notion. "I just want this to be over for you."

"When Vic said he was sorry, I should have said, 'Sorry for *what*?' It's hard to forgive someone who never really asked for it. I think I've forgiven him. I'm trying to, anyway."

"This isn't about forgiveness, Jim." She paused for a moment, and I knew exactly what she was going to say. "It's about *acceptance*."

Ah yes, acceptance—the linchpin of adulthood. Accepting the things we can't change. Accepting our own fallibility. Accepting that a chapter in our life is over. Accepting that there are things we'll never know the truth about.

Back when I was fairly certain Vic had murdered Eileen and gotten away with it, I used to tell people that this book might be my only revenge. But revenge is rarely satisfying in the long run. One day while I was talking to Aunt Pauline about it, I suddenly realized I no longer wanted to use Vic Zaccagnini's real name.

"Oh, Jim, I'm so glad," she said. "That's the right thing. That's what Eileen would want you to do."

Eileen and Vic. They'd had a dream and lost it. Their fairy-tale marriage had gone awry, beset by barrenness, infidelity, guilt, lies, anger, jealousy. Most grown-ups, flush with the wisdom and disappointment that living brings, know that dreams are illusions born to vanish. But Vic and Eileen didn't know that, or refused to accept it. When their dreams began to unravel, their lives spiraled out of control. In the letter Eileen wrote to Mom and Dad the morning of her death, she says she's been through a "nightmare," only to fall back into another dream. She'll "stay home and be a housewife"; she knows what a "prize" she has in Vic. It doesn't matter if Eileen was making a hard-earned decision rooted in her rekindled love for Vic or trying to convince herself that he was an acceptable consolation prize after Hal Boring dumped her. All that matters is, a few hours after writing that letter, she realized the dream was over. And so did Vic.

Murder or suicide? Take your pick.

One thing is certain, you and I and every sentient adult on the planet has done something he wishes he could take back. I'm not talking about something that seems like a bad decision in the long run— dropping out of law school or not marrying your college sweetheart. I mean some impulsive act where you know within a second or two that you've made a horrible mistake, said or done something in a moment of anger or recklessness, cowardice or spite, that you can't undo.

You've set things in motion; now all you *can* do is hold your breath and hope that the damage is not too great. Not fatal.

If Eileen took her own life, I will never stop believing she didn't really want to die. To borrow Darryl's phrase, she just wanted the pain to stop. This may be a rationalization on my part, one that affirms her intrinsic thoughtfulness and lets me believe she never meant to leave us so bereft. She was too kind for that. She loved us too much. If only the gun hadn't been so easy to reach. If only she had fired a shot at the ceiling to let Vic know how close she was to the breaking point. If only she had heard the little boy cry out in fear or confusion. If only . . .

Maybe this was why Vic had so much trouble coming to terms with everything that happened. For him, all the miseries of that entire summer had been telescoped into one bad decision—if only he hadn't tried to call my mother. Everything else became a jumble, most of his memories out of reach, others completely wrong, every word muted by the sound of the gunshot, every image a blur except for the vision of Eileen, kneeling by the bed with a dark spot of blood on her blouse.

What makes the concept of "if only" so heartbreaking—and so difficult to let go—is that you keep reliving that one moment. If only you could go back and do something different. Rewrite history. At times it seems so real you can almost reach out and touch it—some other, better ending.

That is what I have been searching for with Eileen's story, a better ending. It's what we all want—Truth with a capital *T*. I guess that's why we love detective novels, stories that end with a definitive resolution and give us a sense of order in the universe. It isn't simply knowing whodunit; it's a way of ridding ourselves of life's inherent ambiguities, at least for the moment, and affirming our belief that justice will prevail. But real life is hard. The answers we seek rarely come easily, and sometimes they don't come at all.

The subject of Eileen's death doesn't come up much anymore, but some of my friends and relatives still believe Vic got away with murder.

I don't try to dissuade them. I wish I could look them in the eye, as I did with Vic, and say that I'm certain there was no foul play. But doubts creep into my thoughts from time to time, persistent as the bittersweet vines that grow at the edge of our woods. I don't know what to do with those doubts except to weed them out as best I can, and carry on.

As for Vic Zaccagnini, it has been nearly twenty years since we met in that restaurant in Seattle. I never tried to contact him again and he never got in touch with me. He is an old man now and so am I. Sometimes I wonder if he ever thinks about Eileen.

I still have a cache of photos of Eileen in my desk drawer at home, and every now and again I take them out and look at them. In my favorite she is sitting on a bed in a sleeveless flowered dress with her legs outstretched and a sweet smile on her face, holding a framed photo of Vic in his Air Force uniform—a young wife waiting for her husband to return from his deployment overseas. I cherish the thought of her being so happy and so in love. When I look at that photo, I find myself thinking, Thank you, Eileen. Thank you for coming back and tugging on my sleeve. I have spent so much time trying to reconstruct your death. Now, I want to remember how we *lived*. The Fats Domino album Mom would play over and over; the pair of grackles that came down the chimney and chased her around the house. The long johns Daddy wore from October to May, his socks held up with safety pins; the cocoon of warmth and the smell of booze when we crawled in bed with him in the morning. Keith climbing a fence and stealing a tree on Christmas Eve, with Mom standing lookout, because all the lots had closed. You and me searching for Indian Head pennies in Daddy's till; swapping Halloween candy after a night of trick-or-treating like a pair of Bedouin camel traders; taking turns holding the rabbit ears in the perfect spot so we could watch *Dobie Gillis*.

Come back, little sister, and help me remember. Never mind what is fact and what is fiction. I'm done with all that. It's the stories that keep us going. You, me, everyone.

Acknowledgments

Iт тоок more than two decades for this book to become a reality. In that time numerous people have helped sustain me with their love, kindness, encouragement, honest advice, and much-needed criticism. I hope I have found a way to thank every one of them and acknowledge that I owe them a debt that I can never adequately repay.

Darryl Carlson and I remained close friends. Elizabeth and I were able to visit him twice at a retirement home for veterans in Chula Vista before he passed away in 2020. He was such a wise, deeply spiritual man, who dealt with the underbelly of society every day but never lost his faith in mankind.

Cheri Flint is not a licensed P.I., but she has the heart and soul of dyed-in-the-wool gumshoe. Without her relentless pursuit of information, this would have been a much different story.

Bruce Edmands generously pored over the police reports and offered me great insights into them.

From 2003 to 2005, a number of individuals in the San Bernardino Sheriff's Department and the San Bernardino District Attorney's Office, whose identity I have chosen not to reveal, delved deeply into Eileen's case and assured me that my questions and reservations about the original investigation were valid. To a person, they were consummate professionals and treated me with the utmost respect.

Evan Radford and Maura Buchanan are pseudonyms for a lawyer and private investigator whose help was invaluable in pointing me in the right direction.

Don Arbuckle read numerous drafts of this book and talked about it with me for more hours than I can count.

Debra Spark convinced me to take the memoir out of the drawer when I had all but given up.

Adam Schwartz provided extraordinary insights into the storytelling and the structure of the book.

Laura Zigman knew exactly what to leave in and what to leave out as she honed the manuscript into a tighter, more dramatic whole.

Ted Hammett, Ned Hallowell, and Ken Ledeen buoyed my spirits through the rough spots and kept offering up new avenues to keep the project going.

Connie Thomson was my steadfast companion on the first leg of this journey and offered me unwavering emotional support on the second phase of my quest.

Other friends who bucked me up along the way include Jack Herlihy, Andre Dubus III, Jessica Treadway, Joe Hurka, Peter Weinbaum, Dan Roble, Buzz Richmond, Helen Peluso, Jim Bohan, Larry and Bette Smith, Lynn Williams, Jeff and Martha Jordan, Mike Nail, Tom Brown, Cynthia Gitt, Dave and Marna Huber, Beth Hadas, Carlisle Walters, Pete Hogg, Lisa Li, Daniel Statnekov, Lane Hawley, Nat Butler, Gene Meredith, Anna and Larry Allen, Dave Carr, Felicia De Chabris, George Wilson, Joe Toscano, Walter Bode, Christopher Bayley, Leslie Epstein, Bernie Katz, Jonathan Galassi, Simon Lipskar, Vicki and Christopher LaFarge, Aron Steck, Susan Barrett, Paula Hollifield, Greg and Val Huba, Elizabeth Bibb, Debby Smullyan, David and Barbara Webb, Flippy Polikoff, Mark and Susan Bloom, Nancy Prince, Chris Anschuetz, Cynthia Rettig, Lucy and Reynold Sachs,

Joan Scott, Adriana Flores, Jorge Veliz, the late Kim Prince, Pete Rogers, and John Pennington.

Beth Gutcheon became my champion the moment she read the prologue and found out I, too, was from Pittsburgh. She's been a great pal and led me to my agent, Emma Patterson of Brandt & Hochman. When I met Emma, she told me she'd quit and find a new career if she couldn't sell my book. Fortunately, she still has her job. I could not hope to find a better advocate and friend.

Jofie Ferrari-Adler of Avid Reader Press made me feel like I'd won the lottery in our first phone conversation and his enthusiasm for the book has been remarkable. Julianna Haubner is the editor every writer dreams of—insightful, discerning, efficient, and unfailingly upbeat. I am amazed by the thoroughness of Jessica Chin and her team of copy editors at Simon & Schuster, and deeply appreciative of the skill and proficiency of the production team in bringing this book to market.

I could never have undertaken this journey without the love and support of my family—my late aunt Pauline Lott and cousin Mary Guido, Gerry and Cindy Lott, Audrie and Denny Paluselli, Meg Thomson and Patrick Massey, Brian and Danielle McCarthy, Brett and Jodie Thomson, Kelly Thomson and Tim Edwards, and Kevin and Amelia McCarthy.

In our wedding vows I promised Elizabeth I would take her on "ten thousand journeys." This quest in search of Eileen was not the sort of journey either of us had in mind at the time. But she stuck by me through all my dark moods and crazy twists in the road, and the fact that she never asked me to give it up or go it alone is a tribute to her strength and unwavering love. I have been waking up very early in the morning over the past few years. I go to the living room and read and play word games and obsess about the political divide in our country; then, just past seven, I bring Elizabeth a cup of coffee in bed. She thanks me, gives me a sweet smile and a kiss, and all I can think is, *What luck!*

About the Author

JAMES WHITFIELD THOMSON grew up in Pittsburgh and attended Harvard College on a scholarship, after which he served as the navigator of a Navy ship off the coast of Vietnam, then earned a PhD in American studies at the University of Pennsylvania. After a brief stint in academia, he had a successful career as a salesman and business consultant. His novel, *Lies You Wanted to Hear*, received wide acclaim. Jim and his wife live outside of Boston. They have five far-flung children and eleven grandchildren.

Avid Reader Press, an imprint of Simon & Schuster, is built on the idea that the most rewarding publishing has three common denominators: great books, published with intense focus, in true partnership. Thank you to the Avid Reader Press colleagues who collaborated on *A Better Ending*, as well as to the hundreds of professionals in the Simon & Schuster advertising, audio, communications, design, ebook, finance, human resources, legal, marketing, operations, production, sales, supply chain, subsidiary rights, and warehouse departments whose invaluable support and expertise benefit every one of our titles.

Editorial
Julianna Haubner, *Senior Editor*

Jacket Design
Alison Forner, *Senior Art Director*
Clay Smith, *Senior Designer*
Sydney Newman, *Art Associate*

Marketing
Meredith Vilarello, *VP and Associate Publisher*
Caroline McGregor, *Senior Marketing Manager*
Emily Lewis, *Marketing Manager*
Katya Wiegmann, *Marketing and Publishing Assistant*

Production
Allison Green, *Managing Editor*
Jessica Chin, *Senior Manager of Copyediting*
Alicia Brancato, *Production Manager*
Ruth Lee-Mui, *Interior Text Designer*
Erika Genova, *Desktop Publishing Designer*
Cait Lamborne, *Ebook Developer*

Publicity
David Kass, *Senior Director of Publicity*
Alexandra Primiani, *Director of Publicity*
Rhina Garcia, *Publicist*
Eva Kerins, *Publicity Assistant*

Publisher
Jofie Ferrari-Adler, *VP and Publisher*

Subsidiary Rights
Paul O'Halloran, *VP and Director of Subsidiary Rights*
Fiona Sharp, *Subsidiary Rights Coordinator*